the ultimate
hiker's
gearguide

the
ultimate
hiker's
gearguide

Tools & Techniques
to Hit the Trail

Andrew Skurka

NATIONAL GEOGRAPHIC

WASHINGTON, D.C.

contents

introduction

My most successful backpacking trips have been those for which I had honest, accurate, and correct answers to three critical questions: 1) What are my objectives? 2) What are the environmental and route conditions that I will likely encounter during my trip, such as temperatures, precipitation, and water availability? and 3) What gear, supplies, and skills will best help me achieve my objectives *and* keep me safe and comfortable in those conditions?

Accordingly, these questions form the framework for this entire book. The first two are addressed in Part 1, and the last is fleshed out in Part 2. The sample gear lists in Part 3 showcase trip-specific kits that can be used as guides in trip planning.

I wrote this book from the perspective of an unapologetic Ultimate Hiker, which I define as a backpacker who simply loves to walk. We maximize our on-trail comfort by packing light; we move efficiently from dawn to dusk; and we consider the physical and mental challenges inherent in this style as part of our backcountry experience. Our antithesis is the Ultimate Camper, who hikes only a very short distance in order to do something else, like fishing, journaling, or birding. Neither approach is superior to the other—it's simply personal preference—but our contrasting styles have major consequences for our gear, supplies, and skills.

My target reader is one who at least *sometimes* wants to be *more*

like an Ultimate Hiker. You need not take this approach on every future trip or take it to the extreme that I do, but you must want to enjoy the *hiking* component of your backpacking trips more. This book may be most valuable for beginners and intermediates, who are too often relegated to the status of Campers-by-Default. These backpackers lack the knowledge and skills to pack lightly and move efficiently, which makes hiking more strenuous and less fruitful than it should be. To avoid a sufferfest, they instead opt to camp.

I have intentionally refrained from describing this text as a "lightweight backpacking" book. Although weight is an important consideration for the Ultimate Hiker, we must also be concerned with the comfort, safety, durability, efficiency, and best use of our gear. Moreover, it's possible to go "stupid light," whereby desperate weight savings can have adverse effects.

My hope is that this book will become the go-to manual for backpacking how-to, a modern successor to Colin Fletcher's *The Complete Walker*. An original 1968 copy of that classic sat on the corner of my desk for inspiration while I wrote this manuscript. I wanted my book to be credible, informative, and occasionally just a good read. And while my recommendations are based on my extensive hiking experience, I'm not a backpacking guru—remember that you must always exercise your own judgment in evaluating the applicability and utility of the information in this book based on your own ability, experience, and comfort level. I readily admit that there are alternative tools and techniques that will achieve similar outcomes.

At the risk of outdating this text quickly, I felt that it was important to include specific brands, products, prices, and weights. On numerous occasions, I advocate the use of unconventional items—like frameless backpacks, tarps and tarp tents, and alcohol stoves—that are not made by conventional outdoor companies or sold by conventional outdoor retailers. But by focusing on the gear type—not on the specific product—I hope that the information in this book will remain valuable long after the product itself disappears from catalogs and store shelves.

I wrote this book for backpackers who want to enjoy hiking more.

Introduction

why,

when&where

10
ARE YOU A HIKER
OR CAMPER?

16
WHY I'M AN
ULTIMATE HIKER

20
KNOW BEFORE
YOU GO

On every backpacking trip I need clothing, footwear, shelter, a sleeping bag and pad, food and water, and various other items. But my exact selections—whether I take a long-sleeved shirt or a short-sleeved one, an A-frame tarp or a pyramid-shaped one, two 1-liter water bottles or three 2.4-liter ones, et cetera—are informed by two hugely important considerations: 1) My objectives—i.e., Why am I going on this trip? and 2) Environmental and route conditions—i.e., When and where am I going?

If I neglect these considerations, it's difficult to be prepared appropriately. I may pack too much for a hiking-dominated itinerary or too little for a camping-dominated one. I may leave behind items that would have improved my safety, comfort, or fun or carry ones that end up being dead weight.

In this section I differentiate possible objectives for a backpacking trip and demonstrate methods of determining environmental and route conditions that affect gear choices.

Badlands in Anza-Borrego Desert State Park, California

are you a hiker or camper?

It wasn't all going to fit, I finally acknowledged. I stepped back to reconsider my overstuffed monstrosity of a backpack and the plastic grocery bag of items for which I still hoped to find room. Fortunately, it was only 5:30 a.m. on a Tuesday and still dark, so I figured I had some time before anyone else arrived at the Visitor Center at Georgia's Amicalola Falls State Park and discovered my tenderfoot status.

I removed and discarded an extra tube of toothpaste, spare batteries, a small lantern, a full box of blueberry Pop-Tarts, and my fourth pair of socks. A few items were saved by fear of the unknown. "I don't know for sure, but I might need that," I reasoned.

This whittling act dropped the weight of my load from a hulking 52 pounds to a hulking 49 pounds. I squeezed in the remaining items from the grocery bag—and the grocery bag too, just in case I needed it for something—before shouldering my pack and heading toward the summit of Springer Mountain, where I planned to begin a three-month, 2,175-mile journey along the Appalachian Trail to its northern terminus in Maine.

"Should I have expected this to be harder?" I asked rhetorically in my journal entry for that day—May 3, 2002. I described myself as being "in

the hurt shop," with a chafed crotch, sore leg muscles, and aching feet. I had been depleted after covering a mere 15 miles in 7 hours, a humbling distance for a member of Duke University's Division I cross-country and track teams who, during past summers, had logged up to 80 miles per week at a seven-minute-per-mile pace. And for dinner, I was content with a few handfuls of trail mix because "it involves way too much effort to cook anything," even though my planned entrée was ramen noodles, which would have only involved heating two cups of water and adding an MSG-loaded flavor packet.

Over the next week, my misery and suffering only grew. I never put it in these exact words, but many of my nightly journal entries could have been summed up with, "I want my mommy." I was more pointed on Day 7: "This sucks."

Hikers, campers & campers-by-default

On Day 8, I called my parents from the Holiday Inn Express lobby in Hiawassee, Georgia, and explained to them that I had a choice to make. Backpacking, I explained to them, consists of two entirely different activities: hiking and camping. And there are two types of extreme backpackers—*Ultimate Hikers* and *Ultimate Campers*—whose styles contrast in six specific areas:

> Their primary trip objective;
> Their knowledge of the environmental and route conditions they will likely encounter;
> Their pack weight;
> Their skill level;
> Their daily itinerary; and
> Their preferred type of fun—Type I Fun—is fun to do and fun to talk about later. Type II Fun is not fun to do but fun to talk about later. And Type III Fun is not fun to do and not fun to talk about later.

Ultimate hikers

Ultimate hikers could be described as follows:

Their primary objective is to put one foot in front of the other—they simply love to walk.

They are very knowledgeable about the environmental and route conditions they will likely encounter during their trip, either through past experience or through pretrip research. This allows them to take

Encountering a giant Sitka spruce trunk during a 500-mile hike on Alaska's Lost Coast

why, when & where

only what they need instead of taking things "just in case."

They scrutinize each item in their pack to minimize their pack weight. For normal three-season conditions (spring, summer, and fall), their pack—without food and water—usually weighs 15 pounds or less. However, ultimate hikers don't pack "stupid light": They realize that weight is only one important characteristic of gear, and that functionality, comfort, efficiency, durability, reliability, ease of use, value, and cost are all important too.

Their skill level is extremely high, enabling them to remain safe and comfortable despite carrying minimal gear and supplies, some of which demands a high level of skill to use properly. For example, they are able to carry an A-frame tarp instead of a heavy tent because they are adept at choosing campsites and achieving textbook-perfect pitches. And to avoid carrying too little or too much food, they have determined exactly how much they need based on their caloric consumption during previous trips.

Throughout the day they make constant forward progress ("CFP") toward a distant destination. The key is not walking fast but walking efficiently. These "dawn-to-duskers" leave camp early and pull into camp late; after an eight-hour recharge, they repeat. They use their data book, which is a bare-bones chart of distances between key landmarks, to monitor their pace the way runners watch their splits during a track workout.

Their trips are dominated by Type II Fun—not necessarily fun to do but fun to talk about later. They consider the physical and mental challenge of day-long hiking to be a valuable part of their backpacking experience.

Ultimate campers

Ultimate Campers are the antithesis of Ultimate Hikers:

Their primary objective is a non-hiking extracurricular activity such as birding, botanizing, photography, hunting, fishing, reading, journaling, backcountry cooking, befriending other hikers, and/or developing leadership skills.

They may be knowledgeable of the environmental and route conditions, but this knowledge is not critical—they can afford to take more than they need to ensure preparedness against anything that may come their way.

The weight of their gear and supplies is not a huge consideration since they do not carry it far. However, they don't pack "stupid heavy" by taking unnecessary junk that makes whatever hiking they do do much less enjoyable.

They may be skilled campers (or photographers or fishermen, etc.), but their other skills are unnecessary because they can carry gear and supplies that demand few skills to use properly. These foolproof items tend to be heavy.

part 1

Their daily itinerary is relatively relaxed. Although they sometimes jump out of camp in the morning to catch the hungriest fish or the earliest light, they ensure ample opportunities to nap and hang out. If they want to hike anywhere, they will usually drop all their stuff at a base camp and then carry day packs.

They prefer Type I Fun—fun to do and fun to talk about later. For them, backpacking should be leisure, not a challenge.

It was time to commit to one style or the other, I told my parents. If I wanted to stick to my original goal of thru-hiking the entire Appalachian Trail this summer—which would necessitate a pace of about 23 miles per day—I would need to morph into an Ultimate Hiker. For such an extreme goal, an extreme approach was needed. If I wanted to be an Ultimate Camper or to seek a balance between the two extremes, I would need to let go of this aspiration. Whichever choice I made, I was not forever locked into it—on future trips I could change it up.

"I figured you would have to make this decision at some point," said my mom, after I finished explaining my options. "Whatever you decide, make sure it's the right decision for you." Dad was almost out cold in his La-Z-Boy, which is his usual 9 p.m. routine, but he perked up enough to say, "I agree with your mom." As is customary, I told them when I expected to call next, and we hung up.

Campers-by-default

As I walked toward Hiawassee's outskirts so that I could hitch back to the trail, I also pondered how I would define my *current* approach to backpacking. Unlike an Ultimate Hiker, Ultimate Camper, or the happy medium, I hadn't really *chosen* this approach. And because my pack was so heavy, thus far the camping component of my trip had been the most enjoyable. Many of my fellow Appalachian Trail thru-hikers were in the same situation—the experience was more fun when we weren't hiking north.

I decided that I was a camper-by-default:

My primary objective of hiking the Appalachian Trail (AT) screamed "Ultimate Hiker," but I did not understand how this should have affected my approach to the trip in terms of my gear, supplies, and skills.

I had only a vague sense of the environmental and route conditions I would encounter along the trail. I did not know how cold it gets in the Smokies in May, how problematic the black bears are in New Jersey, or when the mosquitoes would hatch. Without knowing the conditions, I couldn't determine exactly what I needed, so I packed for every "what if" and "just in case" scenario, most extremely far-fetched. I erred on the side of caution by taking "everything but the . . . ," which is a much better Ben & Jerry's ice cream flavor than a backpacking load.

A camper (left) packs for in-camp comforts, whereas a hiker (right) packs light.

I did not understand the functions and limitations of backpacking equipment. For example, I didn't understand the nuances of "waterproof," "water resistant," and "waterproof-breathable" fabrics. I was ignorant of the pros and cons of goose down and synthetic insulations. I could not explain what I was purifying and filtering my water against (even though I was doing it) or how effective these treatments were.

Because I knew so little about gear, I had no choice but to blindly trust conventional wisdom while I was gearing up for my trip. I looked as if I had walked out of an outdoor retailer's mail-order catalog. I bought a double-wall tent, water filter pump, hard-sided 1-liter plastic water bottles, a full-length self-inflating sleeping pad, a compass with a sighting mirror, a 40-piece preassembled first aid kit, and an extensive cook set. Naturally, I carried my burden in a burly "bombproof" suspension pack that weighed *seven pounds when empty,* or about the same weight as my *entire kit* for trips in later years.

Outdoor magazines reviewed these products glowingly. Outdoor retail stores stocked them, and their employees never suggested I could wander onto the AT with anything less. Manufacturers appealed to my gullible consumer fears, uncertainties, and doubts with sexy full-page advertisements and rosy descriptions that claimed these were must-have, latest-and-greatest, best-selling products. These items were also the default choice among the outdoor education groups with which I'd been involved, including the Boy Scouts, Duke University's outdoor club, and two summer camps. It never occurred to me that if my backpacking trip involved hiking more than a few miles per day, that conventional wisdom was wrong and that I was being taken for a ride.

My skill level was very low, so my comfort and safety were dependent on the gear I carried on my back, not on the weightless backcountry knowledge I could carry between my ears. Even with all that gear, I still suffered from the mistakes I made. For example, I didn't know how to protect my food from bears and rodents, to find good campsites, to forecast the weather, to read a map, to load my backpack, to address basic health issues like macerated feet and sore muscles, or even how to start a fire.

So I began the AT with 40 ounces of stove fuel, despite knowing I would pass a general store that sold fuel on Day 3. During the climb out of Neel's Gap, I became dehydrated after bypassing the water spigots there and the spring at Rock Gap—I just didn't realize how much water I needed. In the Roan Highlands, I shivered through consecutive nights during an average cold spell. And I developed severe shin splints and knee pain that would have halted my progress were it not for regular 800-milligram doses of ibuprofen.

My daily itinerary was unfocused. I woke up late and camped early. I wasted too much time in trail towns. I hiked too fast in the morning and was burned out by the afternoon.

And my experience was dominated by Type III Fun—it wasn't fun to do, and it's not really fun to talk about now. Only a masochist would enjoy

as much suffering as I endured early in my AT thru-hike.

I was not ashamed of being a camper-by-default. None of my family members or close friends were experienced backpackers who could have reduced the gradient of my learning curve. But I knew that this status was not very compatible with walking a distance equivalent to 83 marathons. The numbers spoke for themselves: Of the roughly 2,000 thru-hikers who start the Appalachian Trail every year, an astounding 85 percent *stop* their trip somewhere short of Katahdin, the high point of Maine that serves as the trail's northern terminus. The field drops off precipitously: Some quit at the first road crossing, 30 miles in; many don't make it to Damascus, a classic trail town in southwest Virginia; and some find sufficient closure in Harpers Ferry, West Virginia, the psychological halfway point.

Some of those who stop prematurely probably discover that they need a more civilized existence that includes daily showers, a soft bed, and daily contact with loves ones. Some realize that they are in fact an Ultimate Camper, so a long-distance hike is not for them. Finally, some remain overloaded campers-by-default, and the task is simply too difficult to continue on. The remaining 15 percent of aspiring AT thru-hikers all realize that to enjoy the hiking component of their experience on their way to Katahdin, they need to become—or become more like—an Ultimate Hiker.

why, when & where

why I'm an ultimate hiker

This book should be relevant to anyone who wants to become — or become more like — an Ultimate Hiker. But it's worth asking oneself the question anyway: Why be an Ultimate Hiker, as opposed to an Ultimate Camper or something in between? My own motivation relates to the most important things in my life — relationships with nature, with others, and with myself.

Relationship with nature

Many assume that by hiking 30-plus miles a day, I must be going "too fast" to see anything. In fact, just the opposite is true. By walking at a comfortable pace of about three miles an hour from dawn to dusk, and by carrying a feather-weight pack, I can penetrate enormous swaths of deep wilderness, days away from the closest towns, roads, and trailheads. This has exposed me to remarkably beautiful scenes, notably the glacier-scoured bowls of Colorado's Front Range as seen from James Peak; the mountain-filled northeast horizon as seen from New Hampshire's Mount Moosilauke; and towering Mount McKinley while skiing down the snow-covered Muddy River.

Perhaps more important, hiking has both sparked and satisfied my curiosity about nature. Thru-hiking the Colorado Trail piqued my interest in the mountain pine beetle and in wildfire suppression. Walking along a service road for the 242-mile Colorado River Aqueduct prompted me to learn about the West's delicate water resources and infrastructure. Traveling off trail in Alaska and Yukon taught me about wildlife travel patterns.

Relationship with others

Solo long-distance trips — generally the type I prefer — admittedly limit relationship building. Still, in my case,

I think my parents and I have a better relationship because of my trips: I check in with them regularly and depend on them for logistical support. I also think that many chance, treasured interactions, with townspeople and others, have occurred because I was not traveling in a multiperson bubble.

But, indeed, multiperson hiking trips are better for developing relationships with others. Members of a group who share a challenging objective and depend heavily on one another for success and survival will bond better than those who don't. On challenging group trips—like the Sierra High Route with Buzz Burrell and the Alaska Mountain Wilderness Classic race with Bobby Schnell and Chris Robertson—my partners felt more like brothers than just teammates.

On a hiking trip, routines like work, housekeeping, and TV watching don't get between people. Earlier this summer, several weekend trips helped to save my relationship with my girlfriend, who rightly felt that this book was getting in our way. Sharing a steaming pot of tortellini and dehydrated cream sauce before retiring to a floorless tarp was not terribly romantic, but it was a refreshing break from the demands that were preoccupying me.

Relationship with oneself

This relationship is actually a prerequisite for the others. If I'm truer to myself, I'm in a better position to give. My trips give me reasons to wake up in the morning. I have maps to study, passes to reach, wildlife to watch. I have a goal that demands focus and energy. My mind and body seem to work in a heightened state—a natural caffeine-like high.

Ambitious itineraries give me a chance to explore my mental and physical limits. Can I walk from Georgia to Maine? Can I average 33 miles a day for seven months? Can I ski, hike, and packraft 4,700 miles around Alaska and the Yukon without making a fatal mistake? I didn't know until I tried. My "game face" is usually broken during these monumental efforts. The most recent example occurred in the Canadian Arctic during a 657-mile, 24-day stretch without crossing a road or seeing another human. After finding the migration trail of the Porcupine caribou, I began to cry uncontrollably, realizing that in this vast and untamed wilderness, I was like them: While being tortured by hellacious mosquitoes, soaked by torrential rains, and stalked by grizzlies and wolves, we were all trying to stay *moving,* and we slept and ate only to continue our constant forward progress.

The skills I have learned out there, like good decision-making and resourcefulness, also serve me well in the Land of the Soft. But perhaps the most important thing I return with is humility—recognition that natural powers are at work that I will never control or fully understand, and that will prevail long after I am gone.

why, when & where

17

tried&true

how to hike "fast"

"Fast" hikers can average up to about 40 miles per day for the length of a long-distance trail. Each of their days can be reduced to the equation *Distance = Rate x Time,* where *Distance = Miles per Day* (MPD), *Rate = Miles per Hour* (MPH), and *Time = Hours per Day* (HPD). To become a fast hiker (i.e., more MPD), then, you must hike quicker or hike longer.

Increase your MPH

To increase my miles per hour, I can:

Work harder. At my *optimal* hiking speed, I am hiking as fast as I can without overexerting myself. This effort is physically sustainable every day, for a trip of infinite length. If I'm below this pace, I can work harder to reach it; but if I'm already at this pace, then working harder is feasible only in the short term. If I continue to overexert myself, I will get injured or become chronically fatigued, or I will exceed my tolerance for Type III Fun, which is "not fun to do and not fun to talk about later."

Lighten up. I hike faster when I carry less, especially in mountainous terrain. So I keep my backpack feathery light and I avoid carrying extra body mass, which is just as much of a spare tire.

Increase your HPD

However, the secret of hiking "fast" is *hiking for many hours per day.* I'm a tortoise, not a hare; my motto is "constant forward progress" (CFP). There are four ways to increase my HPD:

Focus on my pre-trip training. I prepare my muscles, tendons, feet, lungs, and heart for day-long physical activity. If I'm fresh off the couch or just out the office door, I'm instead forced to get in shape "on the trail" by starting slow and building up.

Improve efficiency of nonhiking tasks. I try to leave camp within 15 minutes of waking up. I keep oft-needed items within easy reach so that I don't have to take off my backpack. I've been known to pee while walking. I ship myself food and supplies to avoid time-consuming shopping in towns. And I try to avoid taking days off in towns by limiting my stays to 24 hours, and usually less than 4.

Seize the morning. If I rise early and hike "12 by 10" or even "20 by 12"—as in 20 miles by 12 p.m.—then I have more flexibility in the afternoon. With most of my work already done for the day, I can relax, or I can put in a super-high-mileage day to get ahead of schedule. But if I dillydally, I must spend the rest of the day playing catch-up.

Expect a challenge. A "fast" hike is rewarding and satisfying, but it's not a vacation. It can be very taxing mentally and exhausting physically. I embrace these additional difficulties as an integral part of my trip, on a par with wildlife encounters and scenic vistas.

why, when & where

 To get an extra oomph in your stride, use trekking poles. They allow your arms to help propel you forward and upward during climbs, and to brake on descents.

know before you go

A six-week hike on the Pacific Crest Trail (PCT), starting at the U.S.–Mexico border on June 6, sounded hot to me. But I had spent very little time in southern California and I didn't know exactly how hot, so I didn't know how to prepare. What clothing system and sleeping bag would be best? How much water capacity should I have? Would the daytime heat force me to become nocturnal?

Not knowing where to look for temperature information, I sent questions to the PCT-List, an e-mail forum: "What will be the average high and low temperatures, at the lowest and highest elevations? What about extreme temperatures?" And so on. Ten minutes later, I received a response: "Temperatures, with mean and standard deviation for both highs and lows, can be obtained from a number of stations right along the trail from the Western Regional Climate Center at *www.wrcc.dri.edu.*"

This was not the specific information for which I'd hoped. But in retrospect, this unspecific reply was much more valuable because it forced me to find the data on my own. And that quick lesson in self-reliance has served me well ever since.

Before venturing into an unfamiliar territory or season, I research the conditions so that I can make informed choices that will maximize my comfort and safety. It is obvious in theory that I should prepare differently for a three-day trip in October in New York's Adirondacks than for a seven-day trip in March in Joshua Tree National Park, for example. But by doing some pretrip homework, I can identify exactly how my needs are different, so that I avoid being over-, under-, or mis-prepared.

I consult climate databases, topographical maps, satellite images, guidebooks, backpacking websites and forums, public land agencies, trip reports (both historical and recent), and pictures. I also touch base with knowledgeable backcountry users like park rangers, outfitters, bush pilots, and other experienced backpackers who can share insights that are unavailable elsewhere. By picking up the phone or sending them an e-mail, I might

Renowned Alaskan wilderness hiker Roman Dial summits Aerial Peak.

learn about an unmapped spring, a fast game trail, a surprisingly strong tidal current, or the feasibility of a dicey-looking pass.

Below I've listed environmental and route conditions that affect my gear choices and ways to find information about them. See also Part 3 (pp. 192–215) for a selection of sample gear lists.

Temperatures

I plan most of my trips—that is, all but local and spontaneous outings— long before an accurate weather forecast is available, so when preparing, I instead rely on historical temperature data collected at weather stations near my route. The reliability of a seven-day forecast is often questionable anyway, and quickly becomes irrelevant during a multiweek or multimonth trip. In the United States, this data is held by the National Climatic Data Center (NCDC), a branch of the National Oceanic and Atmospheric Administration (NOAA); it is available from the Center's website or on consumer-oriented websites like *www.wunderground.com*. Regional and local climate centers (e.g., the Western Regional Climate Center [WRCC] and the Mount Washington Observatory) may have additional information.

Before a multimonth trip I collect notes about resupply towns, seasonal water sources, and many other things in a Word document "guidebook."

why, when & where

Factor in elevation

Suppose I was planning a one-week trip to Grand Canyon National Park in early May. Weather Underground shows historical average low and high temperatures of about 30°F and 70°F and extreme temperatures of about 15°F and 80°F. However, these observations were reported at the Grand Canyon Airport, which is on the South Rim at an elevation of about 6,500 feet, and most of my route is planned along the Tonto Platform at about 4,000 feet. Because the temperature changes by about 3 degrees for every 1,000 vertical feet, my route will actually be about 7.5 degrees warmer on average. This would produce expected average lows in the high 30s and average highs in the high 70s.

Suppose my trip also includes a one-night stay at Phantom Ranch, an outpost at the bottom of the Grand Canyon at an elevation of 2,500 feet. Conveniently, there is a NOAA weather station near Phantom Ranch; its recordings are available from the WRCC website. In early May, average temperatures near Phantom Ranch are about 60°F and 90°F, with extremes of 35°F and 105°F.

Precipitation

My clothing and shelter, the types of materials I use (e.g., polyester or wool base layers, goose down or synthetic insulation), and water availability will all be affected by the amount and frequency of precipitation I can expect during a trip.

When conditions might be 35 degrees and raining, I gear up and prepare myself mentally to be cold and wet.

part 1

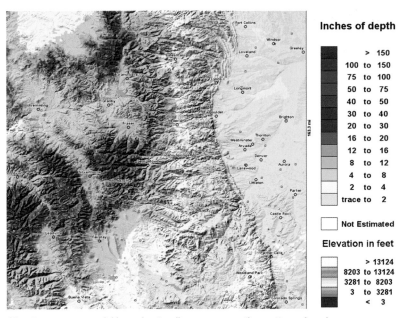

Inches of depth
> 150
100 to 150
75 to 100
50 to 75
40 to 50
30 to 40
20 to 30
16 to 20
12 to 16
8 to 12
4 to 8
2 to 4
trace to 2
Not Estimated

Elevation in feet
> 13124
8203 to 13124
3281 to 8203
3 to 3281
< 3

Climate maps are useful in understanding macro weather patterns for a large area.

Precipitation data is usually available alongside temperature data. At the WRCC website, I see that average precipitation in May at the Grand Canyon Airport is only 0.6 inch, and at Phantom Ranch, a mere 0.3 inch.

If instead of a one-week trip in the Grand Canyon I was planning to thru-hike the Arizona Trail—which runs north–south across the entire state— it would be more informative and time-efficient to view color-coded precipitation geographic information system (GIS) maps of the entire state. These are available in the Climate Atlas of the United States, last published by NOAA in 1983 and now available on CD-ROM. The WRCC has a similar map on its website: *www.wrcc.dri.edu/pcpn/az.gif.* In addition to precipitation maps, the Climate Atlas also has temperature and snowfall maps.

Daylight

On summer trips, there is enough daylight to hike for 15 to 16 hours per day, which I've found to be my sustainable limit. If I'm not hiking at night, I only need a low-powered light for camp chores. And I can depend on my accelerated metabolism to keep me warm, instead of on warm clothing and a sleeping bag. Winter trips call for a high-powered light for hiking after dark, as well as warmer equipment.

Complete sun and moon data for U.S. cities and worldwide waypoints is available at the Naval Oceanography Portal, at the U.S. Naval Meteorology and Oceanography Command website.

why, when & where

Ground cover

I choose different footwear for the East's leaf-covered trails than for the Southwest's soilless rocky ground. My mileage goals are less ambitious if I expect to be stumbling over Arctic tussocks, climbing over fallen ancient redwood trees, or slipping on eastern Montana's gumbo mud. If trail quality, signage, and maintenance are poor, I will bring better navigational aids and more protective clothing. And I may need skis, snowshoes, or crampons for flotation or traction on Colorado's winter snowpack or for lingering snowfields on the John Muir Trail.

Quantitative information on topsoil composition is not very useful, and I've also never found a comprehensive resource for it anyway. Instead, I look at pictures and read descriptions of my planned route. Pictures of the Hoh River Trail in Olympic National Park, for example, show a well-established footpath through a temperate rain forest, the floor of which is topped with abundant and soft forest duff.

The most comprehensive data about snow coverage is found in the National Snow Analyses, provided by the National Operational Hydrologic Remote Sensing Center, a program of the National Weather Service. In the West, additional data is available through the Natural Resources Conservation Service, a program of the Department of Agriculture, which maintains 600-plus SNOTEL (short for "snow telemetry") sensors that collect temperature, precipitation, snow depth, and other data. Most of

the sensors are in remote mountain watersheds, including many prime backpacking locales; real-time and historical data is available. In addition to the SNOTEL sites, California's Department of Water Resources conducts its own snow surveys; current and historical data and data plots are available on its website.

The National Snow Analyses is an excellent resource during the winter. For example, if I want to go cross-country skiing on Forest Service roads in Colorado's high country during the hit-or-miss month of November, I can use the snow coverage maps to ensure that I don't end up skiing on rocks. However, I've found that the Snow Analyses is less useful for predicting early-season mountain conditions, which are extremely dynamic and variable.

Vegetation

For information about vegetation density and types, I look at my topographical maps (which often depict vegetation with green shading), analyze satellite imagery, and find pictures and descriptions posted online. It also helps to have a basic understanding of what types of vegetation are commonly found in an area. When I was planning my first trip to Alaska, I read reports by Alaska Mountain Wilderness Classic racers who had done the Hope-to-Homer and Eureka-to-Talkeetna routes. I scanned Landsat images of the Kenai Peninsula to find walkable beaches and the "brush zone," a quagmire that separates

part 1

When traveling at high elevations and/or on reflective surfaces, sun protection is critical.

why, when & where

forests from alpine zones. And I called Bretwood Higman and Erin McKittrick, who had done a route between Homer and Seward that was similar to the one I was planning.

Sun exposure

During my first trip along the Continental Divide through Colorado, I got scorched. My route was mostly above 11,000 feet and entirely in alpine terrain; it was a sunny weekend in June, and lingering snowfields reflected the sun so well that even my hamstrings badly burned. I wisely wore sunglasses and stayed well hydrated, but I should have worn more clothing and sunscreen.

The amount of sun exposure is a function of cloud cover, vegetation, elevation, surface reflectivity, and the strength of the sun (which depends on the time of day and year). These details can be obtained from topographical maps and other aforementioned resources. Cloud cover data is available in the Climate Atlas of the United States. National maps show that the "mean percentage of possible sunshine" in January is a gloomy 30 to 40 percent in the Great Lakes states, compared to 70 to 80 percent in sunny southern California.

Water availability

Springs and creeks are marked on topographical maps. In the East, water sources are generally reliable, except during exceptional droughts. In the West, however, many water sources dry up during the arid summer months. Before relying on a water source marked on a map, consult someone who has personal familiarity with the landscape, and check guidebooks and online trip reports for past observations.

"Water reports" are available for several long-distance trails, including the southern sections of the Pacific Crest Trail (PCT) and Continental Divide Trail, plus the entire Arizona Trail and Hayduke Trail. In the case of the PCT, the water chart is updated several times a week during peak thru-hiker season by a volunteer who collects observations via e-mail and online posts.

Wildlife & insects

The possible presence of audacious or dangerous animals—like mice, raccoons, bears, and snakes— affects how and whether I protect my food, where I cook and camp, where and when I walk, and whether I carry anything for personal defense. If not somehow mitigated, relentless swarms of mosquitoes, black flies, and no-see-ums (or gnats) can completely ruin a trip. Bites from poisonous spiders, scorpions, fire ants, and disease-carrying bugs and ticks can have longer-lasting and more serious consequences.

If wildlife or insects are a concern, land managers usually post relevant information on their websites. The National Park Service, for example, has posted food storage regulations for Yosemite National Park to help keep bears at bay. The Bureau of Land Management warns about rattlesnakes in Grand

Porcupines and other "mini bears," such as mice and squirrels, will eat gear and food that is left unattended in high-use campsites.

Staircase-Escalante National Monument. And the National Forest Service reports that the black fly season in New Hampshire's White Mountains is between late spring and early summer. For more, or more nuanced explanation, I might call land managers or find other online resources like blogs and community forums.

With particular regard to insects, I've learned there are no hard rules. An unusually cold spring may delay the first hatch, for example. I've also encountered hellacious bugs where other backpackers did not (and vice versa) because I was apparently there at the worst time of the worst day of the worst year.

Remoteness

If something unexpected happens or if something goes wrong—like if I get caught in a freak spring snowstorm, come down with awful diarrhea, or have a group member break a wrist after stumbling on talus—I may need to self-rescue, to depend on others to assist me out, and/or to apply extended medical treatment. Before I leave the trailhead, I should know what types of communication devices have reliable coverage; how likely it is that I will be found by another backcountry user; how long it would take for a search and rescue team to be mobilized; and how far it is to the closest road or town.

To gauge the remoteness of my route, I look at topographical maps and the coverage maps of mobile phone and satellite companies. I speak with land managers, recreation businesses, county law enforcement agencies, and/or other backpackers. I have even researched the frequency of flights over an area. I hope this information never proves valuable, but I would be thankful to have it if the unexpected happens.

Natural hazards

The outdoors is not as dangerous as typically portrayed by sensationalist media stoking fear of the unknown. Nonetheless, people do get sick and injured out there, sometimes fatally. Natural hazards include unpredictable mountain weather, technical rock faces, crevasses, contaminated backcountry water sources, large bodies of water, and avalanches.

Avalanches occur mostly in the West, where the snowpack and terrain are more conducive to them, and mostly between the months of November and April. Several Northeast peaks—notably New Hampshire's Mount Washington—have avalanche-prone terrain, but it's generally a smaller concern there. A list of public and private avalanche monitoring agencies is available at *www.avalanche.org.* Every western state, except for Nevada and New Mexico, is served by at least one avalanche center that produces daily or weekly bulletins discussing current conditions and speculating about future ones; there is also an agency for New Hampshire's Mount Washington.

why, when & where

part ②

tools &

techniques

30 CLOTHING

64 FOOTWEAR

80 SLEEPING BAGS & PADS

90 SHELTERS

112 MAPS & NAVIGATION

122 TREKKING POLES

128 FOOD

136 COOKING SYSTEMS

150 WATER

162 SMALL ESSENTIALS

176 PACKING

On my earliest trips, I struggled to find the most appropriate backpacking tools and to learn critical techniques. But through extensive trial and error and research—i.e., I got geeky—I began to understand hiking gear's underlying technologies, pros and cons, best uses and limitations, plus some associated skills (e.g., how to find a good campsite). In this section I share my experiences and observations, and I recommend specific products that meet my standards for functionality, weight, durability, efficiency, ease of use, and value. But this comprehensiveness should be kept in context. I consider these topics as merely means to 1) achieving my trip objectives and 2) remaining safe and comfortable in the conditions I am likely to encounter (see Part 1).

Northern lights glow over a North American boreal forest.

clothing

As you'd expect in Michigan in January, it had been a long and cold night—almost 14 hours of darkness, and a nighttime low of about minus 20°F. The inside of my shelter and the top of my sleeping bag were coated with frozen moisture from my breathing. I knew even before I unzipped my cozy sleeping bag that the shortcomings of my clothing system would be especially glaring this morning.

I needed my puffy jacket and overmitts to be puffier and warmer, and for the jacket to have a hood. I needed my third pair of pants to be insulated, not merely waterproof. And I needed to find a face mask that would prevent frostbite on my nose and cheeks without restricting my breathing or frosting up.

Almost every time that I have traveled in a new environment, as on this Michigan trip, or by a new style, I have learned what clothing works and what does not through trial and error. On the Appalachian Trail, I learned that "water-resistant" rain gear is insufficient for cold and wet conditions. On my first desert trip, the intense sun baked the skin left exposed by my short-sleeve shirt and running shorts. During a two-day cold October rainstorm in Colorado's San Juan Mountains, I learned the value of warm and waterproof handwear; lacking it, my fingertips tingled for the next four weeks. And while walking along Alaska's Lost Coast, I learned that fleece retains its warmth when wet much better than a synthetic-insulated jacket.

Because I regularly hike for 14 to 16 hours per day, I rely more on my clothing than on any other product category to help keep me comfortable. I can't just jump into my shelter and crank up my stove when conditions deteriorate. I need my clothing to help keep me cool when it's hot, warm when it's cold and windy, dry when it's wet, and sane when the bugs are insane; it also has to protect me against a scorching sun and abrasive brush.

My clothing is also a critical part of my sleeping and shelter systems. By wearing my clothing to bed at night, I can use a lighter sleeping bag. And depending on the vulnerability of my clothing to moisture, I bring a shelter that offers more or less protection.

Layering

All-day and all-night comfort is rarely possible with a single outfit. Instead, I need a clothing system composed of layers that can be easily adjusted in accordance with changes in both my metabolism and the weather. A layering system needs to be comprehensive enough to serve me through huge swings in conditions. But it also needs to be lightweight and packable.

A full layering system has three components, and each component has a primary purpose:

> Base layers (e.g., a merino wool shirt) manage perspiration;
> Insulation (e.g., a down-filled parka) provides warmth; and
> Shells (e.g., a water-resistant wind shirts) protect against precipitation and/or wind.

The chart on p. 32 outlines my entire layering system for a recent summer trip in the Colorado Rockies. You may find yourself asking, "That's it?" The answer is, why, yes, that is it. On another trip, this clothing system might be too little—or too much—but for the conditions I encountered, it was perfect.

Seldom do I *wear* my entire clothing system. Also, sometimes I do not carry a full layering system. For example, if I had gone to Death Valley National Park instead of Colorado, I probably would have left my insulated layers at home and just relied on the warmth of my base layers and shells.

Base layers

Backpacking in the nude has its proponents, but personally I've never found it very comfortable and the conditions oftentimes don't permit it anyway. Instead, I wear a base layer top and base layer bottoms as next-to-skin garments that:

> Manage moisture that originates internally (i.e., perspiration) or

Your clothing system should reflect the environmental and route conditions you will likely encounter during your trip. Here: cool temps, no shade, and lingering snowfields.

tools & techniques

externally (e.g., precipitation or a river ford) by preventing it from accumulating against my skin;

> Protect my skin against sun, brush, bugs, and backpack-caused chafing; and
> Provide some warmth and modesty.

It is remarkable how little clothing I need to wear when I'm warmed up and moving. For example, I have cross-country skied in Colorado and Alaska wearing just a long-sleeve shirt and tights, despite temperatures in the mid-teens. When my base layers alone are not warm enough, I put my insulation and shell layers over them.

A base layer works by wicking moisture away from my skin and dispersing it so that it can evaporate more quickly into the atmosphere, possibly through outer layers first. In *hot conditions,* this process helps to

keep me cool by encouraging evaporative heat loss. And in *cooler conditions,* this process helps to keep me warm by preventing conductive heat loss. If my base layers allow moisture to build up against my skin, I could either overheat (because my skin can't cool down) or I may become chilled (because the moisture is pulling heat away from my body).

To be an effective base layer, a fabric should:

> Be made of hydrophobic (or non-absorbent) fibers;
> Not retain water between its fibers; and
> Permit the passage of water vapor through it, i.e., it should be "breathable."

Base layer garments optimized for *warm conditions* should ventilate

A Sample Layering System: The Rockies in Summer

component	item and description	weight (oz)
base layer	**Long-sleeve shirt:** merino wool (150 g/m²), chest zip	8
	Boxer briefs: polyester/spandex blend	2
	Trekking pants: 85% nylon/15% spandex blend	10
insulation	**Parka:** hooded, 800-fill-power goose down insulation	14
	Gloves: 400-weight fleece	3
shell	**Wind jacket:** hooded, ultralight polyester, water-resistant	4
	Rain jacket: waterproof/breathable, minimal features	8
total:		3 lb 1 oz

What about "extra" clothes?

I never carry an "extra" set of clothes. Instead, I keep my sole set clean through regular washings, and I keep it dry by using my shell garments appropriately.

I do, however, sometimes carry a set of "sleeping" clothes if I am concerned that my daytime clothes could unavoidably become soaked. In this case, the comfort and warmth of sleeping clothes—and a good night's rest—justify the weight.

Don't bring them.

well—via chest zips, loose arm sleeves, and a wide neck—to encourage the exchange of cooler outside air with trapped warmer air. Base layers optimized for *cooler conditions* should minimize ventilation—via a form-fitting cut—to maximize insulation.

Fibers & fabrics

Polyester, merino wool, and nylon are the most popular base layer fibers; cotton is useful in limited situations too. Silk and polypropylene, which were once common, are now seldom used.

Fibers can be mixed. Nylon can be added for durability; cotton for hand, breathability, and odor resistance; and spandex for stretch and fit, though it also noticeably increases the fabric's water retention and dry time, and it tends to lose its elasticity over time.

Despite the claim that "cotton kills," cotton is probably used more often for active pursuits than any other fiber. On my first real hikes—which included climbs of New Hampshire's Mount Washington, the highest peak in the Northeast—I wore an all-cotton outfit. I certainly noticed that this fiber failed

to prevent moisture from building up against my skin, but for these short trips, cotton worked okay. Plus, I already owned a lot of it. But cotton's high rate of water absorption and retention makes it impractical for most extended outings. The one exception is in extreme dry heat, when prolonged heat loss through conduction and evaporation is actually desirable.

In college, I stopped using cotton as a base layer fiber when I discovered polyester; I later discovered merino wool and nylon, too. These three fibers each have pros and cons, and I use them all depending on the situation.

Polyester is a kind of oil-based polymer that is used to make plastic bottles, canoes, LCD displays, and tire reinforcements. It's also the most popular fabric for base layer clothing. Well-known polyester base layer fabrics include Invista's Coolmax, Polartec's Power Dry, Patagonia's Capilene, and Under Armour's HeatGear. I have found that the performance of a polyester base layer—and, for that matter, wool and nylon

tools & techniques

33

too—is mostly dependent on the fabric's weight, weave, and blend, plus the garment's fit and styling. The specific manufacturer is mostly irrelevant.

Polyester has several excellent qualities:

> It will absorb just 0.4 percent of its weight in water (though it can retain quite a bit more than that by trapping moisture *between the fibers*). So it tends to be excellent at wicking moisture away from skin, and it dries very quickly after becoming damp or wet.
> It can be woven into silklike weights, which are perfect when barely-there skin protection is needed, like against a scorching sun.
> It is relatively inexpensive. High-performance polyester T-shirts retail

for just $20, and discounted over-stock is always available.

Merino wool is the main alternative to polyester. It was popularized as an outdoor fiber by SmartWool in the 1990s, and is now also available from Ibex, Icebreaker, and Patagonia. Merino wool is a classification of sheep wool based on its diameter; the wool used in most base layers is 17 to 19 microns and sourced in New Zealand. (A micron is one-millionth of a meter. The average human hair is about 100 microns.) Unlike the coarse wool (25+ microns) used to make carpets and inexpensive sweaters—which leads some to think they have a wool allergy—merino wool is soft and not itchy.

Merino wool has a number of advantages over polyester:

	polyester	merino wool
source	Oil	Sheep
common use	Base layers	Base layers
moisture management performance	Excellent. Fibers do not absorb water. Fabric wicks well, dries fast, and is very breathable.	Good. Fibers absorb more water than poly. But this fabric feels less clammy when wet and is also very breathable.
odor resistance	Awful	Excellent
cold-and-wet performance	Worst. Significant conductive heat loss when wet.	Best. Fibers absorb some water, so moisture is not in direct contact with skin.
cost	Least expensive	Most expensive
durability	Good	Fair

part 2

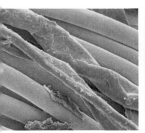 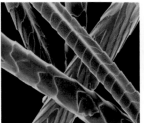 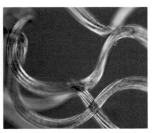

| Polyester | Merino wool | Nylon |

> It is naturally antimicrobial, and therefore much more odor-resistant. That is not to say I don't have noticeable body odor after a few weeks without a shower, but my merino wool layers don't have an offensive odor of their own. By comparison, every polyester base layer I have used—even those with anti-funk treatments—reeks after a mere 30-minute trail run, never mind a multiday outing.

VS nylon

Oil

"Desert" and "travel" shirts, trekking pants

Does not wick or dry as well as poly but better than merino wool. Tightly woven fabric breathes poorly.

Fair

Similar to polyester

Moderate

Best

> It feels less clammy against my skin. This is because of a wool fiber's construction. The cortex (the inner core) absorbs about one-third of its weight in water, but the cuticle (its outer sheath) is hydrophobic. So when merino wool gets wet, the cortex absorbs the moisture (until it is saturated), and the cuticle feels dry against skin. By contrast, a polyester fiber repels moisture, so the moisture stays on the fiber surfaces and between the fibers, where it can come in direct contact with skin.

> Wet wool is warmer than wet polyester because less moisture is in direct contact with skin— it gets absorbed into the cortex. However, wet wool is *not* as warm as dry wool.

In many situations I've been in, staying dry has been impossible, even with the fastest-drying base layer ever created. A tropical storm in Quebec's Chic-Choc Mountains and a splashy packrafting trip down the John River in Gates of the Arctic National Park come to mind. In these situations, wool is the safest, most comfortable bet.

tools & techniques

Merino wool has three main drawbacks:

> It is more expensive than polyester. A simple merino wool T-shirt retails for about $60, and fewer manufacturers unload excess inventory.
> It develops holes with use, especially in high-abrasion areas like around the shoulders. Polyester is slightly better in this regard.
> It cannot be woven into silklike weights, making it too warm for high temperatures. I've heard 80°F used as a cutoff; others insist that polyester is no better above such temperatures.

Nylon, like polyester, is an oil-based polymer. It does not manage moisture as well, but it is more durable and abrasion-resistant. The nylon fabrics used in outdoor clothing are often tightly woven, which improves bug and wind resistance but also makes the fabrics stuffy because of poor breathability. Supposedly, the tight weave also improves sun protection, but the benefit seems negligible—I have never been burned while wearing even a silk-weight polyester shirt.

Fabric weights

Base layer fabrics are available in various thicknesses. Manufacturers may describe the different weights

how 2
choose a base layer weight

1 Determine the warmest conditions that will be encountered during the trip.

2 Consider the amount of body heat produced during maximum exertion, e.g., running versus hiking versus fishing.

3 Choose the fabric weight that will be most comfortable when you are simultaneously at maximum exertion and in the warmest conditions. If you select a layer that is too heavy, you will overheat and need to either slow down or strip down to bare skin. If you select a layer that is too light, then you will always need a secondary layer to stay warm enough. It'd just be simpler to have one layer.

tip Because of nylon's poor ventilation, designers often add mesh panels along the arms and down the torso sides; these are helpful but not as effective as a looser knit fabric.

as "lightweight," "mid-weight," or "expedition weight," or they may use numerical classifications, like Patagonia's Capilene 1, 2, 3, and 4. For an apples-to-apples comparison across manufacturers and fiber types, however, it's necessary to know the exact fabric weight per square area. For example, Capilene 1 weighs 3.4 oz per square yard, and Capilene 4 weighs 6 oz per square yard.

Thicker fabrics provide more insulation than thinner ones. But the fabric's weight also affects its moisture retention. A thicker fabric will retain more water because there are *more fibers* to absorb moisture, and there are *more spaces between fibers* where moisture can be trapped.

However, a thicker fabric will also be more effective in preventing moisture from building up against the skin, because it can "hide" more water than can a lightweight fabric, which will feel clammy against the skin with even the smallest amount of moisture.

skurka'spicks
BASE LAYERS

When it's really buggy, I wear a nylon long-sleeve shirt and nylon trekking pants. Insects struggle to bite through the tight weave, and a permethrin-based treatment like Insect Shield is an added deterrent. My nylon body armor performed admirably in the Yukon Arctic, where the mosquitoes were so intense that I would have eaten food through my head net if I could have. Only about five bugs bit me over a hellacious three-week span.

Nylon pants must fit well: I'm greatly annoyed by a loose waistband, restrictive movement, and baggy lower legs that tangle in brush. Pants with a small spandex content (15 percent-ish) have better range of motion than pure nylon, which has no natural stretch.

If I never expect to remove my nylon pants, I will wear polyester/

This three-piece layering system (base/layer/shell) will keep me comfortable across a wide range of conditions, from sunny and warm to cold and wet.

tools & techniques

spandex boxer briefs. If I may some-times want to have shorts, I wear compression shorts underneath the pants. They are more socially acceptable when used as shorts than boxer briefs are.

If it is not buggy, I wear either polyester or merino wool. For done-in-a-day pursuits like day hikes, trail runs, and bike rides, I usually wear polyester base layer shirts. I can own a drawer full of them without breaking the bank, and I can wash them after every use to eliminate their funk. For a backpacking trip, however, I prefer merino wool.

In temperatures above 50°F or so, I wear a short-sleeve, light-weight merino wool shirt, unless the sun exposure is considerable or I am traveling off trail, in which case I wear a lightweight long-sleeve to better protect my arms. I like both shirts to have chest zippers and a long torso so that they won't ride up and cause my lower back to chafe.

As long as I am hiking on trail and sun exposure is moderate, I wear polyester running shorts with a built-in liner, which is sim-pler and cooler than a separate pair of underwear. They feature superb ventilation; they wick moisture extremely well; they dry very quickly; and they do not inhibit my stride. If I was uncomfortable in such short shorts, I would consider longer run-ning shorts or a hiking kilt (for men) or a running skirt (for women).

If I'm off trail or if the sun expo-sure is intense, I wear nylon trek-king pants.

In temperatures below freezing, I wear a long-sleeve, formfitting, mid-weight merino wool shirt like the **Ibex Hooded Indie** ($92, 10 oz). This shirt's integrated thumb loops insulate my draft-prone wrists, and its integrated hood is more easily accessible and harder to lose than a separate beanie or balaclava.

For bottoms, I wear full-length polyester/spandex tights, which are warmer and easier to layer over than nylon pants, in conjunction with polyester/spandex boxer briefs or compression shorts.

When I travel with a slower moving group in cooler weather, I may take heavier base layers because I rarely reach my maximum exertion level and therefore cannot depend as heavily on body heat to keep me warm.

Insulation

During rest stops and in camp, I wear insulated layers over my base layers to stay warm. Once I resume hiking, I wait until I've warmed up before tak-ing them off. Only once have I regu-larly worn insulated clothing despite being at maximum exertion—dur-ing the first two weeks of my Alaska-Yukon Expedition, while skiing down Alaska's windy Arctic west coast in temperatures as low as -25°F. My insulated layers are also a critical part of my sleep system.

Insulation reduces convective heat loss by trapping body heat within tiny chambers formed by the insula-tion's fibers as it tries to escape into

 **By wearing insulated layers at night too I can take a lighter sleeping bag. An added perk: I don't have to change into cold clothes in the morning.**

the cooler outside air. Note: Insulated clothing and sleeping bags use identical materials and function identically. Instead of repeating this exact information later on in this text, I will discuss both product categories in this section.

Wool & fleece

Coarse wool garments were once the most popular insulating layer, but in the 1980s, they were replaced by polar fleece, which is:

> More thermally efficient, i.e., warmer for its weight;
> Less itchy; and,
> More hydrophobic, because it is made of polyethylene terephthalate (aka PET, the same material from which milk jugs are made).

Like base layer fabrics, fleece is available in various thicknesses. The standard is 300-weight fleece, which weighs about 8.8 oz/yd^2, or 300 g/m^2.

For cold and wet conditions like those commonly encountered in the Pacific Northwest and the Scottish Highlands, fleece is a universal favorite. Its performance resembles a polyester base layer's—in terms of wicking and water retention—but it is warmer. A wind- and water-resistant membrane can be integrated into fleece fabric (e.g., Gore-Tex Windstopper),

but doing so adds weight and cost, reduces breathability, and increases moisture retention.

Fleece is also used to make summer-weight sleeping bags, like the one I used during the hottest sections of my Appalachian Trail hike. These bags are cheap, lightweight, and sufficiently warm.

High-loft down & synthetics

In *purely cold* conditions, fleece and wool are outperformed by high-loft insulated jackets and pants that sandwich goose down or synthetic-fill insulation between lightweight shell fabrics. These "puffies" are:

> More thermally efficient;
> More compressible; and
> More resistant to wind and precipitation.

The thermal superiority of high-loft outerwear is significant. Today's high-end synthetic insulations are about three times as warm as 300-weight fleece per weight, and goose down is about five times warmer. However, moisture can undermine the thermal superiority of puffies, which absorb more water and lose more of their warmth when wet when compared with fleece.

tools & techniques

	wool	VS fleece
thermal efficiency	Fair	Fair
wet weather performance	Fair. It gets heavy because it absorbs moisture, but it retains some insulating ability.	Good. It absorbs little moisture, so it retains most of its insulating ability.
compressibility	Poor	Poor
life span	Good	Good
cost	High	Low

Goose down is a soft and fluffy cluster of filaments that is found underneath a goose's feathers. Down is measured by "fill power"—technically, the spatial displacement (in cubic inches) for a single ounce of down. Hence, one ounce of 700-fill-power down will displace 700 cubic inches. Although 800-fill-power down is considered premium, some manufacturers tout 800+, 850, and even 900 fill power. Low-budget puffies and sleeping bags will feature 600- or 650-fill-power down.

To ensure even warmth, down is contained within a garment or sleeping bag by numerous *baffles,* or chambers between the outside and inside shell fabric. Stitch-through baffles are the simplest and least material-intensive, but heat escapes where the shell fabrics are sewn together; these baffles are commonly found on lightweight jackets and parkas. Sleeping bags and winter-worthy parkas feature advanced-construction baffles like box wall, shingle, and wave.

Synthetic insulations fall into two categories:

> Cut staples, which consist of many short fibers, each about two inches long. The fibers mingle together to create air-trapping pockets. Because the fibers can move independently, these insulations tend to be soft and compressible, but over time, they tend to move around, causing clumps, uneven warmth,

To keep insulated outerwear and bags dry, use a waterproof pack liner. Dry it in the sun every few days and use a shelter with good ventilation.

VS synthetic fill VS goose down

synthetic fill	goose down
Good. Premium brands are comparable to low-grade down.	Excellent. It's up to about 50% warmer than synthetics.
Fair. It's less affected by moisture than down but still loses warmth when wet.	Poor. Its filaments absorb humidity and lose insulating value when wet.
Good	Excellent
Poor	Good
Low to moderate, depending on fill quality.	Moderate to high, depending on fill quality.

and permanent compression. This movement must be controlled by quilting or by using a scrim layer (an ultralight sheet of reinforcement fabric), both of which add weight and bulk.

> Continuous filaments, which consist of an extremely long single fiber that interlocks with itself. These insulations are stiffer and less compressible, but they are not prone to tearing or clumping so their shape and warmth remains more consistent over time. They also do not require extra quilting or a scrim layer, which saves weight.

There are two popular branded synthetic insulations: PrimaLoft, which is known for cut staples; and Climashield, which is known for its continuous filaments. Longtime backpackers might recognize Polarguard, Thinsulate, Quallofil, and Hollofil, none of which is commonly used today in high-loft garments or sleeping bags.

Goose down and synthetic insulations both have strengths and weaknesses. Compared with synthetics, down is:

> More thermally efficient when dry. The warmest synthetic insulations are only as thermally efficient, approximately, as 550-fill-power goose down;
> More compressible;
> Softer; and
> Longer-lasting. I have owned the same down-filled gear for years, while I can burn through synthetic insulations during just one active season.

Synthetics have two advantages over goose down:

> They are less expensive; and
> Their insulating performance is *less affected* by moisture. Still, they do *not* maintain maximum warmth when wet. In my experience, a wet

tools & techniques

During peak daytime temperatures, insulated layers are usually unnecessary for three-season conditions. Once the sun goes down, however, temperatures can drop quickly.

synthetic-filled jacket or sleeping bag is still cold. It's just less cold than a down-filled item.

In some environments, it is impossible to keep down dry. In humid, sunless, and cold environments, I find that down inevitably gets wet from ambient humidity and/or from perspiration that doesn't evaporate into the saturated air. Unless I do something really dumb, it should never get "soaked," just damp. If I cannot be assured of occasional dry air, sun, and/or warm temperatures, the extra weight of synthetic insulations is worth their more reliable performance.

Measuring the warmth of down & synthetic insulation

Down-filled and synthetic garments use distinct techniques to measure their relative warmth.

The warmth of a down-filled garment or bag is determined primarily by its loft, since more loft contains more body heat–trapping air pockets. For example, a down sleeping bag featuring five inches of loft will be warmer than a sleeping bag featuring three inches of loft, regardless of the type of down (i.e., fill power) or the amount of it (i.e., fill weight). Some manufacturers "overstuff" down baffles. This has a negligible effect on loft but it helps prevent the down from shifting around and causing uneven warmth. It is usually more thermally efficient to use larger baffles than to severely overstuff smaller ones.

The warmth of a synthetic-filled garment or bag is not determined by its loft. Instead, it depends on the insulation's fiber size and structure and on the amount of insulation. Thin fibers can create smaller and more numerous air chambers within a given area, trapping more escaping body heat.

Clo is used to measure the warmth of synthetic-filled products. One clo is defined as the amount of clothing required by a resting person to remain comfortable indefinitely in an ambient temperature of 70°F, humidity of less than 50 percent, and a 0.5-mile-an-hour wind. A typical business suit—including shirt, jacket, underwear, socks, and shoes—has a clo value of about 1.0. The maximum clo value is 4.0, which might apply to a clothing system capable of keeping a person warm in Arctic cold.

It can take some digging to find clo values, which I find unfortunate, because clo values are objective and can be used to compare the thermal efficiency of synthetic insulations and synthetic products, in the form of clo/oz. Clo values could also be used to assemble a clothing, shelter, and sleep system of appropriate warmth.

Shell fabrics for high-loft outerwear & bags

Down and synthetic insulations are sandwiched by an outer and inner shell fabric usually made of polyester or nylon. These shell fabrics, which are described in more detail in the Shells section (see p. 46), are the second most important feature of an insulated layer or sleeping bag,

behind only the insulation type and amount. They affect a product in several critical ways:

Weight. Especially in the case of lightweight garments and bags, the shell fabric is disproportionately influential in the product's weight—there is very little insulation between the shell fabrics, but almost as much material is needed as in a colder-weather model. For example, the Western Mountaineering Hooded Flash Jacket ($260, 9 oz) contains just three ounces of 850-fill-power down; most of its remaining six ounces is the shell fabric, with maybe an ounce for the zipper. A lightweight shell fabric can noticeably reduce a product's weight. For example, the 15-degree Western Mountaineering Badger MF ($445, 2 lb 8 oz), which features a 1.0 oz/yd^2 shell fabric, is 6 ounces lighter than the same bag with a 1.7 oz/yd^2 fabric.

Warmth. A shell fabric affects the warmth of insulated layers and sleeping bags due to its weight, air permeability, and down-proof-ness. If the fabric is too heavy, it will compress the insulation, thereby reducing the size and number of air-trapping chambers. Given that lightweight shell fabrics are found even on value-oriented bags today, this is not the

 In the field, actual loft and clo values are less than those provided by manufacturers, because both insulation types are compromised by moisture, dirt, and body oils.

A rare leisurely morning for an Ultimate Hiker, who is usually on the trail before the sun hits her camp.

concern that it once was; heavy cotton fabrics are now found only on cheap bags that are not suitable for backpacking anyway.

A shell fabric must have *some* air permeability so that water vapor can pass through it and evaporate into the atmosphere—otherwise, condensation would form, creating an uncomfortable user experience and wetting the insulation. However, if the shell fabric has too much air permeability, body heat will escape too easily. In other words, body heat is trapped both by the air chambers in the insulation *and* by the shell fabrics. As an extreme scenario, imagine how drafty a jacket or sleeping bag would be if its shell fabric were made of no-see-um mesh bug netting. Thankfully, excessive air permeability seems to be a problem only with shell fabrics that weigh less than 1.0 oz/yd, which is lighter than what is used by major manufacturers. The lightest fabrics commonly used are in the 1.0 to 1.5 oz/yd range.

The source of a fabric's air permeability—specifically, the density of its weave, or the space between adjacent fibers—is also responsible for whether it is "down-proof," or its resistance to losing down plumes. Today's shell fabrics are excellent in retaining *down,* but they are not as effective in withholding quill-bearing plumes, or *feathers.* Because the technology used to separate feathers and down has improved, there are fewer quills in today's high-loft down, and the down-proof-ness of a shell fabric is not as critical as it once was, particularly when using premium high-loft down (e.g., 800 fill). If your layer or bag occasionally loses feathers or even down, you probably do not need to be concerned—a few missing plumes will not noticeably affect its warmth.

Water resistance. Last, the shell fabric can improve the water resistance of an insulated layer or sleeping bag, like against light precipitation or the condensation on shelter walls. However, even a highly water-resistant shell fabric will not keep the insulation dry in wet conditions— it will still absorb ambient humidity and perspiration.

part 2

skurka'spicks
I N S U L A T I O N

When nighttime temperatures drop below 50°F, I consider bringing an insulated top. When nighttime temperatures drop into the 10s, I usually bring insulated bottoms too. However, I usually jump into my sleeping bag shortly after I arrive in camp, so if you tend to lounge around camp in the evening, your temperature thresholds will be higher.

As with my base layer tops, I like insulated tops with long torsos so that my lower back will not be exposed to the cold air when I bend over. I insist that my jackets be hooded. The added warmth is well worth the marginal increase in weight.

In Arctic-like cold and wind, lining jacket and pant openings with animal fur can dramatically reduce convective heat loss. On the first day of my Alaska-Yukon Expedition, the daytime high was -16°F and the peak gust was 22 miles an hour. I am convinced that my nose and cheeks would not have fared well without the coyote fur ruff that my mother had sewn to the perimeter of my hood.

Another Arctic trick: So that I can adjust my jacket even while wearing clumsy mitts, I extend the zipper and hood pull tabs with long cords.

When I expect cold and wet conditions, I bring a lightweight fleece top, like the **Patagonia R1 Pullover** ($120, 12 oz) or **R2 Vest** ($100, 9 oz). A two-day gale along Alaska's Lost Coast and a rainy two-week stretch in the Brooks Range made me give fleece a second look. My Mountain West–based clothing system of a base layer, puffy, and shell had not been up to the task.

Fleece is less thermally efficient than a down- or synthetic-filled puffy, but it loses less of its warmth when wet. It's usually also less expensive.

tools & techniques

To accompany my fleece top, I will normally also bring a synthetic-fill jacket, and possibly pants. The **Patagonia Nano Puff Hoody** ($200, 14 oz) is the current gold standard for three-season puffy jackets. It has ultralight shell fabrics and top-of-the-line PrimaLoft One insulation. The **MontBell U.L. Thermawrap Pants** ($145, 10 oz) share a similar function-driven philosophy. Their three-quarter-length zippers seemed excessive until I found that the pants can be taken off over both ski boots and even snowshoes—a small price penalty for a major convenience and time saver.

For dry climates—like the western mountain states—I do not need fleece, and I prefer down insulations over synthetics. MontBell has an excellent product line, and Patagonia is not far behind.

Shells

The last component of the three-part layering system is a shell, which reduces conductive and convective heat loss by offering a degree of protection against precipitation and wind. I have also used my shells as armor against biting insects in the absence of nylon base layers.

Shell fabrics

Unlike glass, aluminum, or thick rubber, outdoor shell fabrics are *not* waterproof, despite marketing claims to the contrary. Under enough water pressure, they will leak. Some shell fabrics are more resistant to leakage than others—it's a relative definition. Fully waterproof shell fabrics do exist, but they are generally not practical for active outdoor recreation because they are not *breathable,* i.e., moisture cannot pass through them. Breathability is different from ventilation, which is the exchange of air, as through an open zipper.

There are two types of shell fabrics:

> "Water-resistant" fabrics are subtly water-resistant and moderately breathable.
> "Waterproof-breathable" fabrics are moderately water-resistant and subtly breathable.

My experience is that there is an unavoidable trade-off between the water resistance and the breathability of shell fabrics. *You cannot have both.* I will repeat that: *You cannot have both.* Some fabrics offer unexpectedly good breathability given their level of water resistance, or vice versa, but they all are limited by the same technological realities.

Additional shell factors

The water resistance and breathability of a shell is affected by three other factors besides its fabric:

Watertight zippers and storm closures only delay the infiltration of moisture. The fewer closures the better, at least in terms of water-resistance.

Needle holes are created when sewing fabric panels together. To seal these holes, manufacturers use waterproof seam tape. During prolonged storms and over the life of a shell, I have found that seams are usually the first leakage points. A better—but more expensive—construction technique is welding, whereby fabric panels are glued or otherwise bonded together without stitching. Welded garments are marginally lighter and more packable, but their key advantage is that the seams are no less water-resistant than the fabric itself.

Venting features like armpit zippers ("pit zips"), two-way center zippers, and chest pockets that double as chest vents help the exchange of hot and humid air inside the garment with cooler and drier air from outside, which helps to delay overheating and excessive moisture accumulation. Depending on the fabric and the conditions, the ability of a shell to ventilate may be *more important* to user comfort than the fabric's ability to breathe—a remarkable thought, considering the attention given to fabric breathability. Ventilation is especially critical in hot and humid conditions, when the shell's warmth may cause overheating and perspiration can't evaporate into the humid air, as well as during frequent and long-term storms.

Water-resistant shells

There are two types of water-resistant shells:

Wind shells, like the GoLite Dakota ($80, 4 oz), are wispy, ultralight, super

	"water-resistant" shells	"waterproof-breathable" shells
water resistance	Initially good, but ultimately no more water-resistant than untreated fabric	Initially excellent, but will fail over long-term: Moisture seeps in through seams or zippers, or exterior fabric wets out.
breathability	Not as good as a base layer, but good enough for moderate exertion (e.g., running) in cool temperatures	Limited. If users do not get wet from the outside, they will get wet from inside because of accumulated perspiration. Some fabrics breathe better than others, but marketing claims greatly exceed performance.
best use	As second layer for windy summits, dry snow, light drizzle, or warm rain	To delay getting wet during low-exertion activities in cool/cold and wet conditions
cost	Low to moderate	Moderate to high

packable, very breathable, and somewhat water-resistant. I wear a wind shell jacket as a second layer when I'm on windy ridges, in dry snow, or in buggy camps. It is also useful in the East when it's too hot and humid for a waterproof-breathable shell. For day hikes and long trail runs or bike rides, wind shells are barely-there insurance against unexpected changes in weather or my itinerary.

Soft shells, like the Cloudveil Serendipity Jacket ($200, 19 oz), are excellent as outerwear for backcountry skiing and cold weather running. They have good breathability, stretch, and abrasion resistance; they offer adequate protection against wind and dry snow; and they are much more comfortable than a stiff, crinkly waterproof-breathable shell. However, although I adore soft shells for done-in-a-day activities, I do not think they are applicable for backpacking:

> They do not replace waterproof-breathable shells because they are not sufficiently water-resistant.
> They are not as thermally efficient as puffy insulated layers.
> They do not dry quickly after getting wet.
> They are not as versatile as separate garments that collectively offer the same benefits—namely, the weather resistance and warmth—at a similar weight and bulk.

If untreated, wind shell and soft shell fabrics have only enough natural water resistance for sporadic drizzle

how2
restore DWR

1 Launder the garment to remove dirt and body oils;

2 Expose it to heat from a clothes dryer, iron, or even a hair dryer; or,

3 Use an aftermarket spray-on or wash-in treatment.

I have found maintaining the water resistance of a DWR-coated fabric to be time-consuming, expensive, and ultimately futile, especially on long-distance trips when I have limited access to laundry facilities and it's difficult to find specialized aftermarket treatments.

or light, dry snow. So manufacturers enhance their water resistance with a fluorocarbon-based durable water repellent (DWR) coating that bonds to the fabric's exterior fibers. DWR does not impair fabric breathability—it does not seal the fabric's pores like a polyurethane coating does.

DWR can be fairly compared to "new car smell." When DWR-treated fabric is factory-fresh, the DWR is very noticeable: Moisture that contacts the fabric beads up and rolls off. With use, however, the DWR seems to disappear since dirt, body oils, and abrasion degrade it. Eventually, the fabric is no more water-resistant than an untreated fabric. Some DWR treatments are more water-resistant and longer lasting than others, but they all fail inevitably. They can be partially restored, but they are never "as good as new."

Waterproof-breathable shells

When I read marketing copy about waterproof-breathable (WP/B) shells, I often wonder if the individual who wrote the copy has ever used the product. In my opinion, the performance of WP/B shells has been greatly oversold—the product category name, "waterproof-breathable," is itself an oxymoron. My real-world experience is that they fail to keep me dry during prolonged storms, or even during short storms if the fabric has been compromised by dirt, body oils, and/or abrasion, which is unavoidable on a long trip. WP/B fabrics are improving rapidly, especially in the last ten years—becoming more water-resistant, more breathable, lighter, and less expensive—but the products still have not caught up to the marketing hype. A friend of mine is less diplomatic, calling this marketing "a load of hooey."

WP/B fabrics could be the subject of at least a few thesis papers. If you want additional information about fabric construction, testing, and performance characteristics, consult two excellent resources: "Waterproof Breathable Fabric Technologies: A Comprehensive Primer and State

After the durable water repellent (DWR) on my WP/B jacket failed in prolonged wet conditions in the Arctic Refuge, I had to rely partly on a plastic trash bag liner to stay dry.

of the Market Technology Review," by Alan Dixon at *Backpacking Light* online magazine, and "Rainwear: How It Works," by T. D. Wood at REI Expert Advice.

The water resistance and breathability of WP/B fabrics can be measured, but the industry lacks a *uniform* testing system that would generate trustworthy apples-to-apples comparisons. Even if such a system did exist, the results would not necessarily be translatable to a fabric's performance *outside* the lab, because this also depends on personal metabolism, weather conditions, shell-specific features like sizing and ventilation, and the fabric's resistance to dirt, body oils, and abrasion. The results of *proprietary* tests are sometimes presented, but they cannot be blindly trusted. These results are not certified by an unbiased organization, and the results could have been obtained under varying conditions and/or through different tests, producing apples-and-oranges data.

Measuring water resistance. The water column test is the most commonly cited measure of water resistance. The result refers to the height of water that can be vertically suspended over a fabric swatch before it leaks. The result is typically shown in millimeters or in pounds per square inch. A fabric that claims water resistance of 20,000 mm (or 29 psi) means that there was a 66-foot column of water above the fabric before it began to leak. This far exceeds the water pressure exerted by

wind-driven rain (1,400 mm or 2 psi), hurricane-force rain (7,000 mm or 10 psi), and even a fire hose at 30 feet (11,000 mm or 16 psi). There seems to be no consensus on the quantitative standard for a fabric to be technically considered "waterproof." Rather, the classification seems to hinge on the fabric's construction.

Measuring breathability. There are five tests to measure fabric "breathability," which is the layman's term for *moisture vapor transfer rate,* or the ability of a fabric to permit the passage of moisture through it. Four of these tests measure the amount of water (in grams) that passes through one square meter (m^2) of fabric over a 24-hour period. A fabric rated at 20,000 g/m^2/day, means that about 29 ounces of water passed through a square meter of the fabric per hour. For context, the average adult perspires 25 to 50 ounces per hour while exercising and has an average body surface area of 1.7 m^2. The fifth test of breathability, the sweating hot plate, measures a fabric's resistance to evaporative heat transfer (RET), or heat loss, in pascal watts. I have never seen mention of RET or RET-based values in product copy, though peer-reviewed academic articles have correlated RET values with actual field performance using human subjects, which gives them at least some real-world meaning.

WP/B fabrics are laminates, consisting of up to three layers:

> An external-face fabric made of polyester or nylon;

part (2)

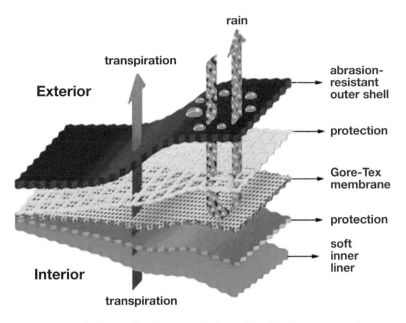

rain

transpiration

Exterior

→ abrasion-resistant outer shell

→ protection

→ Gore-Tex membrane

→ protection

→ soft inner liner

Interior

transpiration

The design of WP/B fabrics—I wish they worked as well as this diagram suggests.

> A "waterproof-breathable" membrane that may be porous or nonporous and that may have multiple layers, one of which is usually polyurethane based; and
> An internal fabric or material that improves user comfort by assisting in the passage of moisture through the membrane,, or at least the perception of it.

A three-layer WP/B fabric has an external-face fabric, WP/B membrane, and internal fabric. A two-layer WP/B fabric has only a face fabric and WP/B membrane. And a 2.5-layer fabric has a face fabric, the WP/B membrane, and some non-fabric material on the inside, like a carbon-based coating. Three-layer fabrics are generally the heaviest and most expensive, but they are also the most durable and comfortable. Two-layer fabrics generally have the opposite superlatives, and 2.5-layer fabrics are in between.

Like water-resistant fabrics, WP/B fabrics also feature a DWR coating. Its purpose is to prevent the external-face fabric from "wetting out," or becoming saturated with moisture. When this happens, the fabric's breathability plummets.

The inevitable failure of DWR, as discussed earlier, is the Achilles' heel of WP/B fabrics. The technology does not work unless the face fabric is dry. If you need your WP/B shell to perform well, you must plan to restore the DWR finish regularly. If this is impractical, and/or if you are not meticulous about your gear, then you might consider an alternative system that offers more consistent and trust-worthy performance.

Types of waterproof/breathable fabrics

There are five distinct types of WP/B fabrics. They are marketed under a dizzying number of brand names, but the underlying technologies are the same:

Polyurethane-polytetrafluoro-ethylene (PU-ePTFE). Branded as Gore-Tex, PU-ePTFE was the first WP/B fabric and today remains the best known. The current prod-ucts—including Pro Shell, Paclite, and Performance—rely on a two-layer membrane consisting of a porous expanded polytetrafluoroethylene (ePTFE, or Teflon) membrane and nonporous hydrophilic polyurethane (PU) film. The original Gore-Tex fabric

did not have the PU film; it was added to protect the ePTFE membrane from the same contaminants that degrade DWR. This addition greatly reduced the breathability of Gore-Tex because moisture moves through it via solid state diffusion—i.e., the PU film absorbs water vapor, which then moves through the film as water drop-lets until it reaches the film's exte-rior, where it can revert to water vapor and evaporate. The popular expla-nation for how Gore-Tex works—that the PU-ePTFE membrane is filled with holes that are too small for water droplets but big enough for water vapor—is incorrect.

Polytetrafluoroethylene-only (ePTFE-only). If Gore-Tex engineers had been able to retain the breathabil-ity of their original ePTFE-only mem-brane without smothering it with a solid PU film, I'm sure they would

Since getting wet in wet conditions is inevitable, I insist that my gear be made of quick-dry materials, and I plan to dry my things out regularly.

have. But this challenge was solved first by another company, BHA Group, Inc. (now owned by General Electric), the makers of eVent fabric, which is renowned for its breathability in both field applications and

Though competing technologies have evolved, the original Gore-Tex remains a market dominator.

lab tests. This porous ePTFE-only membrane features an oleophobic (i.e., oil-repelling) coating that protects it from contaminants without sealing off its breathability-enabling pores. eVent is so breathable that I've heard an employee at my local outdoor retail store complain he can feel the wind blow through it when he's skiing.

Polyurethane-only (PU-only). If a shell is not made of Gore-Tex or eVent, it is probably made of a proprietary WP/B fabric that has a nonporous PU-only layer or coating through which moisture passes via solid-state diffusion. Examples of such fabrics include Marmot's MemBrain, Mountain Hardwear's Conduit, and Patagonia's H2No. Because a PU-only layer cannot be as thin as the PU film in a PU-ePTFE laminate, the breathability of most proprietary fabrics is not as good as Gore-Tex (and not nearly as good as eVent): Water must pass through more material on its way from inside the shell to outside. But PU-only fabrics offer excellent value, and they can be laminated to stretchy and soft face fabrics, instead of being stiff and crinkly.

Polypropylene. Prices of WP/B outerwear are cringe-worthy. Low-end jackets start at around $100, and high-end jackets can cost as much as $500, with $150 to $250 being the norm. One budget-saving alternative for casual users and jobless thru-hikers is microporous polypropylene laminates like those used in O2 Rainwear and Frogg Toggs. These fabrics are lightweight and very breathable (not as good as eVent but better than Gore-Tex and PU-only laminates and coatings). Their wallet-friendly cost is not without trade-offs: The styling and fit of these garments is usually poor, and the fabric is not durable enough for bushwhacking or technical use.

Directional clothing. The final WP/B fabric is Páramo, which has received high praise for its performance in cold, wet conditions. Unfortunately, Páramo is currently available only in the United Kingdom. Páramo consists of a water-resistant wind shell laminated to a hydrophobic mid-weight polyester base layer that replicates animal fur. Because Páramo lacks the membrane or

tools & techniques

53

An umbrella offers good rain protection and excellent ventilation, but it restricts trekking pole use and gets caught by brush and wind.

coating found in other WP/B fabrics, it is much more breathable. But it's reportedly more water-resistant and warmer than a conventional soft shell or the combination of a wind shell and fleece.

Ponchos & umbrellas

Given the shortcomings of water-resistant and WP/B shells, especially in hot and humid conditions, some advocate the use of ponchos or umbrellas, which can offer reliable water resistance and excellent ventilation. Unfortunately, both ponchos and umbrellas have serious flaws:

> They get blown around by the wind;
> They are not as protective in driving rain; and
> They can be snagged by vegetation while bushwhacking.

During most of my Sea-to-Sea Route hike in 2004–05, I used a poncho as my primary rain gear. It worked well on trails and in the warm, humid East, but it did not work well on the windy plains or in the dry western mountain states. During the winter, I used a WP/B shell of about the same weight, because it was warmer.

I have only carried an umbrella—the GoLite Chrome Dome ($40, 8 oz)—once, while walking across Wyoming's sagebrush-covered Great Divide Basin in August. It protected me from the sun better than full-coverage clothing would have, but it was unwieldy. If I held it, I couldn't also use my trekking poles. And it added drag, like the parachutes that shoot out of a drag racing car after it crosses the finish line.

skurka's picks
S H E L L S

You *should* be disheartened after finishing this section. When it's wet outside, remaining *absolutely* dry—both from external and internal sources of moisture—is an unachievable goal. Or, at least this is my conclusion after being caught in hundreds of storms and having experimented with dozens of techniques, technologies, and designs. The question is *not* whether I can stay dry, but how I can minimize my discomfort.

In the East during rainstorms in the hot and humid summer months, I hike in my base layer, possibly with a water-resistant wind shell. A WP/B shell is out of the question; even a highly breathable eVent shell with venting features will be too hot and stuffy. I prefer a shell to a poncho or umbrella, though these are plausible alternatives if I'm staying on trail. After getting soaked, it's worth having a set of dry "sleeping" clothes in my pack for when I reach camp. If it's still raining in the morning, I change into my wet clothes and start hoping for friendlier weather. At the first opportunity—e.g., with a break in the clouds or near a laundry—I dry everything out.

In the desert Southwest—where temperatures are hot and where precipitation is usually predictable, short-lived, and uncommon—a water-resistant shell is also preferable. If I happen to get caught in an afternoon monsoon, I'll stay dryish for a little while, and by the time I'm soaked, the storm is usually over. Post-storm sunshine and body heat, and/or a fire, can dry everything out quickly.

I also wear a water-resistant shell in the winter, when precipitation reliably falls as dry snow. If there's a chance of wet snow or sleet, a WP/B shell is a safer option.

In the western mountain states, a wind shell is suitable for light precipitation, but because being wet in cool/cold conditions can cause tremendous conductive heat loss, I also carry an ultralight WP/B shell (6 to 10 oz) that will offer better water resistance. The lack of venting features on ultralight shells is usually not a problem, because I don't wear the WP/B shell for an extended time and because I'm unlikely to overheat or feel stuffy in the cool, dry air.

Raining and 35°F is the most challenging combination of conditions that most backpackers ever experience. Eric Larsen, a polar explorer also based in Boulder, Colorado, once told me that 35°F and raining is even worse than -50°F. I'm disappointed to report that I have not yet found an effective system for dealing with such conditions, despite traveling through areas that specialize in them, including Alaska and the Yukon, the Great Lakes region, and the western mountain states during the shoulder seasons. Historically, I have used a fully featured WP/B shell made of premium fabric, but after many frustrating experiences during the Alaska-Yukon Expedition, I am still searching.

tools & techniques

The source of my problem is my inability to maintain the water resistance of DWR during long-term trips—and, without a DWR, waterproof-breathable shells are ineffective. If your trip is shorter, a WP/B shell may be a fine solution. I am most optimistic about Páramo, which was designed specifically for cold, wet conditions. I would also like to experiment with a waterproof/*non*breathable shell like the **ORC Hardshell Level 6 Parka** ($67, 16 oz). Inevitably, I will get wet from the inside when wearing such a jacket, but perhaps this will be warmer than chilling rain.

The RBH Designs Lightning Bug Jacket stops perspiration from soaking outer layers, so they maintain full warmth.

Vapor barrier liners

For winter conditions, the three-layer system discussed earlier has drawbacks. Specifically, the breathability results in:

> Heat loss through evaporative cooling; and
> Outer layers getting wet from perspiration, because water vapor reaches the dew point within the layers and turns into liquid moisture. (This is not normally a problem in three-season conditions because the dew point is *outside* of the layering system.)

I use vapor barrier liners (VBLs) on some winter trips—especially frigid and long-term trips—to remedy these two problems. VBLs can be used in a more limited capacity during the cold shoulder seasons. If used properly, I think they can be beneficial to all outdoor winter enthusiasts.

What are vapor barrier liners?

VBLs can be made of any nonbreathable material, like PU-coated nylon; in a pinch, I've made VBLs from a Mylar balloon and plastic trash bags. Waterproof-breathable fabrics like Gore-Tex are fundamentally different from VBL fabrics. Although the breathability of WP/B fabrics is limited, they at least allow the transmission of some moisture, whereas VBLs do not.

Vapor barrier liner clothing and sleeping bag liners are available from

Integral Designs, RBH Designs, Stephenson's Warmlite, and Western Mountaineering. No major manufacturer offers VBL products.

It is redundant and unnecessary to use both VBL clothing and a VBL bag liner. The latter is simpler, lighter, and less expensive, but VBL clothing has three key advantages:

> I can sleep with all of my clothes on, layering as follows: skin, base layer, VBL, other clothes, sleeping bag. If I wore all of my clothes inside a sleeping bag liner (i.e., skin, base layer, other clothing, VBL, sleeping bag), my clothes would be soaked by my own perspiration.
> During the day, VBL clothing keeps my outer layers dry; and, at night, VBL clothing keeps both my outer layers *and* my sleeping bag dry. By contrast, a sleeping bag liner does nothing to keep my outer layers dry during the day.
> VBL clothing is more formfitting than a sleeping bag liner, so I notice quickly if moisture is beginning to accumulate inside the VBL. By contrast, a bag liner could have roomy chambers where excessive moisture can build.

Why I started using VBLs

In the winter of 2004–05, I snowshoed 1,400 miles of the North Country Trail through both peninsulas of Michigan, northern Wisconsin, and northern Minnesota as part of my 7,800-mile, 11-month Sea-to-Sea Route trek. This was my first real winter trip, and a problem that became immediately clear was that my clothing and sleeping system failed to adequately manage perspiration.

If I perspired and then stopped, for example, I would become chilled by the evaporation of my perspiration. A more serious problem was that my outer layers and sleeping bag were getting wet from my perspiration. In the -20°F temperatures, water vapor emanating from my body would turn into water droplets before it reached the outside and could evaporate. My down-filled sleeping bag and puffy clothing became wetter—and less warm—every single day; my footwear was frozen stiff each morning by trapped perspiration from the days before. I also did not notice how much I was perspiring, but I do remember that one morning I steamed when I emerged from my bag.

In frigid temperatures I wear vapor barrier liner socks between a liner sock and an insulated sock to prevent my footwear from freezing solid due to perspiration.

VBLs are suitable only for very cold conditions, like those I experienced in Alaska's Arctic in March, when daytime *high* temperatures were regularly below ten degrees.

If I did not have numerous opportunities to dry my gear—usually one or two times a week, either in homes or laundries—I am certain that I would have shivered through more nights than I did. The utter failure of my most critical equipment was unpreventable with the conventional three-layer system I was using.

Effects & benefits

In January 2007, I returned to Minnesota for a 380-mile, 16-day snowshoe trip I named "Ultralight in the Nation's Icebox." Among my objectives was perfecting my deep-winter gear list, and VBLs were core pieces of my strategy. I brought a VBL jacket, pants, socks, gloves, and balaclava. My VBL system had four effects:

> I became keenly aware of my perspiration rate. If I started to overheat, I immediately noticed the increasing humidity between my skin and the VBL layer, and I would have to reduce my effort or remove a layer.

> Because I was not perspiring as much, I stayed better hydrated, which led to improved circulation and respiratory efficiency. I also didn't need to spend as much time or fuel melting snow for water.

> My clothes did not become sweat-soaked, and my VBL layers prevented evaporation of heat-holding perspiration.

> Last, the warmth of my outer layers and sleeping bag was not degraded by my perspiration. Instead, my perspiration stayed within the vapor barrier liner, so my outer layers remained dry and warm.

When I use VBLs

As with a conventional three-season layering system, there are no set rules about when to use VBLs. It mostly depends on personal experience and preferences. I consider three factors:

Weather conditions. I can use VBLs below about 40°F, or perhaps when it's warmer if it's windy and/or cloudy, if precipitation is falling (particularly cold rain, sleet, or wet snow), and/or if I am walking on or through snow or ice (which is colder than a leaf-covered trail). At the upper end of this range, I can only wear VBLs that are easily removable, like gloves. As temperatures drop into the 20s, I can wear a jacket; and below 10, it's cold enough to start wearing socks and pants, which can't be easily removed or adjusted.

Accumulation period. This is the interval between assured opportunities to dry my insulated layers and sleeping bag. As the accumulation period grows longer, VBLs become more critical in preserving warmth. If I went on a one-week ski trip in Alaska's Arctic in February, for example, seven days of moisture inside my gear would definitely have noticeable effects, whereas on a weekend trip, the loss of warmth would be less worrisome. However, this is not to say that VBLs cannot be valuable during short-term efforts. For example, toward the end of a full day of alpine skiing, when the sun disappears and the temperatures begin to drop, many skiers feel chilled because their boot liners, gloves, and clothing have absorbed sweat during the day. This problem could be solved with VBLs,

and these skiers might be warm enough at 4 p.m. to catch a last run.

Insulation type. Down is more susceptible than synthetics to loft loss when exposed to moisture. Synthetics are vulnerable in the long-term too, but the rate of degradation is lower. Therefore, using VBLs is more important when using down insulations than when using synthetics, though VBLs will be important to maintaining the warmth of both on trips with long accumulation periods.

skurka'spicks
V B L S

A VBL can be worn next to skin or as a second layer, outside a lightweight merino wool or polyester base layer. I prefer the latter, for three reasons. First, the base layer creates a small buffer that eliminates any sensation of clamminess, but without significantly reducing my sensitivity to perspiration, which dictates the adjustments I make to my physical output and my layering system. Second, the lightweight base layer protects my skin from direct contact with frigid winter air if/when I need to ventilate. For example, if my hands are getting too warm, I can remove my VBL mitts without exposing my bare hand to sub-zero temperatures. And, third, the base layer prevents moisture from building up on my skin, which can lead to moisture-related skin issues like maceration.

tools & techniques

59

My VBL clothes must be versatile and adjustable so that I can fine-tune my system to the exact conditions and my physical output. This explains why I like the **RBH Designs Lightning Bug Jacket ($185, 6 oz)**, which is similar to a nonbreathable wind shell. When combined with a base layer and insulated puffy, it is a warmer and more flexible system than RBH's three-layer next-to-skin jacket. I like the **Integral Designs VB Socks ($30, 3 oz)** for the same reason.

For my hands, I trust the **RBH Designs Vapor Mitt ($145, 9 oz)**, which has kept my hands warm down to temperatures below -20°F. As liners under the Vapor Mitts, I use **DeFeet Merino Wool Dura-Glove ($18.50, 3 oz)**.

There are limited options for VBL pants. I made my own out of silicone-impregnated nylon. The challenge is finding a pair that fits snugly without restricting movement.

SP

Headwear

A brimmed hat has many benefits. It:

> Keeps the sun off my face;
> Helps stop rain, snow, and sweat from getting into my eyes;
> Holds the hoods of my base layer shirt, rain jacket, and parka above my face;
> Prevents the bug netting of my head net and bivy sack from being flush against my skin, which hinders ventilation and allows bugs to bite me through it; and
> Makes for a convenient place to clip an LED light.

Since 2003, my brimmed pick has been the Headsweats Supervisor ($20, 2 oz), which has better ventilation and is more versatile than a conventional ball cap like the Headsweats Race Cap ($20, 2 oz). However, for those whose heads burn easily the latter offers more sun protection.

Some of my friends wear cowboy-style hats from Tilley, but they do not fit as well under hoods. When I need more sun protection than the Supervisor offers, I prefer the Headsweats Protech ($26, 3 oz), which is a ball cap with a polyester drape that covers my neck and ears.

Bandanas are very versatile—they can be used as headwear, and for hygiene and first aid. But I have used one of these classic backpacking items just once—in Canada's Yukon as an additional layer of protection against the mosquitoes that were biting my scalp through my head net and mop of hair. In a pinch, a bandana can be combined with a Supervisor or Race Cap for extra sun protection, but it's not as simple a solution as the ProTech.

To protect my face and neck when bugs are intense, I wear a simple head net made of bug netting. Mosquito netting has larger pores than no-see-um netting, so it has better airflow.

When temperatures drop, I need more than just a visor on my head.

**Headsweats
Race Cap, which
offers more sun protection
than a visor for sunburn-prone heads**

My first cold-weather headwear layer is the hood on my base layer shirt. Next, I add a headband or beanie, both of which fit nicely over my visor. In temperatures below about 20°F, depending on the wind and humidity, a full-coverage balaclava helps to keep my neck and jaw muscles warm.

My Arctic headwear system, which I've tested to about -25°F with a 20-mile-an-hour wind, includes the following: balaclava, visor, wool knit hat, sunglasses or goggles, headband, and up to three hoods, from my base layer shirt, shell jacket, and insulated parka, the last of which has a coyote fur ruff sewn to its perimeter.

The biggest challenge of an Arctic-worthy headwear system is finding a way to manage the moisture from respiration. If I cover my mouth and nose with material, moisture builds up on the inside; but if I leave skin exposed, my skin is prone to frostbite. My solution is a merino wool headband—when a patch of it gets uncomfortably wet, I can rotate it around to a dry

I successfully combated the Arctic's fierce mosquitoes with a visor, a bandana, and a head net, in addition to biteproof nylon clothing and DEET.

tools & techniques

patch. Wet patches eventually get rotated to the back of my neck inside my hoods, where they can dry out.

Handwear

When temperatures drop into the 40s—or into the 50s if it's also raining or windy—I don gloves and/or mittens to keep my hands dry and warm. My handwear system is constructed like my clothing system: a base layer (or "liner"), an insulating layer, and a shell. All-in-one gloves and mittens work well for throwing snowballs and scraping frost off my car windshield, but they are not versatile enough for the range of conditions and exertion levels that I encounter during a long trip.

My preferred liner is the DeFeet Merino Wool DuraGlove ($18.50, 3 oz), which has a longer life span than any other glove I have tried, thanks to a grippy silicone pattern and 20 percent nylon content. Abrasive trekking pole and ski pole grips seem to eat liner gloves, and the DuraGloves last 4 to 6 weeks if I use them daily for 10 to 14 hours per day; I burn through unprotected polyester, fleece, and merino wool gloves in half that time. The Dura-Glove fabric is heavier than I typically prefer for a base layer (it's probably equivalent to an expedition-weight base layer), but it's acceptable for this use. If my hands start overheating, it is very easy to remove the gloves (or an outer layer) and store

them in a side pocket. If the fabric were thicker, it would interfere with my finger dexterity.

To protect the DuraGlove liners from precipitation or chilling wind, I add a WP/B shell like the REI Taped Mittens ($55, 4 oz), which are more water-resistant than the lighter Mountain Laurel Designs eVent Rain Mitts ($45, 1 oz) because they feature fully taped seams. The MLD Mitts are best used as wind shells for winter running and as rain mitts in mild conditions, when I'm not overly concerned if my hands get wet.

When conditions demand more warmth than provided by my liner and shell, I take one of two approaches. I may just add fleece gloves or mittens, like the Outdoor Research PL 400 Gloves ($35, 3 oz). Alternatively, when temperatures are reliably below freezing, I trade out my shells for VBL mitts, which are not fully waterproof (the seams are not taped) and therefore can't be trusted in wet precipitation.

DeFeet Merino Wool DuraGloves— the silicone pads make them more durable than conventional liners

part 2

Unless I expect nonstop shade or cloud cover, sunglasses are mandatory equipment.

Mittens may not provide the same dexterity as gloves, but they are much warmer; plus, dexterity is generally not critical to holding trekking poles or zipping up a jacket. I like the RBH Designs Vapor Mitt ($145, 9 oz) for its durability and warmth. The RBH Designs Ultralight Vapor Mitt ($145, 6 oz) is suitable for less cold conditions.

Eyewear

I protect my eyes from bright sunlight, glare, cold wind, and blowing particles (like snow and sand) with sunglasses and goggles. Eyewear is not necessary on every trip. Little sunlight penetrates the East's thick forests, for example, and in northern Alaska, the sun is very weak and the skies are often cloudy.

Sunglasses and goggles may seem outrageously expensive, but I have found that high-end models are worth the price if I use them extensively. The optics are better, and the components (frames, lenses, lens treatments, and rubber nosepieces and earpieces) are more durable. When driving my car, el cheapo models from a gas station or supermarket work fine.

Currently, I wear the Zeal Optics Maestro ($170, 1 oz), with polarized lenses made of NXT polyurethane that is clearer and stronger than standard polycarbonate and low-end acrylic. The lenses are also photochromic, or "transition," so their tint adjusts in accordance with changes in ambient light. The alternative, interchangeable lenses, are a complete hassle. The Maestro also wraps nicely around my face, which improves peripheral vision and blocks incoming sidelight, though I wish venting ports were integrated into the frame to better prevent condensation and fogging.

I have needed goggles only on one trip, when daytime high temperatures were below -10°F and there was a fierce Arctic wind. In warmer conditions, goggles are too good at protecting my face: They fog up because my skin starts perspiring.

footwear

Toward the end of our climb up New Hampshire's Mount
Washington, I had noticed that Joe was walking slowly and delicately, but I assumed this was because of poor conditioning and
a low pain tolerance. Admittedly, it had been a long day—Joe
and I, plus two other high school friends, had unintention-
ally taken a descent route that was twice as
long as we'd planned. Joe always refused
to reveal weaknesses to me, so he kept
his boots on throughout the four-hour
drive back from Pinkham Notch to
my parents' house.

Now here he was—along with his
shredded feet—in the bathroom with
my mom, who was rummaging
through the cabinets for more ban-
dages, moleskin, and tape. His feet
were a complete mess. He had fluid-
filled, dime-size blisters on the tops
and ends of his toes; half-dollar–size
blisters on his arch, forefoot, and heel;
and finger-length blisters along his foot's
outside edge. He also had a few
patches of badly macerated skin where
moisture had built up inside his waterproof boots, which he had outgrown a
year earlier. Fortunately, we were not
hiking again the following day. Instead,
I would drop him at the Nantucket
ferry in the morning, and he'd be back
in his lifeguard chair in the afternoon.

"You really need to pay more attention to the others in your group," my
mom said. She was right, but I wasn't
going to take all the blame. "Well,
they're his feet, and he should have

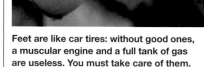

Feet are like car tires: without good ones,
a muscular engine and a full tank of gas
are useless. You must take care of them.

been paying attention to them too,"
I shot back.

Feet are the body's foundation.
Strong and health feet share three
qualities:

> Well-developed muscles and ten-
   dons;
> Biomechanically correct skeletal
   structure; and
> Dry, warm, blister-free skin.

part 2

Footwear needs

Boots and shoes are designed to help keep a backpacker's feet strong and healthy, although the barefoot running crowd has recently been singing the praises of natural conditioning for foot strength and health. The reality for most backpackers probably lies somewhere in between.

Because footwear (along with food) is one of a backpacker's two most personal choices, I've tried to qualify my observations and recommendations. In this chapter, I will simply share what has worked best for me.

What I look for

Regardless of the season, I always want the following from my footwear:

Good fit. Without it, I will quickly forget how many accolades my shoes have won or how discounted the price was. The shoe must be of proper length, width, and volume; it should match my arch; it should not aggravate foot abnormalities like bunions or overly pronounced bones in the hind foot; and it should have some flex and give, so that it comfortably conforms to my foot, not the other way around.

Breathability. If my shoes trap perspiration, my feet will become damp or wet, which can lead to blisters, maceration, and even immersion foot (or "trench foot").

Quick dry. In prolonged wet conditions—e.g., a day of hiking in steady rain or on variable spring snow—my

how2

shop for new shoes

1 Wear your preferred thickness of hiking sock to ensure an accurate fit.

2 Jam your toes into the front of the shoe and try to squeeze your index finger between your heel and the back of the shoe. If you cannot, the shoe is too short and your toenails will get battered and blistered during downhills.

3 After lacing the shoes, try moving your heel up and down, forward and backward, and side to side. A good heel cup and lacing system should lock your heel securely in place and limit this movement.

4 Wiggle your toes. The toe box should be roomy enough to do so, but not so roomy that your foot slides side to side, which will become a problem when side-hilling.

5 Take a short walk to ensure that the shoe allows for a natural stride, foot-plant, and heel-to-toe rotation.

shoes will inevitably get soaked. Even so-called "waterproof" footwear will ultimately fail: Water will enter through the top if I step in a deep puddle or cross a creek, or it will simply run down my legs. Moreover, after moderate use waterproof footwear loses its waterproofness—the sealant on full-grain leather breaks down, and booties made of waterproof/breathable fabrics like Gore-Tex suffer from overstressed seam tape and from degradation by dirt and sweat. If I were to wear waterproof/nonbreathable footwear, like rubber boots, my feet would get soaked by my own perspiration. Instead of trying in vain to keep my feet dry, I now wear footwear that retains and absorbs very little water and dries quickly. Specifically, I look for an upper made partially of a hydrophobic and porous nylon mesh.

Durability. My shoes should, ideally, last 500 to 750 miles—long enough

I swap out my shoes about every 500 miles.

to impact my bottom line and my environmental footprint. To extend the life of my shoes, I fortify their most common blowout points with Aqua Seal glue or additional stitching before I start using them.

Underfoot protection. My shoes need to offer underfoot protection, via a durable plate and/or resilient cushioning (ideally, polyurethane-based foam, rather than ethylene vinyl acetate, or EVA). Runners may be transitioning to ever more minimalist footwear, but they don't carry a loaded backpack, stay on their feet for up to 15 hours per day every day, and hike on such unfriendly surfaces. I have bruised my forefeet as the result of hiking in nonprotective footwear and feel that one or two extra ounces are worth it to prevent months of foot tenderness.

Sensitivity/agility. Underfoot protection cannot be at the expense of the sensitivity and agility of my feet, however. Especially when traveling off trail or in technical terrain (e.g., talus), it's important that my feet feel the surface with which they are in contact. Otherwise, I will not be as confident in my foot placements; I will not anticipate how my feet (or my body, which follows my feet) will move next; and my feet will be unable to adjust correctly to surface abnormalities.

Light weight. Five to six times as much energy is required to move weight on the feet as weight on the back, so wearing two-pound

part 2

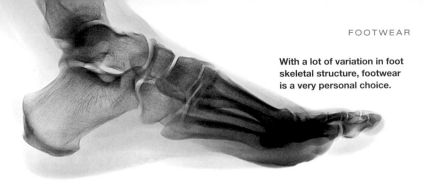

With a lot of variation in foot skeletal structure, footwear is a very personal choice.

shoes—instead of four-pound boots—is equivalent to lightening up your pack by 10 to 12 pounds. (If you are interested in learning more about this topic, read "Energy Cost of Backpacking in Heavy Boots," by S. J. Legg and A. Mahanty, published in *Ergonomics,* Volume 29, Issue 3, 1986, pages 433–438.) Excessively heavy footwear causes premature fatigue and general clumsiness, arguably increasing the likelihood of an accident more so than lighter footwear does.

Depending on the conditions, I *may* want my footwear to have the following features:

Insulation. In cold temperatures, insulation will reduce convective heat loss and keep my foot warmer. Insulation may be in the form of cut staple insulation like Thinsulate, or it may just be full-grain leather as opposed to porous mesh.

No insulation. In warm temperatures, my goal is the opposite: I want to keep my feet cool by wearing shoes that breathe and ventilate, which will result in evaporative and convective cooling.

Waterproof and breathable. A WP/B upper will prevent external

sources of *dry* moisture (e.g., cold snow) from wetting my feet and causing conductive heat loss. The shoes must remain breathable, or else my feet will get wet from the inside because of perspiration.

Stiff sole. When hiking or climbing on hard snow, stiff soles make it easier to kick steps and gain a more secure edge. When the snow is softer, flexible soles are adequate—just ask the hundreds of Pacific Crest Trail hikers who have gone through the High Sierra in June. Crampons have traditionally required stiff soles, but Kahtoola and CAMP both make flexible crampons for less technical applications.

Upper protection. If my route includes a lot of unfriendly ground cover—e.g., glacial moraines, scree fields, and thick brush—then I will want a more protective upper. These uppers are usually more durable too, though they are heavier and less breathable. On foot-friendly, maintained trails, there is less need for a protective upper, though I would still look for a toe guard in the event I accidentally kick a rock or root.

Support and control. I'm fortunate to have good biomechanics; a skeletal system well supported by strong muscles, ligaments, and tendons; and no history of ankle injuries. But if I were not so fortunate, I would probably need my footwear to provide support and motion control via shanks, medial posts, orthotics, and/or high- or mid-cut boots.

If you are prone to ankle sprains, I do recommend wearing high-cut boots. But realize they are not a panacea. You should also wear a brace on the weaker joint(s), use trekking poles, and/or try to improve your muscle strength and biomechanics.

Boots & shoes

Boots and shoes are not easily sorted into well-defined categories; they fall along a spectrum. On one end is the "backpacking boot." It covers the entire foot and ankle and some of the lower leg. Its upper is usually made of full-grain or synthetic leather; it is usually waterproofed with leather sealant like Tectron Sno-Seal or waterproof/breathable fabric. The EVA- or polyurethane-based midsole contains shanks (for stiffness) and plates (for underfoot protection). And the outsole is made of hard rubber, which in high-end boots is usually a branded variety, Vibram.

On the other end of this spectrum is the "trail-running shoe," which was not originally designed for backpacking but which can function well in this application. A trail-running shoe covers only the foot; it leaves the ankle and lower leg exposed. It features a nylon mesh upper that is reinforced, ideally, by a nylon skeleton, an EVA midsole that is shankless and plateless, and a "sticky rubber" outsole that has more aggressive lugs than those on a road running shoe.

In between the stereotypical backpacking boot and the stereotypical trail-running shoe are "hiking boots" and "hiking shoes." Hiking boots could be described as scaled-down backpacking boots, and hiking shoes as beefy trail-running shoes, or maybe low-cut hiking boots. But even backpacking boots and trail-running shoes break ranks. For example, one of the trail-running shoes in my closet has a

Are high-top boots helpful?

Biomechanically, my feet and ankles are designed to adapt to surface abnormalities; they are incredibly nimble and dexterous. In contrast, my knees and hips have a more limited range of motion, as anyone who has seen me dance will attest. By constricting my ankle in a high-top boot, I hinder its natural movements and force less adapted parts of my body (e.g., knees and hips) to absorb unevenness, which makes me less agile. A high-cut boot does not guarantee a sprainless trip: My ankle will still roll. But they can help as a first line of protection.

Not really.

part (2)

Hikers' footwear options fall along a spectrum.

HIKING BOOTS
The conventional choice, despite their discomfort and excessive weight.

TRAIL RUNNERS
An increasingly popular choice because of their weight and comfort.

HIKING SHOES
A happy medium—lighter than boots, more supportive than running shoes.

medial shank and a plastic heel stabilizer, both of which are bootlike features. And my friend owns a pair of mid-cut waterproof/breathable boots that have no shanks or plates, and weigh just two ounces more than my low-cut trail-running shoes. You can see how the traditional classifications get messy.

Backpackers have customarily worn high- or mid-cut boots, often "waterproof." I group such footwear with long-bladed knives, signaling mirrors, bandanas, hard-sided Nalgene water bottles, pump filters, seven-pound "bombproof" suspension packs, white gas stoves, and preassembled first aid kits—gear that novice backpackers think they need but probably do not. (For the record, I started my first long-distance hike with all of those things, and within 500 miles, I had ditched it all.)

Boots are not necessarily obsolete. Mountaineers and ice climbers need the warmth and stiff crampon-compatible outsole, for example. And I sometimes use them too; I also use cross-country ski boots and alpine ski boots.

But for the average three-season backpacking trip, my feet are much happier in a pair of low-cut non-waterproof trail-running shoes. I have worn trail-running shoes on every single long-distance trip that I have made, even on ambitious off-trail trips in the High Sierra, Iceland, Colorado Plateau, and Alaska.

Non-waterproof trail-running shoes have a number of advantages over boots and hiking shoes in three-season conditions:

> They are comfortable right out of the box—unlike a boot.
> They breathe and ventilate well because of their porous and hydrophobic materials.
> When they get soaked, they absorb minimal moisture and dry quickly.
> They generally favor agility and sensitivity over underfoot protection, but there are models that strike a good balance.
> They are about half the weight of a backpacking boot—1.5 to 2.0 pounds

Continued on p. 72

tools & techniques

tried&true

how to care for your feet

Because my itineraries are extremely hiking-centric, I need to care for my feet 24/7. If I fail to notice and remedy a problem, I'll have to spend more time in camp than I want to in order to let my paws recover. I also insist that others in my group be equally vigilant—just one person with battered feet can immobilize all of us.

Foot care

There are four basic themes to my foot care regimen that have served me well over the years:

Preemptive treatment. Spending five to ten minutes now can save hours of lost time (and/or miles of painful hiking) later on. Before I even leave the trailhead or camp, I protect areas where I get frequent blisters with Leukotape. If I notice an emerging "hot spot" after I begin hiking, I protect this irritated skin immediately before it becomes a blister. I keep my toenails short to prevent blisters from forming underneath them, and I keep them devoid of sharp edges that will cut adjacent toes and/or snag my socks.

Clean, warm, and dry. I wash my socks daily (inside and out; no soap) to prevent grit and organic matter from abrading my skin. At least once a day I take off my shoes and socks to let my feet dry and air out. And at night I put on a clean, dry, and warm pair of socks, which helps my feet recover overnight so they can withstand another day of abuse.

Moisture management. When my feet are kept wet, the outer layer of skin absorbs water and becomes pruned (or macerated). Macerated feet are itchy, sore, and blister prone; and they can crack after drying out. However, I know of no technique to keep my feet dry in prolonged wet conditions—I've experimented with every conceivable solution (including waterproof shoes, waterproof socks, and even rubber boots), and they all

fail. Instead, *I hope simply to minimize the effects of wet feet:*

> At night, after my feet have dried out, I coat the bottoms with a hydrophobic balm such as Hydropel or Joshua Tree Climbing Salve. This remoisturizes my skin and serves like a water sealant, which helps to reduce maceration tomorrow. (Note: Hydropel works best when it has had several hours to absorb into the skin—it will not help much if it's applied immediately before your feet get wet.)

> I wear thin socks and non-waterproof shoes made of low-absorption materials, which do not retain as much water as thick socks, conventional boots, or "waterproof" footwear. They also dry much faster.

Miles-proven footwear. Before I trust new shoes and socks on a long trip, I test them during low-risk outings. Generally, I like a small-volume shoe with a secure heel lock, roomy toe box, and generous cushion and forefoot protection but without any "corrective" supports like medial posts. Poor biomechanics and/or a weak muscular system may be partially remedied by orthotics or arch supports. And blisters between toes can be solved with Injinji toe socks.

Get a blister? Lance it. Drain the fluid. Apply a donut-shaped moleskin pad or bunion cushion to keep pressure off it. Finally, cover it with Leukotape.

tools & techniques

per pair (for men's size 9) versus 3.5 to 4.0 pounds, the equivalent in effort reduction to carrying 10 to 12 fewer pounds in my pack.

The lightness of trail-running shoes comes partially at the expense of durability: The most durable models can last about 500 miles, though some ultralight trail-running shoes will only make it 200 to 300 miles. These models are therefore ill suited for long trips through remote areas.

boots VS hiking shoes

	boots	hiking shoes
best use	Mountaineering, backpacking in dry snow	Backpacking with moderate load and/or on rough terrain
comfort	Uncomfortable until "broken in"	Comfortable out of the box
breathability	Poor; leather prevents escape of moisture	Decent, so long as they have no WP/B liner
dry time	Once wet, very difficult to get dry	Better than boots; not as good as running shoes
durability	1,000+ miles	750-ish miles
underfoot protection	Excellent	Good or fair
sensitivity/agility	Poor	Fair
weight per pair	3 to 4 lb	2 to 3 lb
ideal temperature range	Cool or cold	Mild or cool
water resistance	Best, but foot will get soaked in prolonged wet conditions	Minimal without WP/B liner, some with
sole stiffness	Very stiff	Moderate
support	Maximum, but overkill for most applications and users	Good
cost	$150+	$100 to $150

skurka's picks
BOOTS & SHOES

For on-trail trips, my current favorite is the **La Sportiva Electron trail-running shoe** ($115, 13 oz), which protects my underfoot with a plush rock-absorbing outsole. I would like it more if it didn't have a medial post, which provides arch support but restricts my natural form. Its curvy outsole is not suitable for early season travel on snow.

My longtime favorite shoe for off-trail trips was recently discontinued, so I'm currently searching for the perfect shoe. Manufacturers, listen up. I want a shoe that has a glove-like fit and low-to-the-ground design for excellent stability on uneven surfaces; an aggressively lugged outsole that bites into snow, mud, and wet grass while still sticking well on talus and slabs; a stiff forefoot plate that protects against cobbled gravel river bars without materially hindering the shoe's sensitivity; and a durable upper made of a nylon exoskeleton and porous mesh. Its weight should be about 12 ounces, and its life span should be 500 to 750 miles.

For winter conditions non-waterproof trail-running shoes are not suitable—they are not warm enough because they will get soaked from snow. Instead, I wear a mid-cut waterproof/breathable lightweight boot like the **La Sportiva FC 3.0 GTX** ($150, 18 oz), which will dry out faster than a classic full-grain leather model.

VS trail-running shoes

- Trail running and backpacking with light load
- Comfortable out of the box
- Good, so long as they have no WP/B liner
- Fast
- 500-ish miles
- Fair or poor
- Good or excellent
- 1 to 2 lb
- Warm or mild
- Minimal without WP/B liner, some with
- Minimal
- Fair
- $100-ish

Sandals, water shoes & barefoot-like shoes

Most backpackers prefer boots or shoes, but I've seen some using sandals, water shoes, and "barefoot" shoes.

Sandals are excellent in warm weather because they have maximum ventilation and minimal insulation. Because they absorb little water, sandals dry quickly, and they do not get heavy with water weight. I carried a pair on my Appalachian Trail thru-hike, but I concluded they were not worth the weight: I didn't wear them very often because they left my feet too exposed to rocks, sticks, thorns, and abrasive dirt. And they did not fit snugly because I could not crank down on the webbing without avoiding uncomfortable isolated pressure.

Water shoes, like those made by Chaco, Keen, and Teva, are closed-toed and absorb very little water because of their designs and materials. But they are generally not designed for walking long distances. They are best for sitting in a boat, making short portages, and relaxing in camp.

I've read about some backpackers using "barefoot" footwear such as the Vibram FiveFingers, which might be described best as a support-less and cushion-less foot wrap made of nylon and rubber. Most backpackers will probably find that these shoes lack adequate underfoot protection and cushion, especially in technical terrain and/or when carrying a heavier load.

Extra shoes

Frequently I see backpackers carrying an additional pair of "camp" or "river" shoes (e.g., sandals, boat shoes, Crocs, or running shoes). This allows them to slip into something more comfortable than their primary hiking shoes at the end of the day and/or to keep their shoes dry during a river ford or a rainstorm.

During some of my early long-distance trips, I brought two pairs of trail-running shoes (different models), which I would usually swap out once during the day. This had several benefits:

> It forced me to change my stride and foot strike, perhaps helping to avoid repetitive overuse injuries.
> It allowed me to have a dry pair of shoes, which my feet appreciated.
> It gave the cushion in each shoe more of a chance to rebound, extending the shoe's lifespan and improving comfort.

However, I no longer take extra shoes. If I want end-of-day comfort, I may loosen my shoelaces and remove my insole; on a hot day, I may dunk my feet in a cold river, or in cold weather, I may protect my feet from wet shoes with bread bags. I have also learned to cope with wet feet—an inherent part of backpacking, unless I limit my trips to desert environments.

The weight of "camp shoes" is hard for me to justify.

Orthotics & prefabricated arch supports

Shoes and boots come with a non-supportive, generic foam insert that is most accurately described as a "sock liner." To improve foot function, shoe fit, and comfort, you may consider custom orthotics or prefabricated arch supports. These inserts add cost and weight to the footwear, and they may alter the shoe's intended fit. They also cannot solve the source of an injury or pain, such as leg length discrepancies, excessive internal rotation, compensation for past injuries, muscle or tendon tightness, and/or a weak muscular and skeletal system.

Prefabricated arch supports from Superfeet, SOLE, and Spenco are a good solution for backpackers with fairly normal feet who need a little bit of extra support. They cost $30 to $50 and last about one year, depending on the intensity of use.

If you experience recurrent foot problems that are not solved with

Biomechanical flaws may be solved through conditioning or arch supports, or a combination thereof.

more arch support, seek the help of a foot health professional, who may recommend custom orthotics. These are based on a mold of your feet and are most helpful to those with very wide or narrow feet, specific biomechanical issues, or high arches, as well as to very heavy or large individuals. Orthotics cost $300-plus and can last years.

If you use arch supports or orthotics, you should take them with you whenever you go shopping for new footwear.

Socks

In three-season conditions, I wear lightweight socks in order to:

> Prevent blisters by reducing friction between my skin and shoes, and between my skin and debris that has entered my shoes; and
> Prevent skin maceration by wicking moisture away from my skin.

In winter conditions, I prevent trench foot and frostbite by insulating my feet with up to three pairs of socks.

Most socks are made primarily from polyester or merino wool, but they often include spandex (up to 15 percent) for improved fit and nylon (up to 40 percent) for improved durability, especially in high-friction areas like the toes and heel (see the section on base layers, pp. 31–38, in the Clothing chapter for more detailed fabric information). Darn Tough, DeFeet, Injinji, SmartWool, and Thorlo specialize in outdoor socks; many big retailers and athletic apparel companies make socks too. Socks may seem like a generic item, but they are not—their materials, thickness, seams, and construction greatly affect their performance.

The conventional three-season backpacking sock system has two components. A thin polyester *liner sock* is worn next to skin. Its primary purpose is to manage moisture. A thicker polyester or wool *outer sock* provides cushioning and insulation.

Usually, I wear only a liner—specifically, the DeFeet Wooleator ($12.50, 2 oz per pair), which is thin and unpadded; it's made of 63 percent merino wool, 36 percent nylon, and 1 percent spandex. Thin socks:

> Dry faster;
> Ventilate and breathe better; and
> Are cooler in warm conditions.

With my lightweight loads, I don't find padding necessary. I prefer the Wooleator over DeFeet's polyester version, the Aireator, because it smells less and remains suppler. I plan to replace my Wooleator socks about every 300 miles; the pairs I use for training last longer because I can machine-wash them regularly.

Sock thickness affects the fit of shoes. I prefer a single pair of liner socks.

how 2

use sock systems for wet & dry climates

1 **If I expect that my socks will get *wet,* then:** I hike in my "daytime" socks—which get wet and stay wet. After arriving at camp and letting my feet air dry, I put on my dry "sleeping" socks, which I never use during the day.

2 **If I expect that my socks will *not* get wet, then:** I leave camp wearing Pair A, with Pair B in my pack. Around midday, I rotate Pairs A and B. When convenient, I hand-wash Pair A (no soap) and loop the socks through my pack's compression straps so they can dry. When I pull into camp, I take off the dirty Pair B, let my feet dry, and put on Pair A, which is clean and dry. I leave camp in the morning wearing Pair A. When convenient, I wash Pair B, which will be dry and clean by midday so that they can be rotated again.

part 2

In limited situations, I may use a more traditional, thicker hiking sock, like the DeFeet EcoTrekker ($15, 3 oz), which has a mix of materials identical to the Wooleator. The Eco-Trekker absorbs more water and does not dry as quickly as a thinner sock, but it provides more insulation in cold, wet conditions. The EcoTrekker also reduces abrasion if my shoes are regularly filled with grit—along the Olympic coastline, say, or in the canyons of southern Utah. I need replacement pairs about every 600 miles.

On long-term trips in frigid temperatures (i.e., never above 15°F), I use a three-component system:

> As a next-to-skin liner, I use the DeFeet Wooleator Hi Top ($13, 2 oz), which is identical to the Wooleator except for a higher ankle cuff.
> I wear a thin vapor barrier liner sock from RBH Designs or Integral Designs; see the section on vapor barrier liners (pp. 56–60) in the Clothing chapter for details and an explanation of the technology.
> The EcoTrekker is worn over the first two layers, for warmth.

There are two other sock options worth mentioning, besides the conventional two-sock system and my one-sock preference:

> Neoprene socks, like the NRS HydroSkin Wetsocks ($25, 3 oz), are warmer than ones made of polyester or wool in cold, wet conditions, like those encountered year-round in Alaska and in the western mountain states' spring. Neoprene is a nonbreathable synthetic rubber that provides good insulation, even when wet; it is used to make fishing waders and diving wetsuits. Neoprene socks are not to be confused with "waterproof" socks, which are made of a waterproof/breathable laminate and have taped seams. These are not as warm as neoprene, and they don't stay waterproof—I have been disappointed with how quickly the material delaminates.
> Toe socks made by Injinji are excellent for those who tend to get blisters between their toes, though time-consuming to get on or off when wet.

Gaiters

Dirt, leaves, sticks, rocks, sand, and snow can enter my shoes, usually through the gap between the ankle and the shoe. Gaiters seal this gap. Conventional gaiters are made of waterproof/breathable fabric (e.g., Gore-Tex) or coated nylon; they stay positioned with a urethane strap that runs under the shoe and with a metal hook that grabs the shoelaces. Prices range from $25 to $90, and weights range from 5 to 12 ounces per pair.

Unfortunately, these mountaineering-inspired gaiters from Black Diamond, Mountain Hardwear, and Outdoor Research are ill suited for three-season backpacking:

> Their breathability and ventilation are limited, contributing to the

buildup of perspiration and the overheating of the lower legs.

> The gaiters are broadly sized— usually S/M and L/XL—so the fit is often imperfect. The calf cuff can be loose, the body can be baggy, and the hook can be incorrectly aligned with the laces.

> Hiking shoes and trail-running shoes do not have insteps, so any under-the-shoe strap or cord will be severed by the terrain.

A better option is the Simblissity LevaGaiter ($27, 2 oz per pair), which fit without the need for an instep strap or cord and which cost less and breathe and ventilate better than conventional gaiters. They weigh about one-fourth as much as the lightest conventional gaiter. When hiking mostly on trail, I get about 3,000 miles out of a pair; when mostly off trail, the abrasion from brush cuts the lifespan in half. I can improve their lifespan by protecting

how 2

make a fashion statement with your gaiters

1 Visit www.dirtygirl gaiters.com.

2 Place an order for a pattern like Wild Thang, Fetish, Lime Gaiterade Hurl, or Running with the Rockstars. Dirty Girl Gaiters cost $19 and weigh 1.2 ounces per pair.

3 When they arrive, make sure to install the Velcro strip to the back of your shoe. Otherwise they will slip off the hind foot.

Gaiters help to keep dirt, sand, rocks, and sticks from getting into my shoes.

tip | To make overboots for three-pin telemark ski boots, try taking Forty Below overboots with the bottoms cut out and adhering them around the ski boots with glue or Velcro.

the stitching with some Aquaseal glue or restitching them with dental floss.

I have yet to find a gaiter for winter conditions that I can genuinely recommend. My ideal winter gaiter would be made of uncoated stretchy nylon, be mid-height, and have a trim fit. In the meantime, I'll have to be content with mountaineering-inspired gaiters that lack good breathability and an athletic fit.

Overboots

If my feet will not be warm enough with a traditional boot/shoe and sock combination, I may use neoprene overboots for extra insulation. Daytime high temperatures must be colder than 10°F to 15°F for me to consider this option.

When snowshoeing, I use the Forty Below Light Energy overboots ($130, 15 oz per pair), which are designed to fit low-profile shoes, like running shoes or trail shoes; they feature 3-mm neoprene and a top-calf integrated gaiter. Two other cold-weather options are:

> Steger Mukluks, which are made of moosehide and are Native American inspired. They are very warm but not as stiff or supportive as the shoe/overboot combination; they are best for walking around town or on packed trails.
> NEOS overshoes, which have a rubber outsole and waterproof nylon upper, are clumsy and heavy, and I would rather wear waterproof boots than a running shoe/NEOS combination.

NEOS overboots are versatile, but heavier and bulkier than winter boots.

tools & techniques

sleeping
bags & pads

"You looked so cold last night that I considered inviting you into my sleeping bag," said Wild Boar, my sheltermate, when I sat up in the morning. Despite her not being my type and despite having met her just ten hours earlier, I responded, "Yeah, I would have liked that."

A high-pressure front had moved into Vermont's Green Mountains the day before, and a clear overnight sky allowed temperatures to plummet into the 40s. It didn't help that the shelter was located in a deep gorge into which cold air had settled. Six weeks earlier, while farther south, I had exchanged my three-season mummy bag—which was much too hot for the mid-Atlantic's summertime heat and humidity—for a 300-weight fleece blanket. And I had gone to bed the night before resigned to nightlong shivering because this was the unavoidable consequence of having an insufficiently warm sleeping bag, or so I thought.

There were many things I could have done that night to avoid being cold. I could have kept my legs off the

There are many factors that affect your nighttime warmth, like your shelter and tentmates.

part 2

cold shelter floor by putting my backpack under them; worn my rain jacket and used my extra socks as gloves; reduced the draftiness of my shelter; made a big bowl of soup before turning in; and/or, yes, spooned with Wild Boar. But of the tools that can help keep me warm at night, three are disproportionately important: my sleeping bag, sleeping pad, and shelter, the first two of which I discuss in this chapter.

Sleeping bags

A sleeping bag reduces convective heat loss by trapping body-warmed air in tiny pockets so it does not dissipate freely into the atmosphere. These air pockets are formed by high-loft insulation like goose down or synthetic fill, which is sandwiched between two layers of fabric.

A sleeping bag is assigned a temperature rating based on its warmth, which depends on the amount and type of its insulation, its shell fabrics, and its style. Only temperature ratings and styles are discussed in this chapter. Sleeping bags use the same insulations and shell fabrics used in insulated clothing, and they are covered in that chapter.

Temperature ratings

A temperature rating—e.g., "35 degrees"—is generally regarded as the coldest temperature at which the average sleeper will remain warm. Manufacturers rarely explain how they determine these ratings. And, even if they did, it's unlikely that the ratings would apply perfectly to everyone,

how 2

learn the best uses for your bag

1 Use sleeping bags first on low-risk trips in your backyard or on quick overnights so that you can easily bail and avoid the consequences of prolonged failure.

2 Learn your bag's optimal and extreme uses by testing it in a range of temperatures.

3 Discover how your nighttime warmth is affected by using the bag in conjunction with different sleeping pads, clothing systems, and shelters.

given differences in shelters and sleeping pads, gender and body type, metabolism and sleeping style (e.g., side sleeper, back sleeper), clothing system, and/or ambient humidity. In the United States, most manufacturers assign temperature ratings by field-testing and by comparing their models against each other and against the models of competing manufacturers. There is no standard method for determining temperature ratings.

Two bags from competing manufacturers may have the same

temperature rating, but the factors that contribute to it—their insulation type and amount, dimensions, shell fabrics, hood design, draft tubes, and collars—may be notably different. For the time being, at least, product reviews by other backpackers and anecdotal reports from knowledgeable sales staff are probably the best indicators of a bag's warmth.

Europe uses a more scientific method of assigning temperature ratings. Called EN 13537, this standard laboratory test is now making its way across the Atlantic thanks to motivated U.S. manufacturers and to European manufacturers that also distribute in North America.

The European standard assigns four ratings to every sleeping bag, e.g., 60.7, 31.4, 10.6, and 1.8 degrees. The first rating is the *maximum temperature* at which an average adult male will not overheat. The second is a *comfort temperature* at which an average woman will be comfortable. The third is a *lower limit* at which an average adult male will remain warm. And the fourth is an *extreme temperature* at which an average woman will survive but become slightly hypothermic. Still, backpackers in Europe—as in the United States—have to learn how the laboratory settings relate to their personal uses. Firsthand familiarity is far more valuable than manufacturer-determined temperature ratings.

Sleeping bag styles

My first sleeping bag was an inexpensive, flannel-lined, rectangular bag that refused to be contained by any stuff sack. But I was only ten and it was perfect for car camping with my family and the Boy Scouts. In advance of my

mummy VS **top bag**

	mummy	top bag
availability	Widespread	Select manufacturers, notably Big Agnes
thermal efficiency (i.e., warmth per weight)	Poor. Sleeper crushes up to 30% of insulation, and zippers add weight, not warmth.	Can be excellent if not undermined with excessively roomy dimensions.
usable temperature range	Limited. They do not vent well or evenly; fixed girth limits ability to wear clothing at night.	Limited. They do not vent well or evenly; fixed girth limits ability to wear clothing at night.
user friendliness	Good, though twisters and turners get tangled.	Excellent. Very difficult to roll off pad or get tangled within bag.

first real backpacking trip ten years later, I upgraded to a mummy bag.

Mummy bags fully enclose my body and head in a cocoon-like wrap of insulation. Their main benefits are immediately clear: The integrated hoods minimize drafts, and the tapered designs eliminate dead air spaces inside the bag that otherwise I would have to keep warm.

Mummies are all constructed with the same types of insulation, shell fabrics, and techniques. They all also have features like draft tubes, contoured hoods, neck collars, and side zippers. Most manufacturers now offer men's and women's models, to account for gender differences in body dimensions and metabolisms. Men's models (which are usually the basis for unisex models too) are roughly Y-shaped, because men typically have V-shaped upper bodies and ruler-straight legs. Women's models are less tapered, because there is usually less of a difference in width between a woman's shoulders and hips. Extra insulation may be added too, because many women are cold sleepers.

Mummy bags may offer a cocoon-like escape from cold nights, but this design has drawbacks:

> It is easy to become disoriented inside the bag if you twist and turn, making it hard to stay on your sleeping pad, to locate the side zipper for a midnight pee, or to keep your face aligned with the hood's opening. Wide bags are better in this regard, but they are heavier and less warm (because of dead air pockets).
> Mummy bags have limited venting features and are therefore not comfortable across a wide range of

quilt VS wearable

quilt	wearable
Cottage companies	**Cottage companies**
Best. They have no wasted insulation and materials under sleeper; no zippers, draft tubes.	**Highly dependent on design; could be good or very poor.**
Excellent. They can be worn loosely or tightly; variable girth accommodates many clothing systems.	**Highly dependent on design; could be good or very poor.**
Mixed. Simple and flexible, but they can be drafty.	**Excellent. They are much more versatile than other bag types.**

On clear nights I avoid exposed campsites like this one, so I can take a lighter sleeping bag.

temperatures. Their hoods can be easily loosened, but the traditional side zipper causes unequal venting. Chest zippers are better but not widely available. Either way, zippers are an impending disaster when used next to ultralight shell fabrics—they tend to get caught in the zipper's teeth, so I would prefer not to have one at all.

> About 30 percent of a mummy's potential warmth is wasted because it is crushed underneath the sleeper, where it cannot loft and trap body-warmed air in its tiny chambers.

> The girth of mummy bags is fixed, and it is therefore an inflexible component of a sleep system. For example, if my mummy bag is just wide enough for me when I'm wearing a thin shirt and pants, then I can't wear my insulated parka on nights that are colder than its range.

There are three alternative designs to mummy bags:

Top bags are identical to mummy bags with one exception: On the underside, there is a sleeve in which a sleeping pad fits, instead of there being insulation, baffles, and shell fabrics. A top-bag system is lighter and more packable than a comparable mummy bag, and a sleeper cannot roll off the pad because the pad and top bag are securely connected.

Quilts are similar to those found on household beds, though they are constructed from outdoor-worthy fabrics and insulations;

Because of their variable girth, quilts pair efficiently with a range of clothing systems.

part 2

some quilts also have a foot box that extends up to the knees or lower hamstrings. Quilts must be wide enough to cover a sleeper completely and to be tucked partially underneath. Most quilts have webbing buckles on the underside that can be tightened around the sleeper to minimize drafts, or around a sleeping pad to simulate a top-bag experience. However, I've never found the webbing strips to be user-friendly—or crucial—so I remove them.

Quilts are not widely used despite having many advantages in three-season conditions:

> They are more thermally efficient (i.e., warmth for weight) and more packable than other bag styles because they lack zippers, material-intensive hoods, and underside insulation.
> They have a broader comfort range because they are more versatile: In warm temperatures, I can loosely drape a quilt over me; in colder temperatures, I can button up the backside and neck collar; and in camp, I can use it as a shawl. For a winter trip in northern Minnesota, I once used my quilt as an overbag, because my primary three-season mummy bag was not sufficiently warm for the conditions. This saved me the expense of buying a separate winter-grade bag.
> They dry quickly when laid out in the sun because they open up completely; this is possible only with mummies and top bags that have full-length zippers.
> A sleeper does not have to *slide* into a quilt—he can just drape it

how2
minimize quilt draftiness

The advantages of a quilt can be quickly lost if the sleeper does not address its inherent weaknesses: draftiness and no insulation around the head and neck. I try to address these problems by:

1 Wearing hooded clothing at night.

2 Using a water-resistant bivy sack in conjunction with an open-ended tarp, or using a fully enclosed shelter like a mid-tarp (see the Shelters chapter, beginning on p. 90, for more information).

3 Being a calm sleeper. I taught myself to stop twisting and turning at night.

over him—which is a convenient perk for hammock campers.
> They have variable girths, so they can be adjusted in accordance with a clothing system.

Wearable bags make quilts look conventional. Some models, like the Jacks 'R' Better No Sniveller ($270, 21 oz), are enhanced quilts that can be configured as a serape or poncho.

A wearable
sleeping bag
from MusucBag

In contrast, the Nunatak Raku ($619, 30 oz) and Exped Dreamwalker ($300, 35 oz) are hybrids of parkas and mummy bags. A wearable bag is multifunctional. It serves as both a sleeping bag at night and as a jacket in camp and during midday rest stops. Though it can save weight, I question whether a wearable bag functions well as either a garment or a sleeping bag.

skurka'spicks
SLEEPING BAGS

When nighttime temperatures are consistently above 20°F, and ideally above 30°F, I prefer quilts. In dry environments like the Rocky Mountains, the Southwest, and the Pacific Coast states during the summer, high-loft goose down insulation is the clear winner. In these conditions, my picks are the one-season and three-season **GoLite UltraLight Quilts** ($220 to $275, 20 to 24 oz).

In wetter climates like the East Coast, Pacific Northwest, or Alaska, synthetic insulations are a better choice, though they are not "warm when wet" as sometimes advertised. The 30-degree and 45-degree **Mountain Laurel Designs Spirit** ($180 to $195, 13 to 18 oz) quilts are excellent picks for these conditions. I used the 30-degree quilt during my Alaska-Yukon Expedition in temperatures from 20°F to 55°F. The 45-degree quilt would be perfect for all but the hottest summer months. The Spirit features the best synthetic insulation and shell fabric currently available, ClimaShield Apex and Pertex Quantum. The Apex insulation seemed much more durable than other synthetic insulations I have used, but it still does not rival down.

When temperatures are consistently below 20°F, I take a mummy bag instead of a quilt. During the Alaska-Yukon Expedition, I was very comfortable in temperatures down to -25°F, wearing two hooded parkas and two pairs of insulated pants inside a 0-degree mummy bag; I never even needed to zip the bag closed.

Because a winter-rated sleeping bag contains so much insulation, the insulation's thermal efficiency and compressibility become hugely important, or else the bag becomes unwieldy in both weight and size. As an example, consider MontBell's 0-degree mummy bags: The 800-fill down version weighs 2 pounds 13 ounces and compresses to 8 by 16 inches, whereas the synthetic-fill version weighs 4 pounds 8 ounces and compresses to 9 by 18 inches.

This explains why in cold conditions I prefer down insulation, which I prevent from getting wet by using vapor barrier liners, as explained in the Clothing chapter. sp

Sleeping pads

The primary function of a sleeping pad is to minimize conductive heat loss. If I were to lie on the ground without a pad—or a similar barrier—my body heat would freely transfer into the ground until I was the same temperature as it. This heat transfer would be fine if I were napping on warm beach sand, but discomfort, or worse, would be guaranteed during an eight-hour padless camp on snow.

The warmth of a sleeping pad—or, more precisely, the pad's ability to resist heat transfer—is indicated by its R-value. Warm sleeping pads have high R-values, and pads that have minimal thermal resistance have low R-values. An R-value is a linear measurement, so a pad with an R-value of 4.0 is four times as warm as a pad with an R-value of 1.0.

Most sleeping pads are also designed to increase nighttime comfort through added cushioning. If I choose my campsites wisely, however, cushioning is never a necessary attribute. A thick layer of pine needles, moss, grass, and leaves can be just as comfortable—if not more so—as plush sleeping pads that weigh two to four pounds, especially if I "landscape" the surface to better match the contours of my body. Moreover, these organic materials are also less thermally conductive than hard-packed ground or rock, so I stay warmer. If I will be forced to camp in established, high-use, hard-packed sites where natural cushioning is long gone, I will be more inclined to take a more cushioned pad. A good night's rest will easily offset the extra four to eight ounces.

There are two main types of sleeping pads: closed-cell foam and inflatables, which has two subtypes, self-inflating and air chamber. All pads work by preventing the movement of air. But pads differ in how—and how effectively—they accomplish this. Pads also vary in their weight, cost, durability, and comfort.

Closed-cell foam pads

Foam is any liquid or solid with entrapped gaseous bubbles. Solid foams can be classified as either *open-cell* or *closed-cell,* both of which are used in sleeping pads, though only closed-cell is used as a standalone material. Open-cell foams—like those found in couch cushions or dish sponges—have interconnected pores that permit passive air convection; these pores can also fill with water.

tip Sleeping pads can double as "virtual frames" in a frameless backpack for added structure, comfort, and capacity. They can also double as splints in emergencies.

Inflatable Pads

CLOSED-CELL FOAM Reliable, and very warm for the weight, but bulky.

AIR CHAMBER Extremely plush and compactable, but expensive and not as reliable.

SELF-INFLATING Uses open-cell foam to minimize convective air movement within the pad.

In contrast, the gaseous bubbles in closed-cell foam are isolated in small pockets, so the material is essentially waterproof. Closed-cell foam is also stiffer and more rigid.

Closed-cell foam sleeping pads like the Therm-a-Rest Ridge Rest SOLite ($30, 14 oz) are less expensive and warmer for their weight than self-inflating or air chamber pads. Cheaper foam pads are available in the camping department of big department stores and sporting goods stores; Wal-Mart sells a 19-ounce pad for just $12.

Closed-cell foam pads have a number of advantages over inflatable pads. They are:

> Inexpensive;
> Very reliable—they can't leak or puncture, and they don't need to be treated delicately; and
> Easily modifiable, if I want a custom-cut size or shape.

Because of its construction, closed-cell foam is dense and rigid.

Therefore, these pads lack cushioning, and they are not compactable. But they are not everlastingly resilient. I replace a foam pad after about six to eight weeks of use because it flattens out, reducing its insulation and comfort.

Inflatables

Therm-a-Rest dominated the inflatable pad market for many years. In fact, Therm-a-Rest is often used interchangeably with "inflatable sleeping pad." More recently, competition from companies like Big Agnes, Exped, NEMO, and Pacific Outdoor Equipment has helped drive innovation in this product category.

There are two types of Inflatable pads:

Self-inflating pads, like the Therm-a-Rest ProLite Plus ($100, 24 oz), consist of open-cell foam that is sandwiched by two sheets of polyester or nylon nonslip fabric with sealed edges. When a self-inflating pad's valve is opened, the open-cell

part (2)

foam expands and creates a vacuum, which causes air to rush in. In truth, these pads are only "partially self-inflating." They must always be topped off with external pressure, from lungs or a pump.

Air chamber pads share this sandwich-like construction, but they omit the open-cell foam. Inflatable pads are much more comfortable and compactable than closed-cell foam varieties. This is especially true with air chamber pads, some of which could more accurately be described as mattresses. The Therm-a-Rest NeoAir ($150, 14 oz) is a dreamy 2.5 inches thick, for example. This luxurious comfort has earned these pads the devotion of many owners.

Inflatable pads have a tremendous structural flaw, however. The sleeper can be robbed of their warmth by the unimpeded exchange within the pad of body-warmed air with ground-cooled air. Pads that are unable to limit air circulation (e.g., via open-cell foam, goose down or synthetic insulation, or mini air chambers within the larger chambers) are ill suited for cold-weather camping.

Inflatable pads have other problems, too. They can leak because of wear, manufacturing-related defects, and/or punctures; they therefore need to be treated delicately. Air chamber pads filled with down or synthetic insulations must be inflated with a pump, because moisture-filled breaths will adversely affect the insulation's warmth. And in cold conditions, they may need to be reinflated after lung-warmed air cools down.

skurka'spicks
SLEEPING PADS

For most solo three-season trips, I prefer the **Therm-a-Rest Ridge Rest SOLite** ($30, 14 oz), which I cut in half and use as a torso-length pad and as a cylinder-shaped virtual frame in my frameless backpack. I insulate my lower body with my backpack, maps, and sometimes even my trash. A slightly lighter option is the **Gossamer Gear Nightlight** ($32, 11 oz), but the SOLite is less expensive and more widely available.

When camping on snow in temperatures less than about 20°F, I use a full-length **RidgeRest Solar** ($40, 19 oz). I have used this pad in temperatures as low as -20°F, which is definitely not when I want to discover that my pad has a slow leak.

I generally prefer closed-cell foam, but there are two instances when I will carry an inflatable pad. On casual and guided trips, when weight is of less crucial importance, I often take a nine-ounce torso-length self-inflating pad. If/when it punctures, there is ample time to repair it; and I'm not throwing a flattened foam pad in the landfill every six to eight weeks. I will also use an inflatable pad on winter trips that entail extensive bushwhacking, which is even more difficult when a full-length foam pad is perched atop my backpack.

tools & techniques

shelters

The forest was dense and the side of the abandoned logging road was filled with brush and slash piles, so I'd wound up pitching my poncho-tarp directly on the road in a lean-to configuration. "That should do," I remember thinking when I anchored the last guyline and skewer stake with a pile of baseball-size rocks—knowing full well that it might not. The barometric pressure had dropped precipitously in the last 24 hours, and the place I was camping, on Washington's Olympic Peninsula, receives about 125 inches of rain per year. Maybe I was also hoping that Mother Nature would show some mercy. I was only three days away from finishing my 11-month Sea-to-Sea Route hike. Of course, it soon began raining hard; then the wind picked up.

A particularly strong gust at around 5 a.m. yanked a stake from its mooring and my poncho-tarp fell on top of me like a wet blanket. I briefly considered repitching the shelter but opted instead to get moving. I slithered into my soaking poncho-tarp and started running down the road to jump-start my internal heat-producing engine.

When conditions deteriorate, "shelter" can be defined generously.

After about two hours of hiking in the downpour, my situation took a 180-degree turn. I was sipping hot cocoa, wearing a fleecy sweat suit while my clothes tumbled in the dryer, and being entertained at the home of 85-year-old Elizabeth Barlow. She has since passed away, but I will never forget her or her treasure chest of Indian artifacts, historical photos, and even a woolly mammoth tooth that she had found while beachcombing the Olympic coast. Not to mention her purple sweatshirt, which fittingly read, "Can't complain . . . Nobody listens!"

Shelter functionality

It is commonly assumed that back-packers need a "tent," but in reality, most just need protection from precip-itation, wind, bugs, and groundwater. I'd argue that other types of shelters match their needs just as well, with perhaps other advantages like lower weight and more versatility. I evaluate backpacking shelters using four criteria:

> Portability
> Environmental resistance
> Condensation resistance
> Adaptability

Notably missing from this list is a shelter's ability to replicate the com-forts of a permanent home. Instead, I try to be realistic about the poten-tial performance of my home away from home, which often amounts to less than a pound of waterproof nylon, bug mesh, thin guyline cords,

and aluminum stakes. I don't expect my shelter to have a mudroom and ample space, or to keep out grizzly bears and every bug. In lieu of these features, I seek out campsites that will be relatively dry, warm, calm, and comparatively un-buggy; my clothing and sleep system can withstand the inevitable moisture accumulation; and at least occasionally I expect to crawl into a damp shelter wearing damp clothes and to snuggle inside a damp sleeping bag.

Portability

Sometimes it's possible to rely on man-made or natural permanent shel-ters. I've slept in dozens of shel-ters on the Appalachian Trail and in the Adirondacks and have used rock alcoves in the Grand Canyon and in South Africa's Drakensberg Moun-tains. But usually I need a portable house on my back. And to be porta-ble, it must be reasonably lightweight.

The weight of group shelters should be divided by the number of occu-pants, for a per person weight. High-occupancy shelters are generally more weight-efficient than low-occupancy shelters because the marginal increase in weight declines with each additional person. For example, my favorite solo shelter weighs 13 ounces, yet the two-person version (which is identical but proportionally larger) weighs only 16 ounces, or 8 ounces per person.

Environmental resistance

I need my shelter to protect me from environmental threats and

Airflow through an open-sided tarp will help to minimize condensation buildup.

annoyances, namely rain, snow, or sleet—which can fall vertically, be blown horizontally, or cover the ground—along with wind and insects. If exposed to precipitation and wind, I will lose heat through conduction and convection. If left vulnerable to insects, I will struggle to get a good night's rest, at a minimum.

It is *not* necessary to have full-time protection from *all* environmental factors—just the expected and unavoidable ones. For example, in July, I will not camp anywhere in Minnesota without bug protection, but by September, I will; and I do not camp in the Badlands without a fully enclosed shelter capable of protecting me from stiff winds and horizontally blowing precipitation, but I will in the East, since even in a hurricane, I could get out of the wind by pitching an open-ended shelter in a thick cluster of trees or bushes (and then hoping that nothing falls on top of me). To learn how to identify expected and unavoidable environmental factors, refer to Know Before You Go, pp. 20–27.

I do not include cold as an environmental threat against which my shelter must protect me; there are more weight-efficient ways to do this. Consider that four extra ounces of down in my sleeping bag will increase its warmth by about ten degrees, whereas to increase the warmth of my shelter by a comparable amount, I would need to add two to three pounds of material to it.

Condensation resistance

It happens to almost every back-packer. When we wake up in the morning, our shelter's interior is coated in condensation and/or the shelter's exterior is coated in dew or frost. Here, I will attempt to explain why this happens and how it can be prevented.

The amount of moisture that *can* be absorbed by air is a function of the ambient air temperature. For example, air at 86°F can absorb three times more moisture than air at 50°F. The amount of moisture in the air relative to its maximum vapor content is known as relative humidity. For example, if air at 95°F contains 20 grams of moisture per cubic meter, relative humidity is 50 percent, because it is actually capable of containing 40 grams. The dew point is the temperature at which the air becomes oversaturated (humidity exceeding 100 percent) and some water vapor condenses into liquid.

Condensation, dew, and frost form first on the coldest objects, the air around which has the lowest dew point. The coldest part of a shelter is usually the outermost wall—it is not kept warm by the occupants (like sleeping bags are), the earth (like the floor is), or by an outer wall (like an inner wall is).

There are two ways that manufacturers and backpackers can improve the condensation resistance of their shelters:

> Reduce humidity inside the shelter by allowing interior moisture to escape through ventilation or through walls made of waterproof/breathable fabric, as in the case of tarps and single-wall tents. Interior humidity can often exceed atmospheric humidity because of the occupants' breathing and the evaporation of moisture from wet equipment or uncovered ground.

> Keep surface temperatures above the dew point, ideally by choosing relatively warm and dry camps and by camping underneath a radiant reflector such as a leafed tree. Refer to p. 104 for details. Alternatively, a heavy double-walled shelter can be used.

Adaptability

The functions I demand from my shelter change with time and location. For example, I might need rain protection on Friday but none on Saturday, or bug protection in early June and none two weeks and 200 miles later. I might also be forced to camp in a suboptimal location that doesn't permit a textbook pitch. An easily adaptable shelter helps to maintain a high level of performance while minimizing weight, time, expense, and logistical hassles.

Shelter fabrics

A shelter's weight, durability, breathability, and water resistance are greatly affected by the fabrics from which it's made. The two most common are nylon and polyester. Generally speaking, nylon is lighter and more abrasion-resistant than polyester, but polyester absorbs less water and is supposedly more resistant to UV degradation. There is no such thing as a standard nylon or polyester fabric; their performance

Fabric coatings help keep rain outside.

Ripstop nylon with regular reinforcing fibers

characteristics are significantly affected by three factors:

Fabric weight

A single 9,000-meter-long silk fiber weighs 1 denier (or 1D). By comparison, tent floors are usually made of thick 70D fibers in order to improve the fabric's abrasion resistance; the lightest fibers being used are 10D, but 20 to 40D fibers are more common. A fiber's denier is a general indication of its weight per square area. Heavy-duty tent floors weigh 2 to 3 ounces/yard.

Weaving style

Taffeta is a smooth, woven fabric made of fibers with uniform weight. A *ripstop* is basically a taffeta that features reinforcing fibers at regular intervals in order to improve the fabric's strength and tear resistance. The reinforcing fibers create a crosshatch pattern and are usually made of heavier denier nylon or a stronger type of fiber (e.g., Dyneema).

Coatings

Nylons and polyesters can be coated with polyurethane (PU) or impregnated with silicone for enhanced water resistance. These fabrics are described as "waterproof," though they are decidedly not after extended wear. A fabric's waterproofness will degrade more quickly if the fabric is extremely lightweight, stored wet, and/or subject to a lot of abrasion (e.g., shelter floors and those that come in contact with other items in a backpack). Uncoated fabrics are lighter and more breathable than waterproof fabrics, but they are less durable and much less water-resistant. Rainflies, floors, and tarp canopies need to be made of coated fabrics; tent canopies that are protected with a rainfly can be made of uncoated fabric.

Several small manufacturers use "fantasy fabrics" like Cuben Fiber, spinnaker sailcloth, and ultralight silicone-impregnated nylon, which can

tip Shelter walls or floor leaking? Restore polyurethane-coated fabrics with McNett's Tent Sure sealant, and silicone-impregnated nylon with Atsko Silicone Water Guard.

part 2

weigh as little as 0.5 ounce/yard, 1.0 ounce/yard, and 1.3 ounces/yard, respectively. These fabrics tend to be very expensive and their durability can be questionable. For the average backpacker, there are probably other, more economical ways to reduce pack weight.

Tents

I will define a tent as a shelter that includes a fully enclosed tent body (and, in the case of a double-wall tent, a matching rainfly), custom cut and shaped poles, stakes, and possibly guyline cord.

Double-wall tents

The main body of a double-wall tent features a waterproof floor and a non-waterproof nylon canopy that has large panels of no-see-um mesh for improved ventilation. A waterproof polyester rainfly is secured over the top of the canopy for protection from precipitation. Most double-wall tents are freestanding, but some have hoop configurations that need front and rear anchors.

It is easy to understand why double-wall tents like the two-person REI Half Dome 2 ($180, 5 lb 8 oz) are unquestionably the most popular type of backpacking shelter. Pitching them is foolproof; my best friend and I could set one up in a few minutes when we were just ten. They offer full-time protection from all the elements. (Although some models offer the option of just pitching the canopy without the rainfly, or the rainfly without the canopy—in conjunction with an optional nylon "footprint" or floor—to save weight.) And the inner wall is more resistant to condensation buildup because it is insulated by the rainfly and because it is breathable.

Double-wall tents are highly functional, but they have one and a half significant drawbacks. The one: They are the heaviest type of shelter available. A one-person double-wall tent weighs three to four pounds, and a multi-person model weighs two to three pounds *per person.* Even when some of the components are left at home, they are still heavy: a rainfly and footprint setup (which offers no protection against insects) usually weighs 1.5 to

Double-wall tents are full-service shelters, but they are relatively heavy for hikers wanting to travel light.

2 pounds per person. The half: The condensation resistance of double-wall tents is limited in calm conditions. Excessive moisture will be trapped by the nonbreathable rainfly because no dry outside air will flow under it.

Single-wall tents

A single-wall tent like the two-person Black Diamond Firstlight ($300, 3 lb 5 oz) combines a waterproof floor with a canopy made of waterproof-breathable (WP/B) fabric, through which moisture can pass, eliminating the need for a separate rainfly. Because moisture can escape through the canopy fabric, the shelter can be completely closed off from the outside (no vents, no open doors, etc.), which makes it an excellent escape from horrible weather and explains why mountaineers and alpinists commonly use single-wall tents. As a perk, single-wall tents are designed to be pitched from the inside.

Single-wall tents are simpler and less material-intensive than double-wall tents. However, these advantages are offset by the greater cost and weight of the canopy's WP/B fabric.

Single-wall tents are excellent winter shelters, but they may be less

	double-wall tents	single-wall tents	tarp systems
portability/ weight	Poor. One-person models weigh 3 to 4 lb. Multiperson models weigh 2 to 3 lb per person.	Fair. Two-person models weigh 1.5 to 2 lb per person.	Excellent. Fully enclosed one-person system weighs just 1 to 1.5 lb, or less when modular parts not needed.
environmental resistance	Complete protection	Complete protection, usually designed for four-season use.	Poor to excellent, depending on design and components
condensation resistance	Good; moisture usually accumulates only on outer wall.	Fair to good, depending on breathability of fabric and venting features	Good to excellent, depending on size and number of venting features
adaptability	Poor to fair. Most models have fixed pitch; some allow rainfly-only pitch.	Poor; no versatility in pitch or functions	Good to excellent; many pitching options

Waterproof-breathable walls allow single-wall shelters to be sealed shut.

VS tarp tents	VS wp/b bivies	VS hammocks
Excellent; weighs just 1 to 2 lb per person	Excellent; weighs just 1 to 2 lb.	Excellent; weighs just 1 to 2 lb.
Complete protection	Complete protection, though minimal working room inside	Complete protection, though minimal working room inside and not suitable for cool temps.
Poor to fair, depending on design and pitch; very susceptible to moisture accumulation inside.	Poor due to limited breathability of WP/B fabric	Excellent
Poor to fair; no interchangeable components, but pitch slightly adjustable	Poor; can be laid almost anywhere but no pitching or function options.	Good; pitchable anywhere where there are trees; rainfly can be left at home

practical for three-season back-packing because they are prone to condensation buildup—WP/B fabric isn't tremendously breathable, as explained in the chapter on Clothing (see pp. 47–56). The ventilation of single-wall tents may be limited too, depending on the design: If the tent does not have windows and doors that are covered with no-see-um mesh, the shelter must be kept closed to keep the bugs out; if the windows and doors must be closed completely when it's raining, then again there is no ventilation.

Tarp systems

If not used in conjunction with other items, a tarp—which I will define as merely a sheet of waterproof fabric, or several sheets of waterproof fabric that have been stitched together—is useful only as a ground cloth. But with anchors, rope (i.e., guylines), and rigid shafts (e.g., trekking poles, tree branches, or trunks), a tarp can be used as a canopy against vertically falling precipitation, and perhaps horizontally blowing precip too, depending on the tarp's design and pitch. And with additional modular components—like a head net, interior bug nest, bivy sack (imagine a cocoon for your sleeping bag), and/or dedicated ground cloth—I can create a fully functional tarp system.

The per person weight of a tarp system ranges from about 8 ounces to 2 pounds. It *can* offer complete protection against precipitation, wind, and bugs. A tarp system can also ventilate extremely well, so it is more

The poncho/tarp is a classic multi-use item: rain gear, shelter, and pack cover.

condensation-resistant; with just the slightest breeze, dry outside air will take the place of humid interior air. And its modular components are flexible and interchangeable. A tarp system is at least as functional as a conventional double-wall tent.

The most common hang-up with tarps is the concern over being or feeling too exposed. The availability of fully enclosed tarp systems and tarp canopies with 360-degree protection mutes this worry. A more legitimate drawback is that they are not as user-friendly as tents. It requires more knowledge and skill to make them functional and to use them optimally.

Flats

Flat tarps like the eight-by-ten-foot Integral Designs Siltarp 2 ($145, 10 oz) are the simplest and least expensive type of tarp. Because they consist only of fabric, they are also the lightest per coverage area. In skilled hands, a flat tarp is like a sheet of flat paper to an origami genius—the possibilities are endless. Basic pitch configurations include the A-frame, lean-to, and communal canopy (above a cooking or hang-out area). But if it is storming from all directions, the tarp can be pitched to the ground on all sides; if the wind is blowing from just one direction, the pitch can offer more selective protection; if the conditions are mild and humid, the pitch can be maximized for ventilation. The functionality of a flat tarp is limited only by imagination.

A poncho-tarp like the Sea to Summit Tarp-Poncho ($85, 12 oz) is a special type of flat tarp, designed to be used as a shelter, rain gear, and a pack cover. I have extensive experience with poncho-tarps, having used one for about 5,000 miles of the Sea-to-Sea Route and for a thru-hike of the Colorado Trail. Its multifunctionality appealed to me, and at the time, it represented a significant weight savings over a dedicated shelter, rain gear, and pack protection. Eventually, however, I concluded that a poncho-tarp was not a high-performance solution. When used as a shelter, its weather resistance was scant. When used as rain gear, it blew around in the wind and snagged vegetation. And when

how 2

maximize the performance of a tarp system

1 **I must be able to accurately predict the environmental conditions. If the wind blows from a different direction than I expected, my pitch might leave me vulnerable. If I carry a bug nest and bugs never materialize, then I will have carried an unnecessary component.**

2 **I must know how to quickly and effectively pitch my tarp, which is not nearly as intuitive as a pop-up tent. Before I go out with a new shelter, I will practice in a low-risk environment (e.g., my backyard)—pitch, tweak, disassemble, and repeat. I'll read the written directions, watch YouTube videos, and learn the nuances of pitching my shelter, specifically the best order of steps, the optimal pole lengths, and the necessary corner angles.**

3 **I carefully select my campsites because tarps often lack the bathtub floors and 360-degree protection found on conventional tents.**

tools & techniques

it came time to make camp in a rain-storm, I inevitably got soaked. A poncho-tarp is best used in dry conditions, when just-in-case rain gear and shelter are needed.

A-frames

A flat tarp *can be* pitched as an A-frame, but an A-frame tarp like the two-person Gossamer Gear SilTwinn ($140, 11 oz) *cannot* be pitched in any other way because its center ridgeline features a "catenary curve," which accounts for gravity-caused sagging. The catenary curve eliminates this sag (but not the curve), resulting in a more taut pitch, smoother panels, and less wind-driven flapping. A-frames usually also have a tapered cut; they are wider at the head than the foot.

The storm-worthiness of an A-frame is limited by its two open ends. This vulnerability can be reduced through both design and technique. A simple option is to just make the tarp bigger—for an extra three ounces, an additional two to three square yards of material could be added, which would turn a handkerchief-size tarp into a legitimate roof. Another possibility is to partially or completely close these openings with "beaks" or with down-to-the-ground side panels, such as on the MSR Twing ($250, 30 oz) and GoLite Shangri-La 1 ($200, 19 oz).

Unfortunately, beaks and full-coverage side panels reduce pitching configuration options—if it is not pitched as intended, it will sag.

Mids

The sturdiest and most weather resistant tarps are mids, which normally have one apex and are shaped like a pyramid, though some have two apexes and look like a two-pole circus tent. Mids are excellent for winter travel and for harsh three-season conditions. Rain and snow slide down their slanted walls and wind struggles to grab their slanted profiles; also, they can be used as a roof over a cavernous snow pit.

Short and small mids can be pitched with trekking poles, whereas taller and bigger mids need stouter supports like a packraft paddle; an extendable aluminum pole is included with some models. It is possible to tie two trekking poles together to improvise a large mid, but I don't recommend it, as the poles can easily be overstressed.

Mids have several drawbacks:

> They are heavier per person than other flat or A-frame tarps.
> Ventilation is limited, so they are less resistant to condensation buildup. To improve airflow, mids usually have a mesh vent at the

tip | To select an A-frame campsite when it's rainy or windy, I seek out natural windbreaks, like boulders or clusters of trees, that complement the A-frame's storm-worthiness.

I was very confident in my mid shelter during this spring storm in the Alaska Range.

apex(es). If conditions permit, the tarp should also be pitched off the ground and the door should be left open.

> Their pitching configurations are very limited—basically, to one. This inflexibility is partially offset by the availability of model-specific modular components such as bug nests and floors (see below).

Modular components

The tarp is definitely the most important component in a tarp system, but the additional components greatly affect the system's function and its adaptability.

Ground cloths protect against moist ground, snow, and dirt. I have experimented with flat tarps, heavy-duty trash compactor bags, Mylar emergency blankets, picnic tablecloths, and the Gossamer Gear Polycryo Ground Cloth ($4, 2 oz). Instead of carrying a ground cloth, I usually just rely on my foam sleeping pad, plastic pack liner, and/or packraft. Items that need to stay dry, like my camera and maps, can be placed on top of my shoes or food bags.

Footprints are custom-cut ground cloths, ideally made of heavy-duty coated nylon; lightweight fabrics can leak when occupants concentrate their body weight on a small area (e.g., when sitting or standing). Footprints are heavier and more expensive than generic ground cloths, which you can cut to a specific shape with scissors if you wish. A footprint's bathtub floor— whereby the edges are uplifted, for more protection against groundwater—is a nice feature in theory, but it should not be necessary if a good campsite is selected.

Bug head nets, which cover the head and neck completely with bug mesh, provide excellent daytime protection against swarms of bugs, but they are a bit minimalist for nighttime use. If mosquitoes are your only worry, then use a head net made of larger pored mosquito netting, which is less stuffy than the small-pored no-see-um netting.

A bug skirt is a strip of lightweight mesh netting connected to the tarp's bottom perimeter. When it lies flush on the ground, it seals out bugs. The seal can be compromised by wind or a rough ground surface (e.g., high grass) that prevents a snug closure. They are mostly a do-it-yourself feature, rarely found on commercial shelters.

Bug nests, like the GoLite Shangri-La 2 Nest ($100, 1 lb 7 oz), feature a waterproof floor and a canopy made entirely of bug netting. They are designed to be used underneath a

tarp, but they are viable stand-alone shelters on calm, buggy nights. Both A-frame and pyramid bug nests are available; most are designed to be compatible with a specific tarp, but they are often compatible with other similarly shaped tarps too.

Bug bivies, like the Six Moon Designs Meteor ($130, 7 oz), are tube-shaped covers for sleeping bags made of bug netting and a waterproof floor. They are lighter and less model-specific than a bug nest, but they do not have as much interior room. Because bugs can bite through the mesh, you'll need to keep the bivy off your face by wearing a brimmed cap or suspending the mesh above via a thin cord connected to the tarp.

Water-resistant bivy sacks are similar to bug bivies, except the bug netting is replaced with a highly breathable water-resistant polyester or nylon fabric; they retain a small no-see-um bug netting panel (sometimes removable) for ventilation. Water-resistant bivies are very popular among flat tarp and A-frame tarp users for five reasons: (1) They serve as a groundsheet; (2) they prevent spindrift and rain splatter from wetting the sleeping bag; (3) they add five to ten degrees of warmth to the sleep/shelter system by reducing convective heat loss; (4) they provide a seal against flying and crawling insects; and (5) they can be used alone on dry nights to "cowboy camp" (no shelter) without sacrificing

Modular components like this bug nest can be used to create a tarp system.

part 2

Tarp tents are a lighter alternative to double-wall tents, although they can be susceptible to condensation buildup. They are less versatile than tarps.

bug protection, extra warmth, and a ground sheet.

Tarp tents

This category is equivalent to "crossovers" that combine features of SUVs and traditional cars. In the case of tarp tents, their weight and ventilation is comparable to that of tarps, but their enclosed design is reminiscent of tents. For this reason, some consider tarp tents a type of single-wall tent. Large manufacturers have not yet embraced the concept. Instead, all the innovation has come from mom-and-pop companies like Gossamer Gear, Six Moon Designs, and Henry Shires Tarptent.

A tarp tent has panels of mesh bug netting that create a full seal between the waterproof floor and canopy. The canopy protects the mesh panels with awnings and beaks, making weather protection and ventilation simultaneously possible. Most tarp tents are designed to be used with trekking poles.

A tarp tent weighs about half of what a double-wall or single-wall tent does. However, tarp tents are more prone to condensation problems—there is no inner wall to protect the users against a condensation-covered outer wall, and the canopy is not breathable, so moisture inside the shelter will not pass through it. When conditions permit, the canopy door should be kept open to maximize airflow.

Compared with a tarp system, tarp tents are not as adaptable because they do not have interchangeable components (e.g., bug nest) and their pitching configurations are fixed. Tarp tents, depending on conditions, may be heavier—with a tarp system, unnecessary components can be left at home. And users have less control over ventilation. On a calm and humid night, it's not possible to open up a tarp tent like a flat tarp or an A-frame tarp.

Continued on p. 106

tools & techniques

tried&true

how to find a good campsite

part (2)

Out of desperation I have camped in some awful places, including a vault toilet in Montana's Purcell Mountains, a six-foot-by-two-foot bench that I chiseled from a 25-degree slope in Colorado's San Juan Mountains, and a rodent-infested lookout tower in New Brunswick. But usually I am very deliberate and selective about where I camp. A good night's sleep is critical to enjoying tomorrow.

Select a general area

As the end of the day draws near, I identify several potential campsites on my map. I look for general locations that are:

> Flat, where my odds of finding a level campsite are best, though as a soloist I can often find suitable ground on suboptimal gradients, where there would not be enough spots for a group;

> Near natural resources like firewood and water;

> Off-trail, to avoid infringing on another backpacker's wilderness experience;

> Not in the bottom of a valley or canyon, where on a calm night the air will be colder and where dew/frost will be heaviest;

> Not near animal trails or prime habitat, which might lead to an unwanted midnight visitor;

> Not in danger of natural hazards like avalanches, flash floods, and incoming weather; and

> If the bugs are intense, breezy and far from breeding grounds like swampy meadows and stagnant lakes.

Identify a specific location

Once I select a general area, I try finding a specific campsite that is:

> Covered in natural materials like pine needles, leaves, moss, or sand, which will be more comfortable and which will be less thermally conductive than hard-packed dirt;

> Under and next to something—like trees, bushes, or large rocks—that will keep me warmer by serving as a natural windbreak and as a radiant heat reflector;

> Dry, because wet ground is more thermally conductive;

> Not at risk of being flooded by groundwater during rain, as moisture can easily seep through a lightweight floor or an older, heavy-duty floor; and

> Naturally contoured for my preferred sleeping position. I'm a back-sleeper, so I like a raised area for my head, a slight depression for my butt, and a short knoll for the backs of my knees.

Once I have identified a potential spot, I lie down to make sure that it is comfortable. If it is, I mark the location of my feet and head with small rocks so that I can pitch my shelter over this exact location. If it's not, I will try different positions or a different spot. Given the importance of my campsite to my sleep, it's worth being fussy.

tip So that all people in a shelter can sleep well, I have them all lie down on the proposed spot and ask, "Are you comfortable?" If yes, we pitch the shelter.

tools & techniques

Alpine bivy sacks are best used as "emergency" shelters.

Black Diamond

Waterproof/ breathable bivy sacks

The aforementioned water-resistant bivy sacks favored by tarp users are offshoots of waterproof/breathable bivies like the Black Diamond Bipod ($270, 29 oz), commonly used by alpinists who need a lightweight, low-bulk shelter that they can lay down almost anywhere to make an emergency camp—or an intentional camp that would *appear* like an emergency camp to most people. These bivies feature a waterproof bottom made of PU-coated nylon and a top shell made of WP/B fabric like Gore-Tex or eVent. Some models have a short pole to suspend the material above the head, and some feature a removable bug screen.

Three weeks into my first thru-hike, I swapped out my four-pound double-wall tent for a 1.5-pound WP/B bivy in an effort to reduce the weight and bulk of my shelter. So long as nights stayed cool and dry, bugs were minimal, and the skies didn't pour, it was an excellent shelter. Of course, in those conditions, I didn't actually need a shelter.

If the conditions were even slightly suboptimal, however, the bivy was miserable—and I actually have never used this type of shelter again:

> It was unbearably stuffy during the stifling mid-Atlantic summer nights.
> The fabric's limited breathability and the high atmospheric humidity soaked me in my own sweat "from the inside."
> When it rained, my face and ears were inches away from the rain droplets when they splattered on the bivy's exterior—Chinese water torture, bivy-style—and there was no way to cook dinner inside my bivy.
> When it was buggy, mosquitoes whined just inches away from my ears, and they would bite me through the bug netting if I didn't keep it off my skin.
> I needed to regularly revive the fabric's durable water repellent (DWR) finish, which was quickly degraded by my body oils.

Hammocks

I have not yet used a backpacking hammock, such as the Warbonnet Outdoors Blackbird ($160, 25 oz) or

part 2

the Hennessy Hammock Ultralight A-Sym Classic ($200, 31 oz), so my knowledge is admittedly limited. But I would like to test one out soon. These two glowing reviews I found were typical: "[My hammock] offers, quite simply, the most restful and comfortable sleep I've ever had in the backcountry." And, "This single piece of gear has totally revolutionized my backpacking experience."

There are three important differences between a backpacking hammock and a traditional banana-shaped backyard hammock. First, the former feature an asymmetric cut that flattens the sleeping position, to almost as flat as a bed. Second, a rainfly can be suspended above the hammock. And, third, most hammocks have integrated mesh netting for bug protection.

Hammock pros & cons

Hammock proponents emphasize major advantages over other types of shelters:

> Hammocks can be set up anywhere there are trees. It matters not if the trees are rooted in mud, thick brush, boulders, lumpy ground, or even standing water.
> The sleeping position is, supposedly, extremely comfortable.
> In sweltering heat, the user is cooled by underside—as well as topside—convective heat loss.

There are several drawbacks to hammocks, however:

> Trees—or a comparable elevated anchor point—are mandatory.
> In cooler temperatures, the underside convective heat loss becomes problematic, and the solutions are imperfect: Using a sleeping pad is awkward, and placing a lightweight sleeping bag in an underside sleeve adds weight and expense. This makes hammocks best for warmer weather.
> They have less usable space. It's not possible to cook dinner inside, and gear must be stored outside in a waterproof bag.
> And, fourth, pitching a hammock is a skill that takes time to develop and master, which makes it more like a tarp than a foolproof double-wall tent.

skurka'spicks
S H E L T E R S

Since 2003, I have exclusively used tarp systems. They are the lightest, the most resistant to condensation, and the most adaptable type of shelter. And their environmental resistance can be as good as that of any tent. I have confidently used a tarp system to protect myself

tools & techniques

against prolonged rainstorms in the Pacific Northwest, blizzards in Denali National Park, and ravenous mosquitoes in Canada's Arctic.

For most three-season conditions, I use an A-frame tarp in conjunction with a water-resistant bivy sack, specifically the **Mountain Laurel Designs Grace Tarp** ($110, 9 oz) with the **Mountain Laurel Designs Superlight Bivy** ($155, 7 oz). If I wanted more interior volume or needed a two-person shelter, I would use an A-frame with a bug nest because two-person bivies are not widely available. During the West's arid summers, I rarely pitch the tarp. I like the time savings and sense of connectedness that come with sleeping under the stars. I always use the bivy, however. It keeps me off the ground, protects me from bugs, and adds warmth. This tarp/bivy combination is excellent for the wet and humid East, too. The tarp covers a huge area for minimal weight, so it is not as cramped as a tent during rainstorms; ventilation is excellent; and the bivy can be used inside permanent trailside shelters.

When the weather is foul—in winter, during the shoulder seasons, and year-round in extreme locations like the Arctic—I use mid tarps, notably the **Mountain Laurel Designs SoloMid** ($170, 13 oz) or **GoLite Shrangri-La 2** ($225, 26 oz). For its weight, the storm resistance of a mid cannot be beat. If/when the conditions warrant it, optional bug nests are available for these models.

Guylines

A conventional three-season, free-standing double-wall tent can be pitched without guylines, or even stakes. In contrast, you need both to pitch a tarp or tarp tent; without them, it's impossible to get the desired shape and tension.

Pitching system

In three-season conditions, my guyline system works like this:

> I attach three- to eight-foot-long guyline cords to each tie-out point with a bowline knot. The guyline's length depends on the tie-out location.

> For tie-outs that are near the ground (e.g., the corners of a mid tarp), I run the cord from the tie-out to an anchor (e.g., a stake) and back through the tie-out's bowline loop. Then, I pull the cord back toward the anchor until the guyline is taut, securing it with a slippery half hitch.

> For tie-outs that are far from the ground (e.g., the apexes of an A-frame tarp), I use a trucker's hitch, making the bite with a slipknot.

There are several benefits to the two techniques described previously. First, the knots are very secure and easy to adjust. Second, the two-to-one pulley action makes getting a taut line easy. Third, I have flexibility regarding the anchors' location: If there's a rock 12 inches from

Pitching a tarp is a skill that should be mastered first in your backyard.

the shelter, I just move the anchor out another six inches, which would not be possible with nonadjustable fixed loops. Fourth, there are no fixed knots or plastic tensioners that might be prone to becoming entangled with each other. And, fifth, these systems are really fast. I learned them from my friend Forrest McCarthy, who learned them in Antarctica, where pitching a shelter quickly can be a matter of life and death.

On winter trips, I install Nite Ize Figure 9 Small ($2.50, 0.2 oz) rope tighteners to the tie-out points. With them, I can quickly and securely pitch my shelter even when wearing bulky mittens. As with my three-season system, I attach a three- or eight-foot-long cord to the tie-out with a bowline, and I tie the Nite Ize into the bowline loop. The Nite Ize takes the place of the slippery half hitch knot.

Cordage types

Standard guyline cord is inexpensive and can be purchased by the foot or in bulk at outdoor retail and climbing stores. I like Blue Water 3mm NiteLine ($10 for 50 ft, 6.6 g/m), which has a nylon core and polyester sheath. It's cheap, easy to work with (even with gloved hands), and formidably strong (500-pound tensile strength). Plus, its sheath has a reflective strand, which makes it easier for me to find

Silicone-impregnated nylon ("sil-nylon") stretches, especially when wet. So I always retighten my guylines before going to bed and/or after it begins to rain.

tools & techniques

my shelter in the dark when returning from a campfire or a water source.

Some gram weenies use guylines containing Spectra fiber, which is stronger for its weight than standard cord, so a lighter cord can be used. The net weight savings is around an ounce, depending on the total cord length. I've used such cord, but it's twice as expensive as NiteLine and it's not easy to tie or untie knots with it—it is slick and small. I only use it on intense summertime trips, when every ounce matters. A less finicky option is Kelty Triptease ($15 for 50 ft, 2.0 g/m), which has a Spectra core and nylon sheath.

Stakes & anchors

The holding power of a shelter's anchors either enhances or—in the case of most tarps and tarp tents—is critical to its pitch. Anchors are not limited to just stakes; I've also used sticks, trees, branches buried in snow, downed logs, and exposed roots.

The best backpacking stakes are made of aluminum or titanium. Plastic stakes break easily and stainless steel stakes are heavy. Common designs include nails, tubular rods, Y-shaped, and V-shaped; snow stakes are scoop-shaped and have more surface area. A stake's head should have a deep notch or a hook to more securely hold a guyline or stake loop.

A stake's holding power is a function of its design, ground conditions (e.g., dry sand, moist sod, forest duff, and snow), the stake angle, and the pull angle. A stake's holding power can be significantly increased by adding weight (e.g., a rock) atop the stake. For an excellent article on how these variables affect holding power,

A technique to avoid—it bends the stake and loosens the surrounding ground, which makes the stake less secure. Instead, pound in stakes with a baseball-size rock.

part (2)

read "Tent Stake Holding Power: Comparative Evaluation of Various Designs and Lengths" by Will Rietveld, published by *Backpacking Light* magazine.

skurka'spicks
STAKES & ANCHORS

I use three types of stakes, depending on the climatic conditions and my shelter:

On most three-season trips, I use aluminum Y- or V-stakes, like the seven-inch **REI Tri-Stake** ($1, 0.5 oz). This design has earned my trust after staying put during numerous storms, notably a gale in Yukon's Arctic with 30-mile-an-hour winds. Plus, these stakes are cheap, and I can pound them into rocky ground without bending them.

If I'm really counting ounces and conditions are mild, I may bring titanium skewer stakes, like the six-inch **Gossamer Gear Tite-Lite** ($2, 0.2 oz each). These only have about 60 percent of a Tri-Stake's holding power, and they are more delicate; they should be used only for non-critical tie-outs, e.g., not the apexes on an A-frame tarp or the corners of a mid.

When I am camping on snow, I try not to use stakes because they are difficult to retrieve in the morning. Instead, I loop guylines around my skis, snowshoes, and/or ski poles, which I secure by partially burying; I also use deadman anchors made of tree branches that I can leave behind in the morning. **sp**

how 2
make a deadman anchor

1 Dig a hole in the snow, 12 to 18 inches deep, where you want the anchor to be.

2 Lay the guyline across the bottom of the hole.

3 Put two to three forearm-size sticks perpendicular to and atop the guyline, or combine smaller sticks of comparable cumulative size.

4 Bury the guyline and sticks, except for the guyline's end.

5 Pack down the snow on top of the anchor.

6 Wait five to ten minutes for the snow to bond with the sticks; make other anchors in the meantime.

7 Secure the shelter to the anchor using one of the systems previously described.

tools & techniques

maps & navigation

I walked the entire Appalachian Trail, 2,175 miles from Georgia to Maine, without a map or compass. That's not as remarkable as it might seem. The Appalachian Trail is well worn and marked with white two-by-six-inch blazes to avoid any possibility of confusion at trail intersections and road crossings. If I had been incapable of following the AT, I would have needed to find a different hobby. Other long-distance hiking trails, like the John Muir Trail and the Colorado Trail, are also nearly foolproof. Even the Continental Divide Trail, one of the most challenging trails in the country, has frequent signs, cairns, and emblazoned posts.

part 2

My early trips all relied on established trails and their accompanying shelters, designated campsites, guidebooks, and trail towns. But I felt increasingly restricted. Trails limited my destinations, my solitude, my routes, and my skills. So I made a concerted effort to learn to travel *off-trail,* an effort that led me, most recently, on the Alaska-Yukon Expedition, which featured 2,110 miles of off-trail hiking and skiing, plus another 1,270 miles in my packraft on rivers or saltwater fjords and ocean bays.

Finding one's way off trail between Point A and Point B is incredibly rewarding and liberating. But it requires better resources like detailed topographical maps, Landsat images, an accurate compass, and—most important—navigation skills, which are best developed through doing.

As a novice navigator, I learned to orient the map; to match topographical features on my map with those I could see around me; to pinpoint my location based on those features and on dead-reckoning calculations; and to determine the distance and direction to summits, campsites, and valley bottoms. I also learned to stop "bending the map," or convincing myself that visible features matched my map when clearly they did not. Now, as a more experienced navigator, I use maps to discover aesthetically pleasing routes, unmapped water sources, good campsites, and passages through vertical canyon walls and over steep ridgelines; to assess the feasibility and best locations for river fords; to predict vegetation types and the

I keep my maps accessible and refer to them constantly to "stay found."

location of game trails; and to avoid avalanche-prone slopes, ankle-twisting tussocks, and treacherous talus and boulder fields.

Topographical maps

Generally, topographical maps are the most useful for backpackers. They depict terrain features ("relief"), watercourses, vegetation cover, and man-made features like roads, buildings, and hiking trails. The most comprehensive set of topographical maps available for the United States was produced by the United States Geological Survey (USGS). There are government agencies in other countries that produce comparable maps: For example, Canada has the Centre for Topographical Information, and Iceland the National Land Survey.

USGS topo maps

There are *four* USGS topo map series, all helpful, depending on the trip and application:

> For precise navigation in the lower 48, I use *7.5-minute quadrangles,* aka "quads," the borders of which are 7.5 minutes of latitude and 7.5 minutes of longitude apart. The coverage area ranges from about 50 to 65 square miles depending on the latitude. These quads have contour intervals of 40 feet and are at a scale of 1:24,000. This means that 1 inch on the map corresponds to 24,000 inches (or 2,000 feet, or 0.38 mile) on the Earth's surface. There are about 57,000 7.5-minute quads covering the coterminous U.S. states, Hawaii, and U.S. territories.
> These 7.5-minute quads are not available for Alaska, so instead I

use *15-minute quads,* which have 100-foot contour lines and are at a scale of 1:63,360, or one inch to the mile.

> For trip planning and/or straightforward navigation (e.g., following a trail system that is heavily used and signed), I can use the *30- x 60-minute quads,* which have a scale of 1:100,000.

> The *250,000-scale series* is also helpful for trip planning, and I frequently take them along too as "overview" maps in the event I need to bail out or make a major detour.

The USGS topo series is available in *three* forms: as printed maps, as free digital scans, and as commercial software.

Printed maps. The USGS paper maps are the gold standard; their resolution and detail is phenomenal. But at $8 per 7.5-minute map, they quickly get expensive, especially because hiking routes have an uncanny way of using small bits of many maps.

Digital scans. Downloading free digital scans from the USGS website is awkward. And viewing the maps at *MyTopo .com* or as a layer in Google Earth is limiting. The map resolution is low and there are no image exporting features, among other drawbacks. Using digital scans from an online resource is a viable option only for very short trips.

Commercial software. My preferred system for accessing USGS maps is National Geographic TOPO! desktop software, which costs $50 per state. TOPO! is much more user-friendly, time-efficient, and powerful than paper maps or digital scans. It allows me to:

> Seamlessly pan through five levels of maps, including the 7.5-minute and 30- x 60-minute USGS quads

Excuse the shameless cross-promotion—National Geographic TOPO! software.

A few other useful maps

In addition to topographical maps, I may consult other types of maps when planning or when on a trip: 1) Climatic maps reveal weather patterns and are good indicators of vegetation cover. 2) Political maps show boundaries (federal, state, county) and towns; when combined with a road map, they help me to figure out where to "get away" and where to resupply. 3) Land ownership maps help me avoid private property (or get permission to cross it), to obtain backcountry permits, and to contact local land owners/managers, who usually know the most about an area. 4) U.S. Forest Service maps show official trails, recreational sites, campgrounds, and other national forest attractions. 5) Nautical maps are helpful in predicting the strength of tides and the walkability of coastlines. 6) Aeronautical maps, used by pilots, can be helpful overview maps in very remote areas.

when planning or on a trip.

(or the 15-minute and 250,000-scale series for Alaska);

> Measure the distance of my planned route;

> Make notes on the maps; and

> Export map images for printing.

Delorme Topo, Garmin MapSource, and MyTopo Terrain Navigator are products that compete with TOPO! but they are not as detailed, powerful, or economical. TOPO! is only available for the United States, but TOPO!-like programs, such as Fugawi and Memory-Map, are available in other countries; I used the latter for the Yukon portion of my Alaska-Yukon Expedition.

USGS-derived maps

USGS topo data is in the public domain, unrestricted by copyright and intellectual property law. Private organizations are permitted to improve the data and sell their own maps in printed or electronic form. Examples include the National Geographic Trails Illustrated series, Delorme Gazetteers, Earthwalk Press maps of the Wind River Range, Tom Harrison's maps of the John Muir Trail, McKenzie Maps of the Boundary Waters, the Appalachian Trail maps sold by the ATC, and the Superior Hiking Trail guidebook maps.

Landsat imagery

To plan a trip and to navigate, I rely mostly on maps. But I've also found tremendous value in digital photographs of the Earth's surface taken by the Landsat Program, a joint

how 2

make a map set from TOPO!

1 Export maps from TOPO! as 11-by-17-inch image (.jpg) files.

2 Insert the images into a Microsoft Word document.

3 Print the Word document as a PDF.

4 Upload the PDF to a local printer (e.g., FedEx Office)

A four-color, double-sided map set costs about $1.50 per sheet. The print quality is inferior to that of the USGS printed maps, but this is a function of TOPO!'s scanning quality, not the printing quality.

effort of the USGS and the National Aeronautics and Space Administration (NASA). Landsat images can reveal detail that is not depicted on maps, including vegetation density, new roads, unofficial ATV tracks, and recent topographical changes like landslides, receding glaciers, and shifting river channels and deltas.

Google tools

Landsat images can be viewed in Google Maps and Google Earth. Earth offers a 3-D view of landscapes, helping them to "come alive." Atop the 3-D view, I can add "layers" of specialized information like the trail system in Yosemite National Park, my planned route for an upcoming trip (which I can export from TOPO! and convert into a Google Earth .kml file by using a free program named GPSBabel), and the USGS topographical quads (via an add-on from Google Earth Library).

Paper or digital?

Digital mapping and imagery resources are better than paper resources when *planning* a trip, but *in the field,* I much prefer paper maps to the electronic displays on a tablet computer, GPS unit, or smart phone because they:

> Are not susceptible to electronic failure;
> Do not require batteries or recharging;
> Do not break if dropped;
> Are lighter;
> Have better resolution;
> Provide space to jot down notes and thoughts; and,
> Display significantly more information than a digital screen—an 11-by-17-inch paper sheet shows about 30 times more information than the 4.2-inch screen on my smart phone.

part 2

tip | For Landsat imagery, I use Google Maps, which allows me to toggle between road/political maps, shaded relief maps, and the Landsat images.

Navigational devices

I rarely need more than a topographical map to navigate, but most backpackers will need or want more—a watch, a compass, or maybe a GPS.

Watches

Along with its basic time-telling function, I use a watch to:

> Determine my walking speed;
> Estimate my location; and
> Form my schedule.

A simple timepiece is sufficient for backpacking, but an altimeter watch like the Highgear Axio Max ($150, 2.5 oz) is more functional: It features a digital compass, thermometer, chronograph, barometer, and altimeter. The compass is adequate for simple operations, like finding north; the barometer can sometimes be a good weatherman; and the altimeter can help me pinpoint my current location (or help me get to a different one) if I compare its reported elevation with the information my map provides.

Compasses

A compass is helpful when visibility is poor and/or when topographical features are subtle or nonexistent.

Continued on p. 120

Discussing alternative route options with Roman Dial while persistent headwinds raged outside the Chitina Café in Alaska. Large-scale maps are critical for such unexpected detours.

tools & techniques

tried&true

how to packraft

A packraft is a one-person inflatable boat that weighs four to six pounds and rolls up small enough to be carried in or on a backpack. I consider a packraft a critical tool for wilderness travel: I've used one to ferry across glacier-fed rivers in the Alaska Range; to paddle across fjords in Kenai Fjords National Park and open ocean bays on Alaska's Lost Coast; and to float rivers like the Yukon and Copper that were flowing in my desired direction of travel. Packrafts also increase the "fun factor" of conventional backcountry trips. Read *Packrafting!* by Roman Dial and check out the forums at *www.packrafting.org* for more in-depth information.

Equipment

Here's the basic equipment you'll need for an effective packraft system:

Raft. Alpacka Raft makes the most reliable and most whitewater-worthy packrafts. Other manufacturers include Feathercraft, NRS, and Sevylor. I get the smallest (and lightest) boat I can squeeze into because my trips are usually hiking-centric and I don't want to carry the extra weight of a larger boat. The eight-ounce spray deck increases the boat's warmth and whitewater-worthiness.

Paddle. My 215-centimeter-long Sawyer paddle has four pieces—two blades plus a two-piece carbon fiber shaft—and weighs 25 ounces. This paddle hits the sweet spot for me. A stiffer paddle would be heavier and unnecessary, and a lighter paddle would be too floppy and weak.

Personal flotation device (PFD). Conventional foam PFDs are heavy and bulky but helpful or necessary if you go swimming. As an ultralight just-in-case alternative, I use a custom-made double-walled nylon vest that accommodates three two-liter Platy Bottles; the total setup weighs eight ounces.

Basic techniques

Practice these techniques before attempting them in the wilderness:

Inflation. Use the three-ounce pillow case–size inflation bag, and then top the boat off with lung power. Cold water will cause the air inside the boat to compress, so splash it down before putting in and re-inflate, or pull out downstream after the boat gets soft.

Secure backpack to boat. Place your backpack horizontally across the bow and anchor it using two 60-inch-long webbing straps with Ladderloc buckles. Lace the straps through the boat's tiedown loops and the pack's compression and shoulder straps. Cinch tightly; the system will loosen up when wet.

Forward ferry. Point the bow upstream at a 45-degree angle to the current and paddle forward. The boat acts like a hydrofoil, and the river will push you toward the other bank.

Backward ferry. When you need to navigate around obstacles in the river, point the stern upstream at a 45-degree angle to the current and backpaddle.

Backpaddle. When floating through splashy rapids, backpaddle so that fewer waves crash over the bow and fill the boat with water.

Stay drier by learning how to raft conservatively: Avoid waves, ride the edge of wave trains, backpaddle through rapids, and show the boat's bottom to splashy waves.

tools & techniques

When it comes to navigation tools, newer doesn't necessarily mean better.

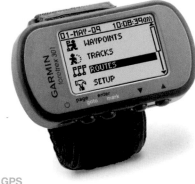

COMPASS
My preferred navigational aid, along with good topographical maps

GPS
An unnecessary gadget so long as I track my location

I was happy to have had a compass, for example, during an early season blizzard in Montana's Absaroka Mountains, during a thick five-mile bushwhack in Alaska's Kenai Peninsula, and during off-road treks across the sparsely inhabited plains of eastern Montana.

If my compass use is infrequent and basic, a lightweight "key chain" compass or the digital compass on my watch will suffice. But if I think I may need to hold a steady course (a "bearing")—through a whiteout or across a frozen Arctic bay, for example—it's worth having a more reliable model. I prefer a lightweight baseplate compass with an adjustable declination scale, translucent baseplate, and a fast needle. Recently, I have used the Suunto M-2 ($24, 1.2 oz), which unfortunately has a sticky needle; someday I may upgrade to a competition-grade model that also has a clinometer to measure slope angle, which would be useful on wintertime ski trips through avalanche terrain. Additional features like

a sighting mirror, global needle, and magnifying lens add weight and cost, and I've never needed them.

GPS units

Many people seem surprised to learn that I can navigate through the wilderness *without* a GPS unit. A GPS (which stands for "global positioning system") unit is very powerful; it can:

> Show my exact location (as I write this, 39.96527N 105.24934W) anywhere in the world, to an accuracy of a few feet;

> Calculate distance to key landmarks, like my car, a favorite fishing hole, or a trail junction;

> Determine how far, how fast, and in which direction I've hiked; and

> Leave "bread crumbs" along my route, so when I get home I can upload and share my route using Google Maps or TOPO!

High-end GPS units feature topographical maps stored on internal

part 2

memory, high-resolution color screens, and even text messaging capabilities.

Map & compass vs. GPS

Despite all of this functionality, I struggle to describe a GPS unit as anything more than a "gadget." With a map and compass, I can do everything that a GPS can do:

> I can pinpoint my location—at least to a relevant degree of accuracy—by noting terrain features, trail junctions, and my pace; in other words, by "staying found."
> I can determine distances, speeds, and directions using a compass and ruler, or my mapping software once I get home.
> I can share my route with my friends by copying key information from my paper map to a digital platform.

Especially for off-trail navigation, a map and compass is actually *more* functional than a GPS. A GPS cannot tell me the best way to get from Point A to Point B. It can tell me the distance and the overall direction, but I still need to look at my map and the terrain so that I avoid thick brush, deep canyons, and unnecessary vertical gain and loss.

And there are significant advantages to this old-school navigation style. A map and compass:

> Are lighter;
> Do not require batteries, or extra batteries;

> Work as long as the Earth has a magnetic field;
> Are not prone to water damage or physical shock; and
> Are much easier to read than a two- by three-inch digital screen, especially in bright sunshine. A tablet computer is more eye-friendly, but its battery limitations are even more pronounced.

skurka'spicks
N A V I G A T I O N

Clearly I have a strong preference for a map and compass. Still, I recognize that a map and compass can be more skill- and time-intensive and more susceptible to human error, and I think that having a GPS as a *backup system* can be appropriate for unskilled navigators and/ or for skilled navigators in challenging environments like the open ocean or the Antarctic ice cap. Look for a simple, lightweight, inexpensive unit, such as Garmin Foretrex 301 ($150, 2.3 oz), that can give latitude/longitude and provide directional advice to preprogrammed waypoints. I do not recommend using a GPS-enabled sports watch as a GPS unit—they lack the functionality and they guzzle batteries. I also don't recommend installing a GPS app (such as TrekBuddy) on your smart phone. Again, this device is not as powerful as a stand-alone GPS unit and its battery life is very limited.

sp

trekking poles

Like most college students, I was frugal, erring toward cheap (and, proudly, still am). But when I rolled into the Nantahala Outdoor Center near Bryson City, North Carolina, on Day 8 of my Appalachian Trail thru-hike, I quickly handed over $100 for a pair of trekking poles to replace the stout tree branches that I had been crutching on since Day 4, in an attempt to relieve stress on my worsening shin splints and aching feet. Since then, I've used trekking poles on every one of my overnight trips and on many extended day hikes as well.

Primary benefits

The *primary* benefit of trekking poles—which are very similar to alpine ski poles—is to give arms an opportunity to assist legs in propelling me forward and upward and to help with braking on descents. This helps to prevent overuse injuries and to delay fatigue; one academic study found that trekking poles reduce the stress on legs by about 25 percent. I notice their benefit most in mountainous terrain and/or when carrying a heavy pack—basically, when I am working hardest against gravity. But I have also seen my stride get some extra oomph courtesy of my arms while walking down the flattest-of-flat roads in eastern North Dakota. Trekking poles have other benefits, too:

> They provide extra traction on soft and slippery surfaces, like "gumbo" mud in eastern Montana, sandy washes in Escalante National Monument, and lingering snowfields in Glacier National Park.
> They offer a third and fourth point of contact when crossing snowmelt-filled rivers or tripping over tree roots in New England or tussocks in Alaska.
> They are useful in probing questionable surfaces like quicksand and rotting snow bridges and checking the depth of silty puddles.
> They save the weight of bringing dedicated shelter/tent poles since I use them to pitch my shelters.

I have also used trekking poles to defend myself against aggressive Doberman pinschers in Maine, wild javelinas in Arizona, and even a grizzly bear in Alaska's Arctic National Wildlife Refuge.

part 2

Lacking trekking poles, my Alaska Mountain Wilderness Classic teammate Chris used stout willow branches to help in crossing swift creeks and powering up climbs.

Drawbacks & solutions

Not every ultimate hiker uses poles, however. One notable exception is Scott Williamson, who has hiked the 2,650-mile Pacific Crest Trail 13 times. I recognize the drawbacks, too: Poles can get tangled in brush; their grip is unreliable on hard rock; they cannot be conveniently stowed; they obstruct hand function; and they can cause further harm to high-use trails. But I have found these drawbacks to be either solvable or negligible. For example, when I want to eat on the go or take a photograph, I just hold both poles under one arm.

Pole weight

As with footwear, the weight of trekking poles is disproportionately important compared with other items in my pack. It takes much more energy to *swing* a six-ounce pole thousands of times per mile than to merely *carry* a six-ounce jacket in my pack over that same distance. With a lightweight pole, it is easier to have proper poling technique—that is, to match every step with a pole plant—and to catch myself quickly if I stumble or lose balance. I often see backpackers with poles that are too heavy, and they end up dragging the poles behind them, lashing them to the outside of their packs because their arms get tired, and/or walking in irregular sequence (e.g., three pole plants for every four steps, instead of one to one). Backpackers who look as discombobulated as newborn giraffes would benefit from ditching their poles—which are only getting in the way—or, better yet, finding a pair they can use correctly.

Shaft materials

Trekking pole shafts are made of either aluminum or carbon fiber. Carbon fiber models are generally more expensive (by $30 to $50) and less durable than aluminum models. But they are lighter (by 2 to 4 ounces per pair) and stiffer; they aren't cold to the touch in cool temperatures; and they have better shock absorption, which translates into a less jolty ride for hands and elbows.

When overleveraged, a carbon fiber shaft will snap; it can sometimes be temporarily repaired with a splint, duct tape, glue, and/or guyline cord. An aluminum shaft will usually bend—and remain partially functional. I have broken both carbon fiber and aluminum models, and I've concluded that durability

is more a function of *product care* than material. During my Great Western Loop hike in 2007, I used a carbon fiber model for 5,000 miles before breaking one of the shafts when it jammed in a root as I was falling down a creek bank. And during the tough-on-gear Alaska-Yukon Expedition, I successfully used a pair for 2,000 miles before losing one during a river ford.

Pole types

The lengths of most trekking pole models are adjustable, via telescoping sections that can be secured together with clamp- or twist-style locking mechanisms. The "usable length" of my poles is 25 to 51 inches (62.5 to 130 cm).

Collapsible/ adjustable poles

These types of poles are very convenient. They can be:

> More easily packed in a checked bag for air travel (airline security sometimes requires that all hiking poles be in checked baggage);
> Shared among family or friends, and/or used for multiple activities (hiking, snowshoeing, or skiing);
> Adjusted quickly if changes in the terrain warrant a different length, or if my shelter requires an exact pole length for optimal pitch; and
> Collapsed and lashed to the side of my back during prolonged technical travel (e.g., boulder fields) so that I can use both hands. This is rarely necessary when hiking

how2
size trekking poles

1 | When you hold the grip, your elbow should be at a 90-degree angle and your forearm should be parallel to the ground.

2 | For open stretches of trail (e.g., a beach) and for winter travel, go with a longer pole.

3 | For steep climbs and snowfield traverses, choke up instead of shortening the whole pole.

Trekking poles are adjustable in two ways.

FOLDABLE
Sections stay
connected with
a Kevlar cord.

COLLAPSIBLE
Complicated locking
systems add weight,
cost, and opportuni-
ties for failure.

on trail, and I try to avoid such stretches when hiking off trail.

The adjustability of collapsible/adjustable poles comes at a price, of course. The overlapping shaft material, locking mechanisms, and complex construction add expense and weight. When poles near their maximum usable length, the joints become very wobbly. And the locks are susceptible to failure, especially the twist-style found on older Leki and Komperdell models (the latter sometimes branded under REI). In wet and/or cold conditions, I've found that the internal plastic expander nut tends to slip. The clamp-style locks first used by Black Diamond—and now also used by most of the other manufacturers—are more secure.

Some adjustable/collapsible poles feature an internal spring to damper shock ("antishock"). These models are even heavier and pricier than normal adjustable models—by up to 4 ounces and $20 per pair. A shock sounds good in theory, but it makes for squishy and insecure pole plants, and the shock is prone to rattling and squeaking.

Foldable/ nonadjustable poles

Foldable/nonadjustable poles were recently introduced by both Black

Diamond and CAMP. These four-piece poles are designed similarly to avalanche probes. Instead of twist- or clamp-style locks, they have a coated inner Kevlar cord and push-button release/lock. These models are very light and compact; the 120-centimeter version of Black Diamond's Ultra Distance ($150, 9.5 oz) collapses to just 16 inches. Unfortunately, the length of these poles is not adjustable. More important, the weight savings seem to be at the expense of structural integrity. When stressed, these poles bend almost like wet noodles, and their joints wobble noticeably. Ultra-runners will love these poles because of their weight and collapsibility, but I prefer a stouter pole, especially for snow travel and off-trail travel.

When I travel by air for a short trip, I prefer these Black Diamond collapsible poles instead of simpler and lighter fixed-length poles.

Fixed-length poles

Unfortunately, fixed-length poles are not currently sold by any mass manufacturer, which is mystifying and infuriating to me because these same manufacturers already sell fixed-length ski poles. All things being equal, fixed-length poles are stiffer, lighter, quieter, and less expensive than their adjustable and foldable counterparts.

However, I had to learn some tricks to get around the structural inconveniences of fixed-length poles. I protect them from airline baggage handlers with a stiff cardboard tubular box and "Fragile" labels. When the terrain has me wishing that my poles were a few inches longer or shorter, I instead choke down on the shaft or hold onto the grip's top.

Grips & straps

The best grips are made of cork or high-density foam. They glide smoothly in my hand, prevent perspiration buildup, are lightweight, and are thermo-neutral (i.e., they don't make my hand colder in cold temperatures). Low-end trekking pole models have rubber and plastic grips, which are heavy and abrasive.

Loops of nylon webbing—straps—are attached to the tops of trekking poles; they are usually adjustable and integrated into the grip. I can only speculate that the straps are relics from Nordic ski poles, where they are critical in pushing off. I remove these straps from my trekking poles for a number of reasons:

> It shaves one to two ounces off the pole.

Poles give you an extra "pop" when jumping over creeks or between boulders.

> Without the straps, it's much easier to grab (and let go of) my poles, which I do constantly—to take a photo, to look at my map, to scramble over rocks, and so on.

> When wearing large mittens, straps are particularly cumbersome because the loops are not large enough for mitts to fit through.

> I find that I am less likely to break a pole if my hands are not tangled in the straps. If the pole tip gets wedged or stuck, I can easily let go of the pole before my momentum torques it too far.

Because cross-country skiers put more pressure on the strap than the grip, the grips on cross-country ski poles are very narrow—only slightly wider than a pole shaft. By contrast, trekking pole grips and alpine ski grips are thicker and knobbed, for a more secure hold. I have

part 2

been told that the narrow grips work well for backpacking too, though I have no firsthand experience.

Tips & baskets

Two other features to consider when shopping for trekking poles are pole tips and baskets—though I have limited use for the latter.

Trekking poles have extremely wear-resistant, replaceable/removable carbide tips. I replace them only once every 1,500 to 2,000 miles, depending on the terrain (rocky, more often; soft dirt and snow, less often). These tips can be planted very securely in soft and broad surfaces (e.g., a wide dirt trail) but they cannot be used as confidently on hard pinpoint surfaces (e.g., granite talus), so be very wary of placing too much faith in your poles in those situations. Instead, pick your poles up, stay low to the ground, and be prepared to catch yourself with your hands.

Many cross-country ski poles and alpine ski poles have blunt aluminum tips instead of carbide tips. If you use such a pole on any surface other than snow, you should buy replacement carbide tips ($15) for improved durability and grip. The new tip will add a few centimeters in length to the pole.

Trekking poles usually come with two-inch-wide "trekking baskets" that are supposed to prevent the pole from becoming jammed between rocks. For improved float on snow, trekking baskets can be replaced with four-inch-wide "snow baskets." I use the trekking baskets for soft ground like Arctic sponga (soft, squishy tundra) and beach sand; and I use snow baskets for winter trips. Otherwise, I remove baskets to improve swing weight.

skurka'spicks
TREKKING POLES

When performance is paramount— as on one of my multimonth solo trips—I strongly prefer fixed-length carbon fiber poles. The only trekking-specific fixed-length pole currently available is the **Gossamer Gear LT3C** ($110, 5.8 oz for 115 cm length), but I'm weary of the thin shafts and would happily invest one to two extra ounces per pole for added durability and rigidity. Next time I need a fixed-length set, I will probably make my own, using golf driver shafts (with Extra Stiff flex), **Gossamer Gear Pole Grips** ($23, 1 oz), replacement carbide tips, and Gorilla Glue.

Fixed-length carbon fiber ski poles are available from major manufacturers like Fischer, Swix, Black Diamond, Goode, and Leki. Adult-size cross-country poles, which start at 135 centimeters, are too long for trekking. Juniors'/kids' sizes are sometimes available, though they may not have a suitable grip or tip.

For less intense trips that require air travel—e.g., many of my guided trips—I take adjustable carbon fiber poles. My current favorite is the **Black Diamond Alpine Carbon Cork** ($140, 16 oz), which has the best combination of weight, stiffness, and lock reliability.

sp

tools & techniques

food

I found my treasure on a gravel bar near the Kongakut River in northeastern Alaska: a 25-gallon drum containing all my food for the next two weeks, along with maps, stove fuel, and new shoes. Kirk Sweetsir of Yukon Air Service had dropped it there for me two weeks earlier and had sent me the waypoints via e-mail. Because I didn't have a GPS and because I only had 1:250,000-scale maps (an inch of which depicts four miles) for this area, I was both ecstatic and relieved to find it. I yelled into my camera, "Do you know how nerve-wracking it is trying to find a barrel of food in the Brooks Range when you're 300 miles from the closest town in that direction and 300 miles from the closest town in the other direction?"

The cache was a good place to lay over for the night. It was raining; I had not rested since my last resupply, in Fort McPherson, Northwest Territories (NWT), 11 days earlier; and there was a nearby cluster of wind-buffering willows. I pitched my canary yellow mid tarp and started counting out my meals, Scrooge-like. Day 1: Breakfast, five snacks, dessert, dinner; Day 2: Breakfast, five snacks, dessert, dinner; and so on, until I had 14 days of food parceled out. I started consuming the leftovers; they were not as satisfying as a burger, but I wasn't going to be fussy.

A dietitian might have screamed in horror to see my fuel for the next two weeks—many more bags of Reese's Pieces, cookies, and Fritos than dried vegetables, cheese, and foil packets of salmon. Meanwhile, some thru-hikers may have thought I needed more standard hiking fare, such as ramen noodles

and Pop-Tarts. Like footwear, food is a very personal subject.

How much
The voraciousness of my appetite seems to be driven primarily by two factors: trip duration and physical intensity.

Trip duration
On trips shorter than about 14 days, I bump up my caloric intake only marginally from my civilian norm. But mine is an *active* norm: Because I run, bike, and/or ski every day, backpacking is not a huge shock to my body. Beyond this two-week threshold, however, my appetite spikes and my engine demands more fuel. The explanation, I think, is that my body initially offsets a caloric deficit with body fat, but after 14 days, as these natural stores become depleted, it starts telling me: "Eat more." A hiker's appetite can be

Cereal with powdered milk is a fast and yummy breakfast, good cold or hot.

the stuff of legend: After I emerged from the Smokies, my then-girlfriend's father fed me two grilled steaks, two chicken breasts, two baked potatoes, and a half-dozen cookies before I was full; in Unalakleet, Alaska, I ate a 20-inch supreme pizza in one sitting. Once my appetite jumps, it remains elevated until shortly after the trip concludes.

Physical intensity

I need more calories when putting in long days, hiking through mountainous terrain, and/or carrying a heavy pack. I remember being chronically starved when I hiked the southernmost 1,700 miles of the Pacific Crest Trail in 44 days, covering an average of 38 miles per day. Despite my best efforts, I couldn't consume more calories than I was burning. By contrast, I was able to remain calorically fulfilled—at least by long-distance hiking standards—during a 30-day trip across the Colorado Plateau in February and March. The short days limited my mileage to about 25 per day, and the route was much flatter.

Depending on trip duration and physical intensity, I usually pack 3,500 to 5,000 calories of food per day, which equates to 1.5 to 2.5 pounds per day, assuming a caloric density of 125 to 150 calories per ounce. During an intense summer trip in the mountains, a 5,000-calorie diet is probably 1,000 to 2,000 calories short of my actual caloric expenditure, so I offset the difference by relying on body fat and on occasional feasts in trail town cafés. Still, on a multimonth trip, I expect my 170-pound athletic build to shed up to 15 pounds.

Lean, hard-charging thru-hikers may have caloric needs comparable to mine, but most backpackers need far fewer calories. I have found 3,000 calories per day per person to be just about perfect on my guided trips. Everyone is satisfied, but we finish the trip with little extra food (or, ideally, none at all). I sometimes bring slightly more or less than 3,000 calories per hiker if the group's demographics are tilted: Children and petite women eat less, and muscular adult males eat more. If you are unsure about how much food to bring on your trip, I recommend starting with this

3,000-calorie target, and then making adjustments next time if you were hungry or if you finished with extra food.

How I eat

When I'm putting in long days and consuming copious calories, a conventional three-meals-a-day menu is impractical. Instead, I eat six to eight meals per day: breakfast, four to six snacks, and dinner. This approach sustains my energy level because I am regularly feeding my body calories; it avoids post-meal food comas; it allows for better digestion; and it prevents prolonged hunger.

Normally, I eat my first meal while breaking down or walking out of camp; a three-ounce calorically dense energy bar with some coffee bean–infused chocolate squares does the trick. If I'm not trying to leave camp within 15 minutes of opening my eyes, I enjoy hot or cold cereal with powdered milk, or butter-laden Cream of Wheat or oatmeal.

I eat my snacks—400 to 500 calories each—two or three hours apart, depending on trip length and physical intensity. I don't have "lunch"; my 1 p.m. snack is calorically comparable to my 9 a.m. and 6 p.m. snacks. I get about two-thirds of my total daily calories through these snacks.

Immediately upon arriving at camp, I have a small predinner dessert, which holds me over until my meal is ready and injects sugar into my depleted system. On unexpectedly long days, this dessert can also serve as an extra snack. If the days are short and my camps are long, I may plan a "midnight snack" between dinner and tomorrow's breakfast, which helps me to stay warmer throughout the night.

Considerations

The menu for a simple day hike is very flexible. Classic gorp is an option, of course, but I'd personally prefer leftover pizza, a peanut butter and jelly sandwich on fresh bread, and/or a few pieces of fruit. On a multiday backpacking trip, however—and

Hiking for weight loss?

Weight loss is a fair motive for hiking, but don't intentionally starve yourself of calories. This approach tends to backfire. When I've been chronically undernourished (not intentionally, but as a result of the circumstances), I've become obsessed with food and have overcompensated once the trip ended, gaining over the long-term. And it's difficult to be cheery and energetic when rabidly hungry.

This approach tends to backfire.

especially on a long-distance back-packing trip—my list of food options is much more limited: Leftover pizza would spoil; the sandwich would get crushed; and the fruit would provide insufficient calories considering its weight. I consider 11 factors when meal planning, their importance varying depending on the type and length of the trip:

Caloric density (calories/ounce)

One ounce of fat contains 240 calories; one ounce of carbohydrates or proteins contains just 100 calories; and water has zero calories. If I need 5,000 calories per day to function, I could save a lot of weight by packing 1.3 pounds of butter instead of 3.2 pounds of instant rice, dehydrated beans, drink mixes, tortilla shells, Skittles, and gummy bears. On a one-week trip, this would amount to a weight savings of 12.8 pounds! Of course, a diet consisting entirely of butter would be entirely unpalatable, and I'd much prefer a better balance of fats, carbohydrates, and proteins with a caloric density of at least 125 calories/ounce, and preferably closer to 150 calories/ounce.

Spatial density (calories/volume)

Consider a one-week ration consisting entirely of Snickers bars (270 calories each) versus larger Thomas' bagels (also 270 calories each). Without a spatially dense food load, I would have to carry a larger (and heavier) backpack, or risk not having enough volume to fit it all.

Stockpiling calories in a resupply town

Portion-ability

Calories are a precious commodity in the wilderness. Portioned packages clearly delineate the calories that can be consumed on a particular day and at a particular time. Without portioned meals, I tend to overeat today and starve tomorrow. Bars come prepackaged; I repackage other foods in sandwich- and snack-size plastic storage bags.

Taste

When I'm calorically deprived, just about anything tastes good. But I try to avoid being chronically starved, in which case only one food item infinitely satisfies: chocolate. Having a mix of flavors (sweet, salty, spicy), textures (chewy, crunchy, soft), and spices can help delay the onset of caloric boredom.

Burn time

Foods that are loaded with simple carbohydrates—including sports bars, gels, and drink mixes, plus Pop-Tarts and gummy bears—are by design absorbed rapidly by the body. The quick energy they provide is desirable when completing a marathon or triathlon, but when backpacking, I prefer fat-laden foods that have more staying power, like nuts, Fritos, and olive oil–based pesto sauce.

Nutritional value

My preferred foods are notably lacking in vitamins and minerals, yet I do not feel as if I have been adversely affected. Still, when practical, I make healthy choices, and when in trail town grocery stores, I fill my arms with fresh produce before visiting the ice cream aisle.

Shelf life

Rather than buy food en route, I purchase most of it before I leave and have it shipped via USPS. These mail drops save me time, ensure that I eat what I like, and make it possible to resupply in towns with very limited services. However, the food must be very shelf-stable, because it might not be sent for months after being purchased.

Thermal resistance

Some foods are not suitable for hot and/or cold environments. For example, energy bars with corn syrup and candy bars with caramel can break teeth in the cold. In a pinch, I've thawed them in my armpits and in my underwear, but in persistent cold, they are not a palatable choice. At the other end of the temperature spectrum, I've seen M&Ms and Reese's Peanut Butter Cups reduced to molten chocolate. If temperatures will be extreme, I pack foods that will not be adversely affected.

Pre-trip prep time

When I need to assemble and package food for a multimonth trip, I ply helpful family and friends with dinner, beer, and as many M&Ms as they please. Still, it's a labor-intensive task, even though I buy dehydrated and premixed ingredients.

In-field prep time

Prosciutto and cheese is a tasty backcountry delight, but this meal requires that I sit down to prepare and eat it. In contrast, I can get a bag of cookies from my pack and eat them immediately—without ever taking my pack off or even breaking stride. During a hard-charging trip, I can be seen doing the latter much more often than the former.

Cost

When I buy several months' worth of food in the span of a few days, there's a noticeable cost savings if I bulk up on plain instant potatoes, couscous, chocolate candy, and salty chips ($2 to $5 per pound) versus energy bars, beef jerky, and freeze-dried dinners ($8 to $10 per pound). Given my expected income during the trip—nada—it's in my interest to be cost-conscious.

What I eat

And now the good news: America might "run on Dunkin'," but I hike on chocolate.

My chocolate-centric diet

I've experimented with many other foods, but chocolate is the only thing that endlessly satisfies me. It took years for me to become comfortable with a chocolate-centric diet. Pop-Tarts, ramen noodles, and granola were my main staples when I was a cheap college student and long-distance backpacking novice. During the Sea-to-Sea Route and Great Western Loop, I adhered to the "bar diet": During the day, I exclusively ate candy bars, granola bars, and Balance Bars (one of my first sponsors). After tiring of the monotony, I experimented with homemade trail mixes, dried and preserved meats, salty snacks like honey mustard pretzels and corn nuts, dried fruit, and yogurt-covered pretzels and raisins. Finally, ten weeks into my Alaska-Yukon Expedition, after enviously watching Roman Dial eat Cadbury bars for a week in Wrangell-St. Elias National Park, I decided it was okay to feed my body what it craves most. From

Nutrition, caloric density, and shelf life are among the considerations when I buy food for a trip.

Cordova, Alaska, I called my mom and instructed her to send more chocolate and less of everything else in my upcoming supply boxes.

Hot meals

At the end of a long day, I enjoy a hot meal, but I insist that it require minimal prep: Boil water, add carbs, let reconstitute, and then add a fat or sauce to improve flavor and caloric density. Instant potatoes, instant rice, instant beans, couscous, and angelhair pasta cook quickly. Butter is my preferred fat. It's cheap; it makes everything taste better; and it can be securely packaged in two freezer bags, even in mild temperatures. Olive oil and coconut oil are messier and more expensive.

Where I shop

For 30 days of rations or less, I find it most convenient to buy everything at one or two stores. Check the weekly circulars of your local stores online to see where the best prices will be. Whole Foods, Trader Joe's, or Sunflower Market have better bulk bins and more creative snack foods.

For a longer trip, or a short trip with a large group, retail warehouse clubs like Costco, BJ's, or Sam's Club have much better prices on core items like instant potatoes, instant rice, pasta, energy bars, and beef jerky; or, if I'm buying retailer-size quantities of a particular item, I may call up the manufacturer to see if I am eligible for wholesale pricing or a volume discount.

how 2

make some of my favorite dinners

1 Loaded potatoes. Reconstitute three ounces of plain instant potatoes and then add one ounce of crumbled bacon, one ounce of cheese, and one ounce of butter.

2 Rice and beans. Reconstitute two ounces of instant rice and two ounces of instant beans, and then add 1.5 ounces of cheese and 0.5 ounce of taco seasoning.

3 Ramen and pesto. Cook a three-ounce package of ramen noodles; do not add its flavor packet. Then add two ounces of pesto sauce that consists of 1 ounce of olive oil, 0.5 ounce of Parmesan cheese, 0.3 ounce of garlic, 0.1 ounce of basil, and 0.1 ounce of "spicy spaghetti" mix.

4 Southwest polenta. Boil three ounces of polenta and then add one ounce of crumbled bacon, one ounce of cheese, and 0.5 ounce of chipotle spice.

part 2

tip

In cold weather, add extra water and make all your dinners into soups—instant potato soup, couscous soup, and so on. Soups will help to warm you up and rehydrate you.

Prehike weight gain

As the starting date of a multimonth trip approaches, I tend to become less disciplined about my fitness. Last-minute trip planning—and a few farewell get-togethers—leave little time for rigorous workouts, and I feel somewhat entitled to enjoy foods that I'll crave during the ensuing months, like lasagna, guacamole, and home-made baked goods. But I avoid packing on pounds because this added weight has nearly the same effect as adding rocks to my pack.

Unless your body fat is dangerously low, I would actually recommend that you consider losing weight before your hike. Your body will be under less strain, and you will move more comfortably and quickly. The beginning of a trip is always a tough adjustment, and a leaner physique will make it easier.

I can think of only a few trips when it has made sense to gain weight beforehand, but these trips have had nutty objectives. For example, in 2006, Roman Dial walked 600 miles in 24 days across northwestern Alaska without a resupply; at one point, he was 119 miles away from the closest village or road. Roman figured the effort would require about 130,000 calories, and he supplemented his 45 pounds of rations with about 20 pounds of body fat, which offered about 3,000 calories per pound. Polar explorers and alpinists often take the same approach.

Bulk bins usually have a good selection and reasonable prices.

tools & techniques

cooking systems

In an attempt to travel fast and light, Roman Dial and I decided to carry my 1-liter, 4.5-ounce titanium pot instead of his 4-quart, 16-ounce aluminum pot during a three-day, 115-mile trekking and packrafting trip across Gates of the Arctic National Park. The travel was phenomenal: We cruised 50 miles down the splashy Class II+ John River, followed caribou trails up Wolverine Creek, and were charged by a grizzly bear in Pingaluk Creek.

But our breakfasts and dinners were painfully slow because we could heat up only one liter of water at a time. I remember watching enviously as Roman sipped his coffee ten minutes before my pot was ready, and as he ate his last spoonful of freeze-dried lasagna before my water was even boiling. (Roman is 25 years older than me, and more accomplished, so out of respect, he got his hot water first—plus, the pot decision was mostly mine.) On our next trip together, we agreed, we would take a cook system better suited to our needs.

A cook system has four components: a heat source, cookware, ignition, and at least one utensil. The optimal system depends mostly on group size, meal types, frequency of use, fuel availability, and local regulations. Other considerations like weight, fuel efficiency, and cooking time should be secondary factors.

Heat sources

The most elemental need in any cooking system is an adequate heat source, of which there are many options.

Open fires

Personally, I love open fires, especially for their primal comfort, security, and warmth. Even after being pinned down along Alaska's coast by a gale or being chased all day by ferocious mosquitoes in Yukon's Arctic, a nighttime fire can magically make me believe that, "It's going to be okay." Open fires have the added perks of being free (no stove or fuel expense) and burning a renewable resource that I don't need to carry. Open fires are excellent for groups, too. They provide the heat output of several stoves, and they offer a communal gathering spot.

There are some valid criticisms of open fires, however. In high-use areas like national parks and in environmentally sensitive areas like deserts and

Portable stoves are more suitable than open fires in ecologically sensitive areas like the desert.

alpine areas, they consume scarce wood resources and can ignite a wildfire if not properly monitored; fire rings, ash pits, and scorched rocks left behind by others impede a wilderness experience. Fuel—or easily combustible fuel—is not always available, and it takes time to gather it and then feed it to the flames. Pots become covered in soot, which will rub off on other equipment inside a pack if left unbagged. And starting a fire is more skill-intensive than using portable stoves, especially when it's windy and/or when the fuel is suboptimal.

Portable stoves

Before I describe the types of portable stoves and their respective pros and cons, I want to credit three excellent resources. A great deal of what I know about stoves, particularly liquid and canister stoves, I've learned from Roger Caffin through his website, Australian Bushwalking FAQ, his articles in *Backpacking Light* online

magazine, and my personal correspondence with him. Another valuable resource is a two-part article in *Backpacking Light,* "Comparative Fuel Efficiency and Carry Weight for Six Lightweight Backpacking Cooking Systems," in which author Will Rietveld analyzes the overall efficiency of stoves. Finally, *www.ZenStoves .com* contains a wealth of stove information, including many make-your-own directions.

Wood stoves. Fritz Hande's Bushbuddy Ultra ($115 CAD, 5 oz), the OC Outdoors Fire-Spout-Mini ($45, 12 oz), and other wood stoves are more environmentally sensitive and fuel-efficient than open fires. They better protect the fire against wind and precipitation. And they cause minimal environmental damage. The fire does not scorch the ground; no fire ring is required; and the ashes can be easily scattered afterward. Homemade versions can be assembled using coffee cans, cook pots, chicken wire, and battery-powered fans.

However, woodstoves have many of the same drawbacks as open fires. The strongest case for using a woodstove would be on a long, unsupported trip through an area that is environmentally sensitive and/or that has limited fuel availability—like a month in the Arctic National Wildlife Refuge, where fire-resistant willow is the most reliable combustible material.

Liquid fuel stoves. The two most popular types of backpacking stoves are liquid fuel stoves and canister stoves. All liquid fuel models will burn white gas (aka, Coleman fuel), and some are also designed to burn kerosene, unleaded gasoline, and diesel. Check the user manual; usually the stove's jets must be changed to avoid a puttering, smoky flame. These fuels are functional in extreme cold temperatures, readily available throughout the world, and relatively inexpensive.

	open fire	wood stove	liquid fuel stove
best use	Abundant fuel, remote areas, large groups	Extended unsupported trip with limited fuel resources	Winter camping when canisters for canister stoves are unavailable
ease of use	Poor; requires fuel collection, building of fire ring, fire maintenance, and so on	Poor; requires fuel collection and fire maintenance.	Fair; fuel reeks, stove clogs up, and its fireball is scary.
fuel availability	Dependent on location	Dependent on location	White gas is commonly available. Gasoline, diesel, and kerosene are widely available.
prep and boil time	Fast once it's going	Fast once it's going	Some pre-use assembly, then fast
cold weather performance	Excellent	Excellent	Excellent
expense	None	Expensive stove but no fuel cost	Expensive stove but low fuel cost
weight	Zero	5+ oz but no fuel weight	8 to 14 oz for the stove plus fuel

During the Alaska-Yukon Expedition, I was able to easily purchase gasoline in off-the-grid native villages; even with the price of gasoline at $8 per gallon, my fuel cost was only about 10 cents per quart of boiled water.

But liquid fuel stoves have considerable downsides. At 11 to 16 ounces for the stove, fuel pump, and fuel bottle (empty), they are the heaviest type of stove. Petroleum-based fuels easily contaminate other things nearby, like clothing and food. The construction, assembly, and usage of liquid fuel stoves create many opportunities for mechanical failure and human error, which makes field maintenance inevitable. I've had to clean fuel lines after they clogged, and have had to send replacement fuel pumps via overnight mail after they busted. The simmering function is limited.

Finally, I find liquid stoves downright scary. A foot-high fuel-wasting fireball is common when starting the stove, and I really dislike sitting near a hot

VS canister stove	VS alcohol stove	VS solid fuel stove
Winter use, large groups	1- to 2-person groups, 3-season conditions	1- to 2-person groups, 3-season conditions
Excellent; extremely fast and intuitive	Excellent except in windy conditions	Excellent except in windy conditions
Poor. It is limited to outdoor stores and cannot be easily shipped.	Excellent. Carried by most hardware stores and gas stations.	Poor. Not all outdoor stores will even carry fuel tablets.
Fast setup and boil	Fast setup, slow boil	Fast setup, slow boil
With liquid feed, excellent. Without, poor.	Fine, but not suitable for melting snow	Fine, but not suitable for melting snow
Moderate stove cost, then high fuel cost	Super cheap	Cheap stove, moderate fuel cost
2 to 8 oz	<1 oz	1 oz

tools & techniques

open flame that is just several inches away from a pressurized fuel bottle.

Canister stoves. A simpler, cleaner, and lighter alternative to a liquid fuel stove is a canister stove, which attaches to a prepressurized nonrefillable fuel bottle. They come in three varieties:

> Upright, such as the Snow Peak LiteMax ($60, 2 oz), whereby the stove's base screws into the top of the canister;

> Remote, whereby the stove is connected to the canister with a hose; and

> Integrated, like the Jetboil Personal Cooking System (PCS) ($100, 15 oz), a very fuel-efficient subcategory of upright stoves that includes a dedicated pot, wind-protected burner, and heat exchanger.

Compared with liquid fuel stoves, canister stoves heat water just as quickly (or faster) and do so with less fuel, partly because no fuel-consuming priming is needed. Also,

canister stoves are easy to operate, like a backyard gas grill: Open the valve and light it with a match or its auto-igniter. The simmering capabilities are excellent. Canister stoves rarely break or need maintenance, and they are odorless.

Upright and remote canister stoves perform comparably, but uprights are about one-third the weight of remote models, which in turn are more stable, making them better for larger pots. Integrated canister stoves are incredibly convenient and fuel-efficient, but in terms of weight and cost, they don't pay off unless used by large groups and/or on long-term outings.

The major drawback of canister stoves is the canister. The standard U.S. version contains a mixture of n-butane and/or isobutane plus propane (15 to 30 percent), all pressurized into their liquid states. Butane and propane are both extremely powerful fuels. But these canisters are difficult to ship, to fly with, and to

Canister stoves are fast and fuel efficient, though lighter options exist.

UPRIGHT CANISTER Very user friendly and relatively light, at two to three ounces without canister.

REMOTE CANISTER More stable for large pots, and suitable for winter use via liquid feed.

purchase anywhere other than an outdoor retail store. They are expensive and heavy. A 12-ounce canister, which weighs four ounces empty and contains eight ounces of fuel (sufficient to heat about 30 pints of water), retails for $6. They are not user-fillable. So even if I only need three ounces of fuel for an upcoming trip, I may have to take a new 12-ounce canister. Likewise, once a canister is empty, it's trash, or recyclable if sent to specialized facilities.

INTEGRATED Superior fuel efficiency pays off only when used extensively.

how **2**

use a canister stove in the winter

Canister stoves are not customarily recommended for winter use because, without a few tricks, the gas-in-liquid state will not boil off as well (or at all) in cold temperatures. If it does not boil, no gas will come out of the canister for the stove to burn. But here are a couple of tricks that will help:

1 | **Keep the canister warm: Store it in a parka** before using it; insulate it from the snow by keeping it on a foam sleeping pad; and deflect some heat from the stove back to the canister using a windscreen.

2 | **Use a "liquid feed" by turning the canister** upside down so that liquid fuel—not gas—comes out of the canister.

A liquid feed can be done only with remote canister stoves, and can be done safely only with stoves featuring a "preheat tube," which will vaporize the liquid fuel into a gas before it emerges from the jets.

tools & techniques

Hybrid liquid/canister stoves. The Brunton Vapor AF ($150, 16 oz) and Primus OmniFuel ($165, 16 oz) hybrid stoves can be fueled by both butane/propane canisters as well as liquid fuels. This is a convenient feature, but it would be lighter and equally economical to own a liquid fuel stove and a canister stove.

Alcohol stoves. Among many long-distance and ultralight hikers, alcohol stoves rule. It's unlikely that you'll find an alcohol stove at your local retailer, because they can be made easily and cheaply at home, replicating any of the hundreds (no exaggeration) of designs online. The Pepsi can stove is probably the most popular model, but I strongly recommend the Fancy Feast stove ($1, 0.3 oz), which can be made in ten minutes from a three-ounce aluminum cat food can using just a paper hole punch (see Tried & True, pp. 144–145).

For a solo, long-distance hiker, alcohol stoves have tremendous advantages over other stove types:

> They are ridiculously lightweight. An entire cook system can weigh as little as 3 to 5 ounces, which is lighter than most liquid fuel and canister *stoves* (just the stove, and nothing else needed to cook with it).
> Most designs are fail-proof, with nothing to break or clog. If you accidentally step on it, you can just bend it back into place and fire it up.
> They hardly make a sound, and operation is extremely easy. Pour some fuel into the well and light it with a match.

Fancy Feast stoves run on alcohol.

> The fuel is widely available and inexpensive. The paint department of any hardware store will have denatured alcohol ($6 per quart, enough for about 45 one-pint dinners), and every gas station in northern regions will have gas line antifreeze like HEET ($3 per 12-oz bottle, enough for about 15 one-pint dinners). The fuel can be stored in any plastic bottle, and you can take precisely as much as you need.

Alcohol stoves do have limitations:

> They are difficult to turn off. They can be smothered or blown out, but neither technique is as convenient as a valve adjustment. It's best to learn exactly how much fuel the stove needs for a given amount of water, and then let it burn out.
> Their efficiency is greatly reduced by wind, making a windscreen imperative. A foldable, inexpensive 0.3-ounce screen can be made with Reynolds Wrap;

alternatively, you can improve the stability and fuel efficiency of your system with a Trail Designs Caldera Cone ($35, 1 to 3 oz, depending on pot size).

> Their boil times are slow—six to eight minutes, depending on the model, water temperature and volume, and windscreen. I find other things to do while waiting, like stretching and looking at tomorrow's maps.

> The fuel has low potential energy for its weight, making it inefficient for melting snow, long unsupported trips, and communal cooking for groups of more than two people.

> The flame is invisible during daylight, which has resulted in at least a few skin burns and brush fires.

> Last, most designs lack a simmering feature so it is difficult to "cook"

with them; they are best for hot drinks and for dinners that reconstitute in hot water (e.g., freeze-dried meals).

Solid-fuel stoves. ESBIT, or solid-fuel, stoves are mostly unknown beyond the long-distance and lightweight backpacking communities. These ultralight stoves—platforms, really—burn 0.5-ounce cubes of hexamethylenetetramine, which will boil roughly two cups of water in seven minutes. In many regards, they are comparable to alcohol stoves in terms of weight, efficiency, energy output, speed, and wind vulnerability. But ESBIT cubes are about five times as expensive as alcohol, and only slightly more available than fuel canisters. Plus, they leave a sticky residue on cookware.

Continued on p. 146

The fuel efficiency of this solid-fuel stove could be improved with a windscreen.

tools & techniques

tried&true

how to make a Fancy Feast alcohol stove

part 2

Of the hundreds of homemade stove varieties, I prefer the Fancy Feast stove, which can be made in five minutes out of a three-ounce aluminum cat food can using just a paper hole punch. It weighs a mere 0.3 ounce, costs less than $1.50, and does not need a separate pot stand.

This stove is suitable for soloists and two-person groups who eat boil-only meals: freeze-dried packages, angel-hair pasta, instant beans and rice, hot drinks, et cetera. It is not suitable for large groups or for small groups that want to cook.

To maximize its efficiency, use a one-liter pot that is wide and short, not tall and skinny. Also, an aluminum windscreen is mandatory.

For fuel, I use either denatured alcohol or a yellow bottle of HEET; the former is available in most hardware stores, and the latter at many gas stations. I keep the fuel in an 8- or 12-ounce plastic bottle and budget about 0.7 ounce of fuel per meal.

Stove assembly & usage

Remove the cat food and wash out the can.

Flatten any sharp edges around the rim with the hole punch.

Just below the can's lip, make a ring of holes with the hole punch. Leave a gap of about one-eighth inch between the holes.

Below the first ring, make another ring of offset holes. This lower ring should have the same number of holes as the upper ring.

Pour fuel into the stove. Do not pour more than is necessary. The stove does not have an OFF switch, and it is difficult to blow out.

Light it with a match and wait 20 to 30 seconds for the fuel to start boiling.

Place your water-filled pot on top of the stove and surround the stove/pot with the windscreen (see below). It will boil 1.5 to 2 cups of water in about seven minutes.

Windscreen assembly

Cut a length of aluminum foil that is about four inches longer than the circumference of your pot.

Fold the sheet of aluminum foil in half lengthwise.

Fold over the outer quarter inch of the windscreen twice to increase the rigidity and tear strength of its edges. Avoid trapping air inside the windscreen: It will expand when heated and damage the windscreen.

Surround the stove and pot with the windscreen, leaving a quarter-inch gap between the pot edge and the windscreen, on average. The ends of the windscreen should overlap by 1 to 1.5 inches.

To protect the stove and windscreen during transport, I store both inside the pot and fill the remaining space with food to prevent them from bouncing around. I fold the windscreen in eighths and keep it on the bottom of the pot.

tip

In a pinch, this stove can be made more rudimentarily. Cut a soda can in half with a knife and poke holes in the side. It's delicate and will last only a few meals.

tools & techniques

145

Open fires heat up large amounts of water quickly, and no fuel must be carried.

Cookware

On my first backpacking trip ever—a solo overnight in Yosemite National Park in March—I carried a complete cook set: a 1.5-liter pot, a 2-liter pot, and a fry pan. This might be a suitable setup for car campers and backcountry chefs, but ultimate hikers almost universally carry just one pot for heating water, and perhaps a drinking or eating container.

Volume & shapes

Pot volume is the main consideration. In three-season conditions, 600 to 1,000 milliliters of pot volume per person is appropriate. Backpackers who have large appetites and/or who want hot drinks with their meals will be on the upper end of this range. A four-liter pot is about the largest pot that can comfortably fit inside a three-season backpack or a lightweight winter pack; it can hold enough water for up to about eight people for one meal. In winter conditions, when melting snow is necessary and hot drinks are craved, it is much more time-efficient to have two liters of capacity for each person.

Pots also come in different shapes and wall thicknesses. Fuel efficiency is better with short and wide pots, as opposed to tall and skinny ("deep") pots. Fuel efficiency also improves with thin-walled pots because of improved heat transfer; these pots are also lighter.

Handles

Most pots feature handles: Larger pots usually have a swiveling top handle and smaller pots usually have folding side handles. Bails are excellent, especially for lifting a boiling kettle of water out of a hot fire (using a stick). Side handles are not compatible with alcohol or solid-fuel stoves because they interfere with a secure

part 2

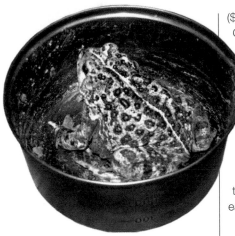

A huge toad hopped through my camp and into my 900-milliliter pot.

($10, 4 oz) or the two-quart Open Country Kettle ($14, 12 oz). Even if you are trying to shed every gram, don't be tempted to use a Wal-Mart Grease Pot or a Foster's beer can—neither is durable enough for a week-long trip, and the Foster's can has horrible fuel efficiency because of its lanky dimensions. For long-distance hikers and avid backpackers, the added cost of titanium is more easily justified.

windscreen seal; I cut them off, which saves some weight too, though not enough to justify this measure to my younger sister, who had given me an expensive titanium pot for Christmas one year. Handles are sometimes insulated with a rubbery coating, which melts. The coating can be preemptively melted off by filling the pot with water and placing it in a fire.

Material

Volume and features being equal, a pot's material is the largest factor in its weight and cost. Stainless steel pots are the cheapest, but they are much heavier than aluminum, which costs only slightly more. Titanium pots are the lightest and most expensive. For the average backpacker who only gets out a few times a year, aluminum pots achieve the best balance of weight and value. Consider the three-cup AntiGravityGear Non-Stick Pot

Ignition sources

You won't get very far (or very full) if you don't have a reliable ignition source.

Matches

Even if my stove has an integrated ignition, as on the Brunton Raptor ($61, 5 oz) upright canister stove, I want a manual way to light my stove, too. Matches are cheap and ultralight, and allow me to keep my fingers farther from the stove when it ignites. I store my matches with my toilet paper in a waterproof zipper bag. I have never found "stormproof" matches to be necessary.

Lighters

A Bic lighter produces a longer lasting and more wind resistant flame than a match, and it can be used to throw sparks even when the fuel is gone. With cold hands, lighters can be difficult to use. Lighters are compatible with most stoves, but using a lighter to ignite an alcohol stove will inevitably result in singed fingertips.

Fire starters

A final ignition option is an old-fashioned magnesium rod and steel fire starter. Fire starters can throw seemingly infinite sparks—my favorite model, the Light My Fire FireSteel Mini ($8, 1 oz), is good for 1,500 strikes—but the accuracy of those sparks is highly dependent on having a stable surface for the magnesium rod.

Utensils

My breakfast items and daytime snacks require no assembly or cutting—everything is contained in a wrapper or a zipper storage bag. Occasionally I pack something less utilitarian, like cheese and salami, and if I need to cut anything, I use my pocketknife or tear it with my hands and mouth. My dinners only require a spoon—the mainstays include instant potatoes, couscous, angel-hair pasta, and soup. Given my voracious hunger by day's end, I want a

Without a full-length handle, my spoon is more packable.

utensil that resembles a shovel, like the REI Campware Soup Spoon ($1, 0.3 oz). Titanium spoons are popular among the lightweight crowd, but plastic utensils are lighter and less expensive, and they don't get cold to the touch. "Sporks" are a classic light-weight multiuse item, but they can't hold the same liquid volume as a normal spoon. If you eat your dinners out of a bag, not your bowl, you can keep your hands clean by using a long-handled spoon.

skurka'spicks
COOKING SYSTEMS

When traveling solo in three-season conditions, I rely on both a Fancy Feast alcohol stove and an open fire. If I want dinner or midday coffee in a hurry, if I want to cook inside my shelter because it's windy and raining, and/or if I'm in a high-use corridor where an open fire would be irresponsible, my alcohol stove gets the nod. I light it with matches and carry the fuel in an 8- or 12-ounce plastic bottle ($1, 1 oz). Open fires complement the alcohol stove. I may start one if I'm projecting a fuel shortage and/or if I need a hot flame, either to boost my morale or to dry out. Since 2004, I have used the 0.9-liter Evernew Ti Ultralight Pot #2 in conjunction with my alcohol stove.

On solo winter trips, I leave my beloved alcohol stove at home in favor of one capable of melting snow for water. I prefer using a

part (2)

Cleaning up food scraps—

Once I've consumed all the calories in my pot, I add some water and scrub the insides with my fingers. I don't use soap. If there is stubborn fat or food stuck to the sides, I will then use something more abrasive, like sand or dirt. In bear country or in arid climates, I usually drink the gray water—otherwise, I disperse it in a wide arc. I eat all my food in my bowl; if you don't, pack it out, eat it later, or give it to a hungry thru-hiker.

I don't use soap.

remote canister stove like the **MSR WindPro** ($90, 7 oz) and a liquid feed. However, because the canisters are difficult to get, I have used liquid fuel stoves for all of my long-term winter trips, when I've had to find fuel en route. If I can reliably obtain white gas, I like the **MSR Simmerlite** ($100, 6 oz), which is a few ounces lighter than the **MSR Whisperlite International** ($90, 10 oz) that will burn other fuels besides white gas.

It's worth carrying a larger and heavier pot when melting snow; I like the 1.9-liter **Evernew Ti Non-Stick Pot #4** ($75, 9 oz). When handling a pot that is full of hot water, a one-ounce pot grip is critical for stability, control, and safety. I also bring a full-length plastic spoon so that I can reach the bottom of the pot without dipping my fingers below the pot's rim.

For three-season group trips, my preferred system depends on the trip's objectives. On a guided trip where teaching clients wilderness skills is a high priority, I've found it beneficial to make two-person cook groups and rotate different stove systems among them, so that everyone can experience the comparative pros and cons. Without an educational focus, it's best to bring a four-quart **Open Country Kettle** ($15, 16 oz) and a powerful stove—like a remote canister (better stability than an upright model) or a liquid fuel stove, depending on fuel availability—which I use as a backup to an open fire. If one four-quart pot is not enough, I will bring a second pot, rather than a larger one. For the sake of hygiene and efficiency, every group member should have their own eating and/or drinking container, like a Fozzils bowl ($10 for two-pack, 0.6 oz each), the bottom of a discarded Platypus bottle, a screw-top Tupperware container, an inexpensive plastic cup, or a wide-mouthed water bottle.

sp

water

At 80 ounces each, the seven bottles cumulatively contained 35 pounds—or 4.4 gallons—of water, also known as transparent gold to someone attempting a two-day, 70-mile hike across Joshua Tree National Park along a route that had no water sources. Magically, I squeezed them all into my tiny 50-liter pack, along with four pounds of gear and six pounds of food. Fortunately, I knew my crushingly heavy pack would lighten by 0.75 pound per hour, and never again for the remaining six months of the Great Western Loop would I need to carry this much weight.

I waited until the sun dropped below the Pinto Mountains before leaving my final water source, the Colorado River Aqueduct. My plan was to hike through the first night and rest during the following day's peak heat to minimize my water consumption early on. After two miles, the abandoned jeep track I'd been following petered out in a wash, so I took a bearing on a distant star and began walking toward it through sparse creosote bushes. The loose sand offered poor traction, and the short sections of hardpan were no better because I kept punching into the rodent tunnels just below the surface.

Fatigue began to set in around midnight. I had already hiked 25 miles that day to reach my launching point; my body was also not adjusted for nocturnal travel. I lay down on the sand, and got up again when I became too chilled to nap. I brushed myself off and hiked for another hour before rewarding myself with another ten-minute snooze. Dreams and reality began to mingle; the hours and miles ticked away. To psyche myself up for a final push into dawn, around 4 a.m., I momentarily stopped hiking, assessed my surroundings, considered what I was doing, and let out an inspired "WAHOO!"

Unexpectedly, I received a response from the north, then the west, and then the southeast. "AWOOO!" howled the coyotes. "WAHOO!" I replied. The conversation continued for a few minutes until silence returned to the desert night.

The importance of hydration

If the human body could be compared to a combustion engine, then food would be gasoline and water would be motor oil. Water helps to keep everything functioning as designed. It is critical in:

At two pounds per quart, water is painfully heavy, but sometimes a lot of it is required.

> Regulating body temperature;
> Protecting organs and tissue;
> Converting food into energy;
> Carrying nutrients and oxygen to cells;
> Cushioning joints; and
> Removing waste.

Risks & perils

Because water is so critical to the body's functions, it's important to maintain your hydration level within an optimal range.

Too little water. I've experienced dehydration before, always when I miscalculated my needs or bypassed a critical water source. The worst incident was in Colorado's Sawatch Range during my first Colorado Trail thru-hike. As an East Coaster, I did not understand that creeks shown on my topographical maps with a dotted blue line were seasonal, and I was there out of season. Dehydration can cause dizziness, fatigue, and muscle cramps, and eventually even heat stroke, which is a life-threatening emergency.

Too much water. In an effort to prevent dehydration, I have also consumed too much water and become hyponatremic. On my first real desert trip, I remember feeling drunk while leaving several water sources, where I'd knocked back three quarts in 20 minutes. The concentration of sodium in my bloodstream was too low, and my body could not effectively absorb all that water. Other symptoms of hyponatremia (also known as "water intoxication") include muscle cramps, disorientation, strange behavior, and slurred speech; severe cases can lead to seizures, coma, or even death. It is most common among ultra-endurance athletes, who lose large amounts of sodium through perspiration (and through urine) and do not replace it. In hot environments, I am especially careful to consume salty foods like Fritos, beef jerky, and ramen; I could also rely on electrolyte supplements from Gu Energy, Hammer Nutrition, and Nuun.

How much

At two pounds per quart, water is heavy, so I try to carry as little as possible while still staying well hydrated. The best indicator of my level of hydration is the color of my urine—I like it to be clear and copious. Depending on the conditions and my physical output, I usually need four to ten quarts per day, though I remember a relentless three-hour climb in 100+°F heat on the Pacific Crest Trail when I drank two quarts per hour and wanted more.

To calculate how much water I should carry, I consider three factors:

> How long and how far it is to the next water source;
> The terrain between my current location and the next water source; and
> Weather conditions.

I should be able to extrapolate future needs from past consumption. Suppose that it will take four hours to hike the 9.3 miles between Turquoise Creek and Slate Creek, that the trail is mostly flat, and that it's 90°F and sunny. If I had consumed 0.75 quart per hour over similar terrain in similar conditions the previous day, I would leave Turquoise Creek with 3 quarts of water.

My water needs also depend on my current level of hydration. If I am dehydrated when I arrive at a water source, I may need to carry more water than normal on my way to the next source—or I may take a short rehydrating break before continuing on.

Almost as an insurance policy, I "camel" water so that I can endure an unexpected dry stretch without becoming too dehydrated. Specifically, I usually consume one to two quarts of water within the first hour of my day, to ensure that I'm well hydrated before temperatures climb and I start working hard. Also, if water sources are frequent, I may "top off" by regularly drinking 8 to 16 ounces so that I stay fully hydrated.

Bottles & reservoirs

There may be a multitude of different water containers available, but my needs are met with just three plastic collapsible bottles. On three-season trips when water is abundant, I usually bring two 1-liter/34-ounce Platypus SoftBottles ($9, 0.9 oz). On three-season trips when water is scarce, I carry as many 2-liter/70-ounce Platy Bottles ($13, 1.2 oz) as needed. I prefer the standard Closure Cap on both Platypus bottles; compared with the HyperFlow cap, it is less likely to leak and has a better flow rate. Finally, on winter trips when I must melt snow for

tip You can use soft-sided water bottles as pillows at night. Fill the bottles three-quarters full with air and water, and then put them inside a stuff sack with some extra clothing.

part 2

water, I bring two 48-ounce Nalgene canteens ($10, 3 oz).

The Nalgene Canteen's wide-mouth spout makes it more suitable than the Platypus bottles for winter trips: It takes longer to freeze shut, it has a wider opening into which I can pour melted snow from my cook pot, and the bottle can be dipped into an open section of river by looping the cap into the strap of a ski/trekking pole.

I prefer to bring two or more smaller bottles instead of just one large bottle. Smaller bottles are easier to hold and fill, and an extra bottle is insurance against losing or puncturing one, which is known to happen. Even when water is abundant, I always carry at least two liters of capacity because it gives me the option to have a dry camp. I use one liter with dinner, and I drink the other liter first thing in the morning to rehydrate.

Bottles vs. reservoirs

A high-volume water reservoir with a remote drinking tube and mouthpiece like the three-liter Platypus Hoser ($23, 4 oz) may allow for hands-free drinking, but overall, I think bottles are a much better option. Bottles can be quickly pulled out of a side pocket and filled. With a reservoir, I must take off my pack, unthread the hose, pull the reservoir out, refill it, slide it back inside my pack, rethread the hose, and put my pack back on. Bottles are also easy to fill, and I can also see how much water is in a bottle.

Hands-free hydration is convenient, but the system is a hassle.

Reservoirs create an uncomfortable bulge against my back. Mouthpieces have a tendency to leak with long-term use. If not sealed correctly, reservoirs will cause disastrous leakages. In cold temperatures, reservoir straws will freeze, even those insulated with a heavy neoprene sleeve. And reservoirs with zipper-style closures are very hard to seal with mittens and/or cold hands.

Collapsible bottles vs. other bottles

There are alternatives to the plastic, collapsible varieties that I prefer, but overall, they don't work as well for backpacking. For durability, stainless steel and hard-sided plastic bottles are best; stainless steel has the added benefit of not leaching chemicals or absorbing flavors. Many thru-hikers

tools & techniques

153

how2

pack water

1 When temperatures are above freezing and water is abundant, I keep a one-liter bottle in a side pocket, empty or full, where I can easily access it.

2 In the desert, I prevent heavy water loads from skewing my center of gravity by counterbalancing bottles in the side pockets or by centering them in the main compartment.

3 In sub-freezing temperatures, I insulate bottles with extra clothing and/or foam cozies, or keep them next to my belly just outside my base layer shirt.

SoftBottle weighs one-sixth as much, and a 1.5-liter Nalgene Canteen weighs half as much as the classic 1-liter hard-sided Nalgene bottle.

> They consume negligible pack space when not in use.

Collapsible bottles have a few downsides compared with hard-sided bottles. Their life span is shorter; they last an average of about two months of daily use. They are prone to puncturing, for example by cacti and campfire sparks. However, I have always been able to seal holes and punctures with fast-drying glue and duct tape. Finally, they do not insulate liquids as well as hard-sided bottles do.

Water purification

On occasion, I have had no option but to drink water from an utterly nauseating source. Among the classics: There was a stock pond on Arizona's Coconino Plateau that was surrounded by cow patties and was the color of urine; a scum-filled water tank above the Missouri River in eastern Montana with dead mice floating on the surface; and Harris Wash in Grand Staircase-Escalante National Monument, where I found a half-decomposed cow that had become stuck in quicksand.

I don't carry testing equipment with me, but it's probable that these water sources were contaminated with something that would wreak havoc in my body. To drink confidently from

use "disposable" bottles, which are lightweight, relatively durable, and free when retrieved from a recycling bin. I use these bottles on occasion too, if I lose my preferred bottle or if there's an unusually dry stretch ahead for which I temporarily need more water.

Collapsible bottles have two key advantages over noncollapsible varieties:

> They are unrivaled in their volume per weight. A 1-liter Platypus

backcountry water sources without risking major repercussions, I first purify it.

Contaminants

It may appear as if that clear spring carries only the purest of water, but the danger of contaminants always lurks.

Pathogens. The contaminants that receive the most attention are pathogens:

> Protozoa like *Giardia, Cryptosporidium, Entamoeba histolytica,* and *Naegleria fowleri;*
> Bacteria like *E. coli, Campylobacter, Shigella, Salmonella, Vibrio cholerae, Yersinia,* and *Helicobacter pylori;* and
> Viruses like *Rotavirus,* Coxsackie virus, norovirus, adenovirus, hepatitis A, polio, and echovirus.

For detailed information about these pathogens and their effects, consult a reliable Internet source.

Most of these pathogens are transmitted by the fecal–oral route (i.e., you ingest water or consume food that has been contaminated by the feces of an infected carrier). The carrier does not need to be showing symptoms to be contagious. For example, more than 80 percent of those infected with *Helicobacter pylori* are asymptomatic, and only 50 percent of those infected with *Giardia* show symptoms. And some pathogens are much more worrisome and/or prevalent than others: Infection by *Cryptosporidium* usually resolves without treatment within two weeks, whereas *Naegleria fowleri* leads to primary amoebic meningoencephalitis, or PAME, which has a survival rate of just 3 percent. Fortunately, it's also extremely rare, with just 300 cases reported worldwide as of 2008, including 30 in the United States since 2000.

The severity of a pathogenic infection depends on three factors:

When in short supply, water contaminated by stock is better than no water at all.

tools & techniques

> The amount of pathogen consumed, which is a function of pathogen concentration and water volume;
> The virulence of the pathogen, or the potential damage it can do to the host; and
> The strength of the host's immune system.

Pathogens in North America.

In a matter of minutes, I can obtain temperature and precipitation data for a planned route, but there is no comparable resource that contains information about the quality of backcountry water sources. Mostly, we have to assume that water sources may be contaminated by *something*.

The protozoa *Giardia* and *Cryptosporidium*, which are common worldwide, get the most attention in North America. Neither is the most harmful or the most common pathogen; rather, they are the most common pathogens that can be harmful. In fact, *Giardia* is the most commonly diagnosed intestinal parasite in North America. Both protozoa have probably been in fresh water for centuries, but we did not seem concerned about them until fairly recently: In a 1996 issue of *Backpacker,* the Environmental Protection Agency's chief microbiologist described *Giardia* as being "part of

the natural flora in drinking water" before water treatment plants were regulated in the 1940s.

Most outbreaks of *Giardia* and *Cryptosporidium* infections are traced to faulty municipal water treatment plants, contaminated swimming pools and water parks, community cookouts, and other non-backcountry sources. The most notable case occurred in 1993, when 403,000 residents of Milwaukee were infected by *Cryptosporidium* that had passed through the municipal filtration system. The number of infected outdoor recreationists is low by comparison. And the number of infections that can be traced to contaminated water is even lower. Some research has concluded that poor group hygiene is more often the culprit.

Viruses are the second most common pathogen in North American water sources. Bacteria are the least common.

But "common" does not necessarily mean "everywhere" or "enough." Tests of backcountry water sources show that water quality can be surprisingly good. For example, in 2000, only 23 percent of tests conducted on San Francisco's primary water source—the Hetch Hetchy Reservoir, which is fed by the Tuolumne River flowing out of Yosemite—tested positive for *Giardia,* and then presented

Use good hygiene to prevent group contamination: Regularly wash your hands with soap, especially after "bio breaks" and before meals.

Is the water ever clean?

In short, you can never be sure. But certainly some water sources are more likely to be safer than others. Water quality should be best at the source—where water first gurgles out of the ground or drips from a snowfield—though it may not be entirely free of contaminants there either. As water flows downstream, opportunities for contamination increase. Wildlife, grazing livestock (namely cattle and sheep), and humans defecate in high backcountry watersheds. And farther downstream, the rivers carry away pollutants from residences, industry, and agriculture.

You can never know.

levels so low that, on average, a person would have to drink eight liters of water just to ingest one cyst, a small fraction of the minimum needed for infection.

Nonpathogen contaminants.
Pathogens are not the only contaminants in backcountry water sources. There are organic and inorganic materials, especially after rain or during spring runoff. There are biological organisms that reside in the water and soil, like larvae and guinea worm. But the most worrisome nonpathogen contaminants are chemical pollutants from industrial, agricultural, and natural sources. In Colorado, I have skipped springs and creeks that were clearly contaminated with heavy metals, probably from mining activity more than a century ago. In southern California, the irrigation canals are polluted with pesticides, herbicides, and fertilizers. In southern Utah I have been disappointed by springs that

were too alkaline (salty) to drink. Most purification methods are ineffective against such contaminants.

Assessing water quality. Besides the distance to its source (see sidebar above), I consider four other factors in trying to assess water quality:

> I think about the water volume in proportion to potential contaminants. If there is a tremendous amount of water—for example, peak runoff in the Cascades after a record-setting winter—contaminants will be diluted. Unfortunately, sometimes just one organism is an effective dose, as in the case of *Cryptosporidium*.
> I consider water turbidity, because some purification methods may be ineffective against microbes that have burrowed into sediment.
> I am cautious during and shortly after rain, which flushes contaminants into waterways.

tools & techniques

157

> I am more inclined to drink flowing water than stagnant water, because pools are one-way collection sites for contaminants. When I drink water from stagnant sources, I take water from the top few inches, which receive abundant UV light, a proven purification method.

Immunity

I drink from unpurified sources regularly. On the Alaska-Yukon Expedition, I didn't carry any form of purification. On the Great Western Loop, I purified only about a tenth of my water. During long runs on Boulder's popular foothills trail system, I drink water directly from springs and small streams. And during a two-week traverse of the Grand Canyon, I tanked up at stagnant potholes without purifying, almost as a test of my body's sensitivity to water quality.

And I've never been diagnosed with a waterborne illness. It is possible that I have just been lucky. It's also possible that I'm a master at identifying clean water sources. But a more realistic explanation is that I have developed antibodies through frequent low-dose exposures to common pathogens. People with AIDS and others whose immune systems are compromised probably would not fare as well. Resistance to contaminants really depends on the individual. After a trip last year through Alaska's Talkeetna Mountains, my friend Don got horribly ill and was diagnosed with giardia; his hiking partner, Alan, drank from the exact same sources and had no symptoms. Furthermore, immunity to some pathogens does not translate into immunity against *all* pathogens. I would probably be sickened by pathogens that are unique to Asia or South America, where I have never traveled.

Purification techniques & recommendations

Purification techniques vary in their effectiveness, speed, cost, weight,

	boiling	filters	iodine
effectiveness	Excellent. It kills everything.	Viruses can slip through filter pores.	It has limited effectiveness in cold water and is not effective against cryptosporidium.
treatment time	Slow	Fast but energy consuming	Slow
weight	Fuel weight	1 lb	<1 oz
expense	Fuel cost	Expensive	Cheap
aftertaste	None, but water tastes flat.	None	Like a medicine cabinet

part 2

durability, ease of use, and effect on water taste. Their complete specifications are available online.

Boiling is a time-tested technique. It kills all biological matter, including pathogens. But it is very time-consuming and fuel-intensive. And just-boiled water is flat and hardly thirst quenching.

Pump filters are very popular, and so it's understandable why I bought one prior to my first backpacking trip. I thought, "If you don't know what you're doing, then do what everybody else is doing, and hope that they're right." Unfortunately, I was misled. The filter did rid my water of protozoa and bacteria, and it may have improved water taste, though mountain water is usually delicious already. But after only a few days of use, I had discovered its drawbacks: Pumping was slow and tiresome; it was heavy to carry; it retained water after use that leaked in my pack and froze in cold conditions; and silty water quickly clogged the filter. Furthermore, I learned that "filters" were not effective against viruses, which are small enough to slip through the filter's pores. I either needed to use a second, chemical-based treatment, or I could buy a filter "purifier." I decided instead to ask other hikers about alternative purification techniques.

Gravity-fed filters like the Platypus GravityWorks System ($110, 11 oz) may not require pumping, but they require patience while water is trickling through the cartridge, and sometimes there are no nearby trees or rocks to create a gravitational force. Plus, they are just as expensive and almost as heavy as pump filters. This option may work well for large groups who spend a lot of time in camp, but it's ill suited to a backpacker on the go. A second chemical-based treatment may still

tools & techniques

VS household bleach	VS chlorine dioxide	VS ultraviolet
Not effective against cryptosporidium.	Excellent. It has a 15-minute kill time, except for cryptosporidium (4 hours).	Excellent in clear water, assuming it works.
Fair	Fair	Excellent
<1 oz	<1 oz	3 to 5 oz
Cheap	Cheap	Expensive
Like a swimming pool	Usually none, sometimes bleachy	None

be needed, depending on the filter/ purifier system.

Squeeze bottles with in-line filters and purifiers, like the Katadyn MyBottle Purifier ($50, 8 oz), are lighter, more time-efficient, and less expensive than pump filters and gravity filters. However, the bottles are heavy and small: The 8-ounce Katadyn bottle holds just 24 ounces of water, as does the 22-ounce Lifesaver bottle. As well, the flow rate is poor: It's like trying to slurp down a Wendy's Frosty with a standard-sized straw. Personally, I like the option to chug, especially when I'm trying to tank up before a long, dry stretch.

Iodine is lightweight, inexpensive, and widely available. However, it is not effective against *Cryptosporidium,* and its effectiveness against *Giardia* and *E. coli* is notably impaired by cold water and turbidity. It also makes water taste like a medicine cabinet. A longer-lasting and more economical alternative to the classic Potable Aqua tablets ($7, 1 oz) is Polar Pure ($15, 3 oz).

Household liquid bleach (sodium hypochlorite) is effective against *Giardia, E. coli,* and viruses; but, like iodine, it is ineffective against *Cryptosporidium.* It also degrades with age, and it makes mountain water taste like a swimming pool. I would use it in the event of a natural disaster or if my local outdoor retailer was closed for the night and I was leaving for a trip in the morning, but otherwise, I'd rather use something different.

Pump filters are slow and energy consuming. Many are also ineffective against viruses.

skurka'spicks
WATER PURIFICATION

My preferred purification method is chlorine dioxide, specifically Aquamira drops ($15, 3 oz), effective against all protozoa, bacteria, and viruses. This two-part solution must be mixed for five minutes before it can be dispensed into water. The manufacturer, McNett, does not recommend "premixing" the solution hours before using it because

its potency may decline, though it is a fairly common practice. Chlorine dioxide inactivates *Giardia* and viruses within 15 minutes, or within 30 minutes for "worst-case water"— i.e., very silty and contaminated water. However, *Cryptosporidium* is more resilient: The recommended dwell time is four hours for worst-case water.

Chlorine dioxide is a proven purifier, but I also like it because:

> It is ultralight, especially if it is decanted into smaller dropper bottles.
> It is reasonably inexpensive, at about $0.50 per gallon of purified water.
> It has no chemical taste—in fact, it actually helps to neutralize unpleasant flavors.

Although I prefer chlorine dioxide liquid drops, I swap to solid **Aquamira tablets** ($15 for 24-pack, 1 oz) in the winter because the drops freeze in temperatures below about 15°F. Tablets are not as flexible as drops, and they are more expensive, but their effectiveness is the same. At the publication date of this book, Aquamira tablets had been approved by the EPA as a "purifier"—i.e., they are certified to kill all potential pathogens and can be marketed as such—but the droplets have not yet been, even though the underlying technology is identical.

Due to the ineffectiveness or delayed effectiveness of iodine, liquid bleach, and chlorine dioxide against *Cryptosporidium,* some recommend that a lightweight filter be used in conjunction.

However, ultraviolet light pens such as the **SteriPEN Adventurer Opti** ($90, 4 oz) would seem like a simpler and faster option than a two-part chemical and filter combination if you are concerned about crypto and are not willing to abide by Aquamira's recommended four-hour dwell time. (For the record, I usually only wait 15 minutes before drinking.) UV light prevents pathogens from reproducing by scrambling their DNA; it neuters protozoa, bacteria, and viruses in 45 to 90 seconds. There are some drawbacks and limitations, however:

> It is expensive, and replacement batteries are an additional cost.
> It can be properly submerged only if the water container has a minimum opening of 1.75 inches, which excludes my preferred Platypus narrow-mouthed bottles.
> Its effectiveness is limited in silty water, possibly requiring a second blast.
> Because the pen occasionally malfunctions, a backup water system is recommended.
> It is not as light as chlorine dioxide.
> Treated water that is exposed to visible light for a long period of time may allow neutered pathogens to recover and become a viable threat again, though lab testing has not shown this to be a serious concern.

small essentials

The title of this chapter was an ongoing debate—I just didn't feel that "Other Stuff," "Miscellaneous," "Odds & Ends," or "Dinky Things" accurately portrayed the importance of these topics.

Toiletries

Items I need during the day are kept in a pocket on my waistbelt; everything else I keep inside a small stuff sack that I keep at the top of my pack.

Toothpaste

Sample-size tubes of toothpaste are light and packable, but I use Dr. Bronner's Peppermint Liquid Soap instead.

Only a few drops are needed per brushing, and it is multipurpose: I use it to wash my hands and clean my pot (if water is not enough), and I could use it for wound care. Its soapiness is an acquired taste. To avoid carrying an entire retail-size bottle, I decant the soap into a small 0.2-ounce dropper bottle, which is enough for 10 to 14 days.

Odds and ends kept in my accessories pouch or in my backpack's waist belt pockets

Toothbrush

Yes, I do cut my toothbrush in half, but mostly because a half-length toothbrush fits better in my accessories stuff sack.

Dental floss

In addition to being critical for oral health, floss is also useful in repairing gear, as it's much stronger than standard thread. I've used it to fortify busted seams in my shoes and to repair rips in my clothing, in addition to removing bits of salami from my teeth.

Toilet paper

When available, I prefer to use natural materials, which reduce my environmental impact. I budget four squares of premium Charmin per day for when natural materials are unavailable or to polish the rearview mirror.

Sunscreen & lip balm

To protect exposed skin, I wear a hat and may also slather on Dermatone sunscreen. In warm weather, the water-based lotions are fine, but in cold weather, I like the additional wind-resistance of balms.

Lubricants

Sportslick is a long-lasting petroleum jelly–like substance containing antifungal and antibacterial agents. Instead of taking an entire tube, I put some in a small balm jar.

Insecticides

Full-coverage clothing—specifically, a nylon shirt, nylon pants, and a head net—treated with permethrin offers the most protection against biting insects. When the bugs are not bad enough to justify such hot and stuffy clothes, and to protect any exposed skin when they are, I carry a small vial of high-concentration DEET in my waist belt pocket.

First aid

A recurring tenet for me is that the more you know, the less you can take. With first aid, the opposite is true. As I've learned more about wilderness medicine, I have taken more first aid items, because I actually know how to use them.

Four principles account for the contents of my first aid kit:

> The items cannot be improvised. For example, I can make a splint from my trekking poles and foam sleeping pad, but I cannot make a CPR mask, latex gloves, or medications.

> The items must be versatile so that they are useful in a wide range of circumstances. For example, tape gauze can be used as tape or cut into squares.

> The items must be relevant to the trip's environment, duration, and activities. For example, on a trekking trip I will bring an extensive blister kit, and if I were to visit the Himalaya I would bring drugs for altitude sickness such as Diamox.

> I only take things that I know how to use. If I didn't know CPR, I wouldn't take a mask. And because I don't know how to stitch up a wound, I don't carry the supplies for it.

tools & techniques

Items that I may take on a trip include but are not limited to over-the-counter medications like ibuprofen, Tylenol, Benadryl, and antidiarrheals; prescription medications like OxyContin (a painkiller) and epinephrine (for allergic reactions); and medical supplies like a CPR mask, duct tape, Leukotape, gauze tape, bacitracin, scissors, and a knife.

Knives & scissors

If you plan to be chopping your way through the Amazon rain forest, killing and gutting your food, chopping wood, and/or cutting rope to make a raft, you may want a big knife. But personally, I have never needed more than the Victorinox Swiss Army Classic knife ($18, 1 oz): I use the two-inch knife for serving food and opening mail-drop boxes; the scissors, for clipping nails, cutting cord, and treating blisters; and the tweezers for removing splinters and cactus needles.

In a multiperson group, I bring slightly more robust tools: the Gerber Ultralight LST ($21, 1 oz), which has a longer and better quality blade; and the Fiskars Premier Blunt-Tip Scissors ($7, 1 oz), which are bigger, sharper, and stronger than the Classic's.

Lighting

Unless I'm traveling in the Arctic or Antarctica during the summer months, when it never gets dark, I always carry a portable light, such as a flashlight or headlamp. Moonlight is romantic but unreliable.

In the early-2000s, flashlight and headlamp manufactures began replacing the traditional vacuum and halogen bulbs with LEDs (light-emitting diodes), which, with few exceptions, are now the standard, even on cheap keychain lights. Compared with vacuum and halogen bulbs, LEDs:

> Are more resistant to physical shock;
> Use batteries more efficiently;
> Are physically smaller and have built-in reflectors; and
> Have an effectively limitless life span—they really don't "burn out."

When deciding which light to bring, I primarily consider two factors:

> The expected frequency of use (e.g., daily, occasionally, or rarely); and
> The expected scope of use (e.g., for camp chores and/or for night hiking).

Expected usage drives the desired brightness, beam type, and position options. On long-term and resupply-challenged trips, a light's power

To avoid carrying extra batteries unnecessarily, look online to see how long batteries last in your light, and then consider how much you'll be using it.

Different beam types disperse their light in different ways.

SPOTLIGHT
Its 100-lumen bulb concentrates light and illuminates objects up to 230 feet away.

FLOODLIGHT
Its four-LED array illuminates more of the peripheral vision.

source and efficiency are important too. If multiple models meet my specifications, I may consider other factors like price, weight, size, glove-friendliness, and current type (regulated or unregulated).

Brightness

A light's brightness can be measured in two ways: maximum light output, aka lumens, and beam distance. *Lumens* measure the total light emitted by the bulb, in all directions. *Beam distance* refers to the farthest distance from the bulb at which there is still "usable light"—or exactly 0.25 lux, which is about the light intensity of a full moon. Lumens and beam distance are loosely correlated. A bulb with many lumens will probably also have a long beam distance, but it ultimately depends on how its beam is reflected and focused.

Beam type

The bulb's light can be reflected and focused in two different ways:

Spotlights concentrate their light on a small area. They are excellent for seeing things far off in the distance—like the next blaze or cairn, or cows on the trail.

Floodlights scatter their light over a wider area. This is desirable when hiking at night because it is visually exhausting to hike in a narrow light tunnel.

The optimal beam type—spot or flood—changes frequently, according to conditions and tasks. Ideally, manufacturers would simply make the primary bulb more versatile, adding a flip-down "diffuser" lens or twistable light housing that focuses or spreads the beam. Unfortunately, most models come equipped with spot and flood both. This two-in-one approach seems to add unnecessary weight, complexity, and expense.

Position options

Headlamps are convenient for backpacking. They free up my hands to

tools & techniques

pitch my tarp and use my trekking poles, among other things. But for night hiking, an eye-level light is very poorly positioned:

When illuminated from above, the ground looks two-dimensional. Without shadows, there is no way to tell whether a rock in the trail is a no-big-deal two inches high or a stumble-causing six inches high.

When it's snowing or raining, and/or when I'm walking through high brush, the headlamp fails to illuminate the ground. Instead, it lights up whatever is in front of my face.

A flashlight held at waist level is better positioned for night hiking, but it is a liability in camp: Unless I hold it in my mouth or rest it on something, it binds one hand.

Power source

Most headlamps and flashlights are powered by inexpensive, widely available AA or AAA batteries. Lithium batteries—which are more expensive, more powerful, and more cold-worthy than traditional alkaline batteries—can be used in some models; check the user manual for compatibility, or risk damaging the light's circuitry.

Smaller, ultralight lights sometimes use coin cell batteries, which are harder to find and fairly expensive. Equally inconvenient—at least for backpacking—are the rechargeable battery packs for heavy-duty mountaineering/caving lights.

A multimode light—that is, a light capable of *multiple levels* of light output—has better battery efficiency,

because its brightness can be fine-tuned to the exact usage required.

LEDs have either *regulated* or *unregulated* output. A regulated LED will maintain consistent brightness until there is no more battery power, at which time its brightness falls off a cliff. In contrast, the brightness of an unregulated LED will slowly decline until the batteries are completely drained.

skurka'spicks
L I G H T I N G

On summer trips, when there are more hours of daylight than hours I can physically hike, I only need a light for camp chores or for midnight emergencies, like going to the bathroom or scaring away a Snickers-craving Sierra black bear. A simple, inexpensive, lightweight light with a minimum brightness of about ten lumens is adequate for these trips. My favorite is the **Fenix LD01** ($40, 1 oz), a three-inch flashlight that can be attached to my visor's brim with its pocket clip. It uses one AAA battery; it's lithium compatible; and its output is regulated. The LD01's firepower is unsurpassed in its weight class: It can throw an 85-lumen spot beam for an hour, or a 28-lumen spot for 3.5 hours, or a nine-lumen spot for 11 hours.

When the days are shorter, my lighting needs increase. For these trips, I prefer a two-light system: an eye-level spotlight that illuminates my line of sight, and a waist-level floodlight that increases my peripheral vision. When walking, I mostly need only the flood beam; in camp, the reverse is true. Both lights should have at least 30 to 50 lumens, depending on the color, reflectivity, and texture of the ground surface. For example, less power is needed to illuminate a snow-covered meadow than a leaf-covered trail in a thick forest. The spotlight should have multiple levels of output, so that I can see far down the trail when necessary but conserve battery power in camp for less demanding uses.

This two-light system is heavier, more expensive, and more complicated than a one-light system. But night hiking with inadequate light is unsafe, slow, and mentally taxing. It's telling that this system is popular with ultra-runners, who often race through the night.

For the eye-level spotlight, I again use the Fenix LD01. For the waist-level floodlight, I rethread a traditional headlamp with a 40-inch-long belt of nylon one-inch webbing. My current choice is the **Mammut Lucido TR1** ($35, 2.5 oz), which has a 50-lumen four-LED array. Formerly, I used a Petzl model, but the swivel range on the second-generation unit is very limited and it is no longer functional for this purpose. It points aggressively downward, and when placed at waist level, its beam extends only five to ten feet out, a not uncommon problem when

headlamps are used in this fashion. But LED technology is improving rapidly, and I am optimistic that brighter floodlights will become available soon.

Firearms & bear spray

Prior to my first trip to Alaska, I received an e-mail from a gentleman in Denver who began following my adventures after attending a slideshow. He pleaded with me to take a gun for defense against grizzly bears, and when I told him I didn't know how to shoot a gun and that I was leaving in a few days, he offered to take me shooting if I made it back alive.

Well, I made it back alive, we went shooting, and I still don't take a

Bears can be problematic, but guns aren't the only means of protection.

firearm when traveling in grizzly country. Firearms are heavy, expensive, and sometimes not permitted on public lands. Plus, in order to take down a bear with one bullet, you need to be a good shot and to have a big gun. I'm not the former, and I don't want to carry the latter.

A better alternative is capsaicin-based bear spray from manufacturers like UDAP and Counter Assault. A potent irritant, capsaicin is the same compound that gives chili peppers their heat. Bear spray is lighter, less expensive, and more widely available than firearms. It's a glorified aerosol can that has a 30-foot range and presents no risk to life and limb for its user and other humans in the vicinity. Research shows that bear spray is actually more effective than firearms in preventing injuries from bears. Studies by the U.S. Fish and Wildlife Service and by a Brigham Young University researcher, Thomas Smith, have found that bear spray is effective more than 90 percent of the time in avoiding a bear attack, whereas firearms are only 50 to 70 percent effective.

Communication devices

It's romantic to clip the tether of modern communications, but I've never found it very practical, convenient, or safe. Groups split up, plans change, and emergencies happen. For the weight of a few Snickers bars, communications devices can save time, effort, and even a life. Just as important, they can also help to calm the worries of those back home.

Staying in touch

Every solo traveler should have a tool or a system for getting help. Before I leave for a trip, I always share my plans with someone, usually my mother. Sometimes it's just a simple e-mail that contains the basic trip info, but before my big trips, I give her printed copies of my itinerary and route, plus an emergency plan with key contacts. There are two ways that my mother can realize that something has gone wrong and that I might need help: if I do not return when I said I would return, or if I contact her from the field. In deciding whether to carry a communications device, I mainly consider the location and the environmental conditions. I almost always carry one now if I am going to be in a remote area and/or if the conditions could present exceptional risks.

A communications device capable of reaching the outside world is not as important for a group. If one person goes down, in theory, other members can assist and/or run for help. But this approach wastes time, and it might not be effective if a patient's problems are beyond the medical training of group members or if the messenger doesn't make it out. Groups may also want a way to communicate with each other if they intend to split up.

Contact with the outside world is not a panacea; there is no such thing as a fast search and rescue.

Even in the foothills outside Boulder—within view of the city—evacuations conducted by Colorado Mountain Rescue (CMR) are often half-day affairs. Once a call for help is placed, it takes a few hours just for CMR volunteer members to be mobilized and reach the scene, and another few hours to evacuate an injured patient on a backboard.

Group communications

It is as important to be able to stay in touch with your group as it is with the outside world.

A whistle is no louder than a scream—both are about 100 to 120 decibels—but it's possible to blow one for an extended period of time without getting hoarse. Plus, whistles are a universal sign of distress, and blast sequences can be defined beforehand and easily interpreted in the field (e.g., "Two short blasts means, 'Stop and wait.' Please respond with one long blast to confirm that you heard me.") Many backpacks feature a sternum strap buckle with an integrated whistle.

Two-way radios, realistically, have a range of about two miles—despite rosy estimates of up to 18 miles under "ideal conditions"—but they make it safer and more convenient for large groups to split up. I learned the value of two-way radios the hard way on a radio-less trip in Wyoming's Wind River Range. Near the end of the second day, our group intentionally split up during a long climb, and we agreed to rendezvous and camp at Ink Wells Lake. The lead group misread the map and camped at a different lake nearby. I figured they were okay, but I would have slept easier and we could have rejoined

From anywhere in the world, I can make a call or send a text message using a satellite phone.

tools & techniques

20+ mi into headwind. 5-star camp.
Last Updated by Andrew on Sep 10
9/7/11 11:21 PM

Directions   Search nearby   Save to map   more ▾

A short message sent using a SPOT Connect and smart phone at the end of a four-day trip

faster in the morning if the other guide and I had had radios.

Cellular phones

The lightest and least expensive (because almost everybody has one already) communications device is a cellular phone. Check your provider's service map to determine whether it will be reliable where you'll be traveling.

Even if a cell phone is not reliable for emergency purposes in the backcountry, I still often carry one to use in town. Pay phones are increasingly rare, and—if given the option—I'd rather be checking my e-mail and catching up on news while filling my belly at the café than waiting for computer time at the public library.

Satellite communications

Wild country that is beyond the range of cell towers is not beyond the range of orbital satellites. A growing number of devices tap into these networks, notably:

> SPOT Satellite Messengers;
> Personal locator beacons (PLBs); and
> Satellite phones.

SPOT satellite messengers are the most practical satellite-based solution for most backpackers. They are dependable, lightweight, relatively inexpensive to own and operate, and battery-efficient. SPOT taps into the 44-satellite network operated by Globalstar, its parent company; the network covers most of the Earth's landmasses.

The SPOT Satellite GPS Messenger ($170 + $100/year service plan, 5 oz) is a one-way communicator capable of sending four messages: "SOS," "Help," "OK," and a customizable message. For an extra $50 per year, there is also a tracking service that will record its location every ten minutes.

The SPOT Connect ($170 + $100/year service plan, 5 oz) is like a one-way satellite modem for a smartphone. Using the SPOT Connect app, I have the same four-message capability as the GPS Messenger, but I can also update my Facebook and Twitter pages, and send short e-mail and text messages.

When an "SOS" message is sent from a SPOT device, it gets relayed instantly to the GEOS International Emergency Response Coordination Center (IERCC), which delegates the response from there. The other messages are sent via e-mail or text message to people whom I specify. To make the "Help" message less ambiguous, before I leave I instruct my family and friends to interpret it as: "I am not in mortal danger but something has gone wrong. I will keep moving if possible; otherwise I will stay put. Please send help. If my situation changes, I will send a different message."

SPOT devices have helped save lives, but most users conclude that their greatest value is in alleviating the worries of those back home and in sharing a trip real-time. After my mother offered to buy me a SPOT for Christmas, I told her that good decision-making, not a SPOT, keep me alive in the outdoors. She replied, "It's not for you—it's so that I can sleep better." My mother greatly anticipates the daily "OK" e-mails, but she also looks forward to exploring the area around my most recent coordinates (included in the e-mails) and looking at pictures taken nearby.

A personal locator beacon (PLB) like the McMurdo Fast Find 210 ($250, 5 oz) might be considered a primitive SPOT. It can be used only to

transmit a distress signal to Cospas-Sarsat, a satellite-based international search and rescue detection and information distribution system. Each PLB sends a unique signal, so it can be traced to an individual; units that have an embedded GPS will simultaneously send location information to speed up recovery operations. Unlike SPOTs, PLBs cannot be used to send "OK" or "Help" messages, or for tracking.

However, PLBs do have worldwide coverage, better water resistance, and a battery that is operable to -20°F. There is also no service fee. Before SPOT devices came along, I owned a PLB, but I subsequently sold it because its advantages are not relevant to my normal trips.

A satellite phone is heavier, more expensive to own or rent, and more breakable than a SPOT device or a PLB. However, it's a much more powerful communications tool—like the difference between the telegraph and the telephone. Some models are capable of sending text messages, which is a good way to transmit information and minimize expensive talk time.

Even on "remote" trips in the lower 48—including difficult treks across the Colorado Plateau and the crest of the High Sierra—I have carried only a SPOT unit. The reality is that I'm never that far from help, even if I try to be. In truly remote places, however, like northern Alaska and northern Canada, I carry a satellite phone. Fortunately, I have never had to use one for an emergency. A friend of mine did, however, when he ripped several tendons in his ankle while north of the Brooks Range. When he called a bush pilot, he was told that he'd have to hike another 80 miles on a floppy foot to reach the nearest landing strip. That conversation could never have taken place with a SPOT or PLB.

A satellite phone is helpful in preventing emergencies as well. During a 48-hour snowstorm in the Alaska Range, I called my friend Roman Dial to discuss alternate routes that would be less avalanche-prone than my original route. During a windy September rainstorm that prevented me from paddling four miles across Kobuk Lake, I called home on several occasions to get weather updates.

The current crop of satellite phones is exemplified by the Iridium 9595A ($1,400 + about $1/minute, 13 oz), which is about as big and bulky as cell phones from the 1980s and which has a user interface that's equally archaic. So I am encouraged by the new TerreStar Genus ($1,150, 5 oz), which is the first satellite phone with the features of modern smartphones, like e-mail and Internet access.

Gear maintenance & repair

No matter how durable you think your gear is, occasional field repair or inter-trip repair should be expected.

Shoes & clothes

Before I wear my shoes, I fortify their most common blowout points (which I've observed in previous pairs) with Aquaseal, a urethane-based glue. On trail running shoes, the most vulnerable points are the crease of the toe box and the outside near the pinky's knuckle, which is a high-abrasion area when kicking steps in snow and/or walking through brush. If my shoes start to fray in the field, I normally use Krazy Glue because it dries almost immediately.

In the field, I also hand-wash my clothes (every few days) and socks (daily) to remove salt, dirt, and gritty particles, which degrade the fabric's performance and cut apart the fibers.

Repair tools

Needle and thread (or dental floss) can be used to repair rips in clothing and equipment. I normally do a baseball stitch and then protect and waterproof the stitches with Aquaseal glue, a trick I was taught by fellow adventurer Bretwood Higman. Stitches are longer lasting than self-adhesive fabric patches, which I also take along for a fast temporary solution.

The Speedy Stitcher Sewing Awl has been around since 1909, and it is great for thick fabrics and materials like webbing, leather, and padded shoulder straps. I have never carried a Speedy Stitcher on a trip, but I often use it before I leave, for things like adjusting the length of my pack's waist belt and for cutting my ski skins.

McNett makes a series of products to restore the performance of outdoor equipment, including waterproof-breathable and water-resistant shells, polyurethane-coated nylon, and full-grain leather boots.

Photography

Before I started my Sea-to-Sea Route trip in the fall of 2004, I purchased a digital SLR, the Nikon D70. Its image quality, depth of field, low-light capabilities, and range of manual controls were far better than anything offered by the point-and-shoot models of that era. I don't regret carrying that camera—it was a trip of a lifetime and I wanted beautiful pictures of it—but the camera was indeed a nuisance. It weighed two pounds, and it was too big and too expensive to carry outside of my pack.

The features and quality once found only in high-end SLRs have now trickled down to smaller models. For Facebook, slideshows, and perhaps some small prints, there is no need to look beyond the point-and-shoot models. These cameras are small and light, can be stored in a side or chest pocket, and are relatively inexpensive.

My current favorite is the 10-megapixel Canon Powershot S95 ($400, 7 oz), which has a fast f/2.0 wide-angle lens, 720p HD video, RAW capture, excellent image quality, and good range of manual controls. If you want better features and are willing to carry more weight and bulk, consider the Sigma DP and Canon G series, or a Micro Four Thirds (MFT) camera, which has interchangeable lenses that are smaller than those on conventional SLRs.

Batteries

I began my Appalachian Trail thruhike with a solar-powered battery charger for my camera. But I realized that the charger weighed about as

A small camera is not an "essential," but I always take one to record my experiences.

tools & techniques

much as two months worth of batteries, and I've never carried one again. About every week, I drain a battery for my Powershot S95, so on any outing longer than a week, I need at least one extra battery. On a long-distance trip, fresh batteries are sent to me in my mail drops by my logistics coordinator (my beloved mother), and I send dead batteries back to be recharged. Inexpensive, non-OEM (original equipment manufacturer) batteries are available at *BestBatt. com*—they are not as long lasting but they are a better value.

Memory cards

A similar rotation system could be used for memory cards. You could receive a blank card in the mail and send a full one home, and then a logistics person could download the files and send it back. If you don't have a support person, there are two approaches. The first is to buy enough memory cards for your entire trip. Another option is to "bounce" a standalone data storage unit—like the Digital Foci Photo Safe II ($150)—from post office to post office along your route, so that you can download your data when your card is getting full. When you ship memory cards, pay extra for a tracking number; when you back up memory cards, back them up on two different drives. I've lost cards and data before, and it's heart-wrenching.

Tripods

Tripods are useful for self-portraits and long-exposure landscapes. Small, inexpensive, lightweight tripods are made by Pedco and Joby (my preference); they cost $15 to $30 and weigh two to four ounces. I rarely carry a tripod, however, preferring instead to use rocks or trees if I really need a stable surface.

Journaling

Nine years after my first thru-hike, I vividly recall few of the shelters I slept in, the thru-hikers and townspeople I met, and the look and feel

Keeping your camera safe

The aforementioned cameras are not waterproof, so during rainstorms or packrafting sections, it's wise to protect them. I put my camera inside the waterproof liner inside my backpack, or I store it outside in a 1-liter Sea to Summit Ultra-Sil Dry Sack ($10, 0.5 oz) or a waterproof 6.75-by-6-inch Loksak Aloksak ($7 for a three-pack, 0.3 oz). The Dry Sack is preferred for packrafting because I can secure it to my pack in the event that I flip.

. . . and dry.

part 2

Journaling takes time and mental energy, but it's nice having a written record.

of a particular section of trail. Photos and video are helpful in jogging my memory, but I find far more joy in rereading pages from the 20-ounce spiral-bound journal I carried from start to finish that summer. For my Sea-to-Sea Route trip, I found a lighter system: I cut 8.5-by-11-inch sheets of nice résumé paper in half, and sent blank pages to myself in my mail drops.

By 2006 and 2007, the faster-farther-lighter mantra—climaxing in the Great Western Loop—had made me ditch the paper journal and pen. At the end of 15-hour, 40-mile days, I was too exhausted to spend another 30 minutes writing. So instead, I used a digital voice recorder (DVR), like the Olympus VN-6000 ($40, 2.2 oz), which worked wonderfully: I was able to record much more material than I

would have ever been able to write down. However, the digital files lack the aesthetics of handwritten entries.

I've since returned to writing down my thoughts, on the margins and unimportant spaces of topographical map sheets, or even on blank sheets of paper when particularly inspired. On map sheets, I like how my notations and ramblings are adjacent to the topographical features of my route.

As far as writing instruments, I carry two pens—usually one black and one red, both medium ballpoints. Gel inks are smudge-prone and pencil lead fades. In cold temperatures, ink freezes. Using a pencil is one possible solution, but I prefer rotating two pens, keeping one in my jacket while I write with the other, then swapping when the ink begins to freeze.

packing

I said goodbye to my generous hosts at the highway mainte-
nance camp and began hiking into Canada's Richardson Mountains
via rain-swollen James Creek. Ahead of me was the most challenging section of my entire Alaska-Yukon Expedition: a 657-mile, 24-day
stretch across Yukon's Arctic and the Arctic National Wildlife Refuge
during which I didn't cross a road or see another human being.

I knew this section would be memo-
rable, but I didn't know that I would
encounter Porcupine caribou during
their fall migration; that I'd experience
mosquito swarms so intense I began
hearing their high-pitched whine even
when they were not around; or that
I'd be charged by grizzly bears on
three occasions, including one when
the bear came so close that I threw
a trekking pole at it before reaching
for my pepper spray. (The bear left
behind a 20-foot-long streak of berry
poop as it ran away.)

What I did know as I slogged up
James Creek, however, was that
this was the essence of backpacking. It was liberating—and humbling—
to know that my safety, comfort, and
success were fully dependent on
what I was carrying between my ears
and inside my backpack.

Backpacks

Intentionally, I've not discussed backpacks until now. To have done so
without first discussing the gear
and supplies whose weight and volume dictate the pack's load-carrying

capacity and volume would have
been putting the carriage before
the horse.

Backpacks are often categorized
by the trip length for which they are
traditionally used, but these classifications tend to incorrectly state true
needs. For example, conventional
wisdom would have me carry a
7-pound, 80-liter "extended outing"
pack for my long-distance trips, but
normally my needs are met with much
less. For loads weighing about
30 pounds or less, I use a 2-pound,
50-liter pack; for loads weighing up
to 55 pounds, which would include
a packraft and two weeks' worth of
food, I have used a 3-pound, 75-liter
pack. I may be an extreme case, but
most avid hikers will find that traditional guidelines are not applicable to
them either.

Load-carrying

Backpacks come in two basic
flavors: Frameless and framed (or
"suspension").

Frameless packs do not contain
a rigid structure, save for perhaps a

To increase my hiking efficiency, I organize my pack to minimize how often I take it off.

closed-cell foam backpad. They are an unconventional choice for backpacking. In the late-1990s, an ambitious startup company, GoLite, came up with the 13-ounce Breeze, a glorified daypack that didn't even have a waist belt. After adding other lightweight gear, food, water, and some odds and ends, GoLite argued that the entire kit was light enough that a conventional suspension system was unnecessary.

Framed packs have a rigid chassis that can more effectively transfer weight from the shoulders to the hips. Weight is best carried by the hips because hips are supported by large muscle groups—namely the gluteal and quadricep groups—and because hips are closer to an adult's center of gravity. In contrast, the shoulders are supported by weaker muscles.

The Kelty Yukon ($120, 4 lbs 14 oz) exemplifies the earliest framed packs. These *external frame* models, which have a separate harness, aluminum frame, and pack bag have been almost entirely replaced by *internal frame* packs, in which these components are integrated. External frames are still thought to carry heavy loads best, but they are not as stable, travel-friendly, or streamlined as internal frames.

There are three commonly used support structures in internal frame models:

> A stay is a flat aluminum rod, usually about one inch wide, that runs parallel to the spine and spans the pack's length.
> A framesheet is a semirigid precurved pane usually made of plastic.

	frameless	VS framed/ suspension
weight	8 oz to 2 lb	3 to 8 lb
expense	$100 to $200	$150 to $400
volume	Generally smaller	Generally larger
load-carrying capacity	Limited to less than 25 lb to 30 lb	Capable of more than 25 lb to 30 lb
comfort	Excellent as long as load-carrying capacity is not exceeded	Can more comfortably carry heavy loads, but heavy loads are inherently uncomfortable regardless of a pack's features
durability	Depends on fabrics and construction quality	Depends on fabrics and construction quality

part (2)

> A **peripheral rod** borders a pack's perimeter and is made of aluminum or semirigid nylon.

Stays and framesheets are sometimes removable, which is convenient for times when the load does not justify the weight of these suspension features. Peripheral rods cannot be removed.

Framed vs. frameless packs.

The load-carrying capacity of *framed* backpacks can be enhanced by using more than one support structure. Stays can be attached to or embedded in framesheets, and peripheral rods can be added to packs with framesheets and/ or stays.

The load-carrying capacity of *frameless* backpacks is more limited than framed packs, but it too can be enhanced beyond its design by:

> Better distributing the load with a quality hip belt, back pad, sternum strap, and shoulder straps.
> Fortifying the pack with a removable "virtual frame." I normally use a torso-length closed-cell foam pad, which gives my frameless thru-hiking pack a nice cylindrical shape. But I've also used a pack-raft and a Snowclaw Guide ($20, 6 oz), a semirigid disc that I

tip Downsize to a frameless pack. The discomfort of loading gear into a frameless pack will force you to become disciplined about your load's weight and volume.

use primarily to dig my shelter footprint and to collect snow for melting.

Some niche backpacks are actually designed to be used with a virtual frame. The classic Gossamer Gear G4 ($125, 16 oz), for example, has a sleeve that fits several types of sleeping pads. Virtual frames are not as effective in transferring weight as conventional systems because they are not as stiff, but they can help.

Because frameless packs lack the complicated stays, framesheets, and peripheral rods featured on their framed cousins—plus the other bells and whistles that seem to be customary on these models—frameless packs are both lighter and less expensive. Prices range from $100 to $200, and weights range from 8 to 32 ounces, compared with $150 to $500 and 3 to 8 pounds for framed models.

Framed packs lock my back into a fixed position (straight and upright) and limit my hips' range of motion. A frameless pack allows for a more natural stride and greater agility while crossing boulder fields and smashing through alder. Some frameless packs have no waist belt, which I suppose allows for maximum agility, but I like the modest load stability and weight transfer that a hip belt offers.

The consensus—with which I mostly agree—is that loads of less than 25 to 30 pounds can be comfortably carried in a frameless pack. Frameless packs can be exceedingly comfortable—*as long as they are not overloaded.* Plus,

I have never understood how a 40- or 50-pound load could ever be described as "comfortable," even if supported by the most advanced suspension system.

In determining whether a frameless pack is necessary or overkill, it is important to consider the weight *source* in addition to the total weight:

> Gear does *not* get lighter during a trip; but
> Food is consumed, at a rate (for me) of about two pounds per day; and
> Water rapidly disappears.

how2

learn how framed packs transfer weight

1 Put on a framed backpack.

2 Take your arms out of the shoulder straps.

3 Put on a frameless backpack and repeat Step 2.

The framed pack will stay upright and the weight will stay over the hips, whereas the frameless backpack will flop backward once weight is removed from the shoulders.

tools & techniques

When my pack is light and well balanced, I barely notice that it's on.

On a desert trip, then, it might be worth loading a frameless pack with 30 pounds—or maybe more—because the weight will quickly drop to a more manageable level.

Volume

A heavy load is usually big, and a light load is usually small. But there are many instances in which this correlation does not hold. For example, my wintertime load is light but big, because I have a warm sleeping bag, a full-length foam sleeping pad, and a 2-liter or 4-liter cook pot. And my desert load is usually heavy but small, because I have to carry a lot of water.

Compression systems. To extend the usable range of their packs, manufacturers install compression systems—consisting of nylon webbing, bungee cords, and/or hook-and-loop devices—that reduce the pack's effective volume. My 70-liter frameless pack, for example,

compresses to an amazing 25 liters, which is comparable to the volume of my minimalist overnight pack. However, because the compression system does not proportionally reduce the pack's volume, the main compartment is very restricted in some places and very bulbous in others. Statistically, its compressibility is a great marketing story, but its usability is more limited in reality. A pack can probably be compressed only by about one-third before its performance is adversely affected.

Fit

Backpacks are sized according to spine length, which is imperfectly correlated with height. If a backpack is too long or too short, it will not fit right—it may hang too low (or ride too high) on the hips, or place no weight (or too much weight) on the shoulders.

Back lengths. The back length of conventional framed packs is adjustable, allowing users to precisely match the pack's harness length with their spine length. However, this feature adds weight and cost.

All frameless packs and many lightweight framed packs, on the other hand, have fixed back lengths. Depending on the manufacturer, most models come in two or three sizes, and each size accommodates spine lengths within a two- to three-inch range. For example, my 50-liter thru-hiking pack, which is sized medium, fits spine lengths of 17.5 to 19.5 inches. When on the cusp between two sizes, I prefer sizing down because I prefer my pack to ride higher on my hips. That way, it doesn't restrict the movement of my hips as much, and lightweight loads tend to float upward to my waist anyway, which is my torso's narrowest point.

Waist belts. A properly sized waist belt is crucial to carrying comfort. If it's too big, the load sways and can't be transferred to the hips; and if it's too small, it's constricting and uncomfortable. The robust waist belts found on conventional frameless packs are usually interchangeable, because they are extensively padded and can only accommodate a narrow range of waist sizes. The waist belts on Osprey packs, for example, have four-inch ranges, e.g., 30 inches to 34 inches.

Frameless packs and lightweight framed packs normally do not have interchangeable waist belts, but their belts are designed to fit a wide range of body types. My 50-liter thru-hiking pack, for example, fits waists sized 27 to 52 inches.

Women's packs. Women-specific packs are now widely available. They share the same features as men's models but they are better fitted, courtesy of narrow shoulder widths, shorter spine lengths, shorter and more ergonomically shaped shoulder straps, and angled waist belts that better fit women's waist-to-hip ratios.

Fabrics

If several packs offer the load-carrying capacity, volume, and fit that I need, I make a final decision based on secondary considerations like fabrics, features, and loading style.

A backpack is constructed mostly of nylon, sometimes with ripstop or mesh construction. These nylons usually have a polyurethane or silicone coating, which makes the fabric (but not the pack) waterproof; with enough use and UV exposure, these coatings peel off anyway. To achieve a desired level of durability while also saving weight and cost, designers may use "bombproof" fabrics in wear-prone areas like the pack's base.

Continued on p. 184

tip

Your spine length is measured from the C7 vertebra (the knob at the base of your neck) to the iliac crest (the top of your pelvic bone below the side of your rib cage).

tools & techniques

tried&true

how to pack a backpack

part (2)

On solo trips I aim to be walking down the trail within 15 minutes of waking up. To do so quickly I can't just stuff everything into my backpack randomly, however. It must be packed so as to minimize the load's effect on my center of gravity and maximize organizational efficiency.

Maintain your center of gravity

The location of one's center of gravity depends on gender and body type. For a normal adult male, it's around the sternum; for a normal adult female, it's above the belly button. A backpack of any weight will affect my center of gravity (and a heavy pack much more so) and I will need to compensate for that with an unnatural walking form, hence the forward lean. My goal is simply to minimize the effect, specifically by:

> Placing the heaviest items (e.g., food, water, and stove fuel) against my back, so I don't have to lean forward as far.

> Cinching the pack's compression straps, which help to pull the weight closer to my back. (Removing compression straps is a classic "stupid light" move.)

> Keeping all or most of the weight below or level with my sternum to prevent swaying, which would make me less nimble and could possibly be dangerous on technical terrain.

> Centering the weight along my spine so that the pack does not tilt to the left or right. This can be achieved by packing the heaviest items against the spine or by counterbalancing the weight.

Keep your pack organized

An unorganized backpack is frustrating and inefficient: I can't find what I need, and I waste time looking for it. To organize my pack I keep:

> Oft-needed items within easy reach. In my hip belt pockets I keep my water purification, DEET, head net, camera, lip balm, and/or sunscreen. In my side pockets I keep my water bottle(s), maps, and perhaps a beanie, bear spray, and/or gloves. I attach my insulated overmitts to my shoulder strap with a small carabiner, which is more secure than my side pockets. And I keep my sunglasses atop my visor when I'm not wearing them.

> Occasionally needed items inside my pack, at the very top. These include my accessory pouch (which contains my LED light, fire starter, toiletries, chewing gum, etc.), a quart freezer bag with my day's rations, layers of clothing (e.g., wind shirt, rain gear, and puffy jacket), and additional bottles of water if I'm in a dry stretch.

> Items I won't need until camp or during future days—like my sleeping bag and my food for the rest of the trip—at the bottom.

tip Because my food and water supplies change daily, I arrange my belongings slightly differently every morning, but I always follow these general rules.

tools & techniques

The current standard for light and tough pack fabrics is a 210D 4-ounce nylon that has a quarter-inch rip-stop grid of Dyneema, which is the world's strongest fiber, at 15 times the strength of steel on a weight-for-weight basis. Since 2004, my thru-hiking packs have been made primarily of this fabric. I've seen it rip just three times, always thanks to abrasion against sharp crystallized rocks. The tears were only one to two inches long and easily repaired with a needle, thread, and Aquaseal glue.

In an effort to save weight, some Ultimate Hikers are willing to carry packs that are made of shelter fabrics like silicone-impregnated nylon or spinnaker sailcloth. Personally, though, I prefer less delicate fabrics because my trips tend to involve more remote areas, off-trail travel, heavier loads, and pointy winter gear (e.g., metal-edged skis). I'm happy to carry an extra pound to allay concerns of overstressed seams, fatal tears, or structural malfunctions.

Pack features

Manufacturers load backpacks with a range of add-on features—some are useful, some are not.

Pockets add weight and cost, but they are very convenient. In side pockets, I store my water bottle, map, glove liners, and/or bear spray. In hip belt pockets, I keep my camera, water purification, bug repellent, head net, and sunscreen/lip balm. And in a back pocket, I may keep a wind shirt, rain jacket, or wet tarp; I try to

My go-to thru-hiking pack since 2004: the GoLite Jam, made of Dyneema fabric

avoid putting heavy items in the back pocket because it skews my center of gravity. I prefer pockets made of a durable nylon, as they are less susceptible to snags and abrasion than mesh pockets.

Back panels can be made of mesh and/or feature "air flow channels" that supposedly reduce clamminess and help prevent overheating. This adds weight and expense, however, and it can affect the user's center of gravity by pushing the load away from the back.

A hydration sleeve, which accommodates a drinking reservoir, is usually the first feature that I remove when I get a new pack. I much prefer using bottles, so the sleeve is

part 2

unnecessary weight. Plus, if it is not removed it tends to snag items as I push them into my pack.

Zippers are usually the first blowout point on any outdoor product, and I avoid them when possible. When a zipper is truly functional, I prefer large-toothed zippers with protective flaps to water-resistant zippers, which seem especially vulnerable to failing and jamming. Plus, the sole benefit of water-resistant zippers is undermined by the remainder of the pack not being waterproof.

I use compression straps, which are lengths of webbing located on the side of a pack that can be tightened, to improve load stability and my center of gravity and to secure skis, paddle shafts, trekking poles, and oversize water bottles to the outside of my pack. Compression straps with buckles are more versatile than straps with fixed fasteners.

Top lids are separate bags that sit atop the pack, usually fastened with webbing, that are, unfortunately, found on most packs. They tend to fit sloppily in real-world conditions and they add one more step to accessing the pack body. I suppose that top lids are useful in storing oft-needed items like sunscreen, food, and water purification—but I just keep these items at the top of my pack or in external pockets.

Daisy chains & ice ax loops are seldom used by backpackers. I usually cut them off even though the weight savings is minimal.

After washing my socks I loop them through my pack's compression straps to dry.

tools & techniques

Climbing or keychain carabiner clips seem to be popular ornaments on backpacks. They may be useful in lashing stuff to the outside, but it's better to have everything inside the pack, where it can't sway annoyingly from side to side. I have found only one worthwhile use for a carabiner. In the winter, I use one to secure my insulated mitts to my shoulder strap. The alternate location, a side pocket, is intolerably risky because I probably would not notice if one fell out.

Loading style

Most backpacks are loaded from an opening in the top ("top-loading"), though many large-volume models have an additional entry point along the main pack body ("panel-loading") and/or a separate sleeping bag compartment at the base. I prefer a top-loading-only design: It avoids the blowout-prone zippers and extra weight of secondary openings, and it's easier to balance and organize a pack from one entry point.

I suppose that panel-loading designs are convenient for accessing items that are buried deeply in a pack, but I avoid having to dig through my pack by keeping my load small and well organized, with items I need often at the top or in exterior pockets.

skurka's picks
BACKPACKS

I backpack often, and I have good relationships with several backpack manufacturers. Even so, I own only four backpacks.

For long day trips and minimalist overnights, I use the 21-liter **GoLite VO24** ($90, 1 lb 5 oz). More often, though, I use it as my everyday pack for grocery shopping, post office drops, downhill skiing, air travel, and as a computer bag.

For most solo three-season thru-hikes, my go-to pack since 2004 has been the 50-liter **GoLite Jam** ($150, 1 lb 13 oz). For solo winter trips, I bring the 70-liter version. The Jam has gained weight with each new iteration, but I generally like the improvements: padded hip belts, hip belt pockets, and more durable side pockets. However, I could do without the breathable mesh back panel; a Dyneema pane would be stronger and lighter, and it would not collect debris.

For guided trips and packrafting trips, I like the **ULA Epic** ($275, 40 oz), which has dual aluminum stays and a unique sandwich-like harness system that can securely hold a pack bag, packraft, paddle, and personal floatation device (PFD). The Epic now comes with a

To shave up to 8 oz from the GoLite Jam, remove the hydration sleeve, foam pad and pad sleeve, ice ax loops, and outside/rear pocket.

part (2)

10-ounce 65-liter waterproof dry bag made of heavy-duty thermo-plastic polyurethane (TPU)-laminated 420D nylon. I once loaded the Epic with about 55 pounds of gear, supplies, and food. It is impossible to make this load "comfortable," but the Epic did a pretty good job in light of its 2.5-pound weight.

Waterproofing

Backpacks are not waterproof. Some pack fabrics are waterproof, but there are still several ways moisture can get inside: through the seams (which cannot be completely sealed with glue or tape because of the complex construction); through the zippers; and/or through the top opening.

Keeping your pack dry

There are four ways to protect the contents of a pack from precipitation:

Pack liners. Place a pack liner inside of the empty pack; all the pack's contents go inside it. I normally use a 20-gallon trash compactor bag or a bag made of 2-millimeter poly-ethylene film. These liners will last one to two months before becoming irrep-arably torn or punctured.

The only drawback to pack liners is the lack of a secure closure. But by using a bag that is bigger than my pack's volume, there is enough extra material leftover to seal it through twisting.

Waterproof stuff sacks. These sacks from Granite Gear, Outdoor Research, and Sea to Summit are

A plastic trash compactor bag is an effective and inexpensive way to waterproof my pack's contents. I prefer this method over waterproof stuff sacks or a pack cover.

tools & techniques

seam-sealed and have a waterproof closure. Available volumes range from 1 liter to 55 liters; they cost $10 to $40 and weigh 0.5 ounce to 5 ounces. They can be made of silicone-impregnated nylon, which is the lightest but least durable; PU-coated nylon, which is heaviest and most durable; and/or waterproof/breathable fabric (e.g., eVent), which is of moderate weight and durability, but which is expensive.

On a packrafting trip, when my pack will likely get soaked and even submerged, I use a large-volume PU-coated nylon waterproof stuff sack. It functions like a pack liner, with the added perk of a waterproof closure. I avoid the silicone-impregnated nylon sacks—constant abrasion destroys their waterproof quality after about a month.

Pack covers. The least effective way to protect the contents of a backpack from moisture—yet one of the most commonly seen—is a pack cover, which fits over the outside of the backpack and is secured with an elastic cuff. They are made of PU-coated nylon or silicone-impregnated nylon, cost $25 to $40, and weigh four to eight ounces. Pack covers have a number of fatal flaws:

> They do not protect the entire pack, so precipitation seeps inside after dripping down the user's neck and back.
> They add effort and time in accessing the contents of the pack, which must be partially removed; side

pockets are oftentimes blocked.
> They are prone to being caught by the wind and by brush.
> In a drenching storm, water can pool in the bottom of the cover, adding weight and soaking whatever is at the bottom of the backpack (probably a sleeping bag).
> They offer minimal protection during a river ford, when the pack might be entirely submerged.

Ponchos. A variant of the pack cover is the poncho, the backside of which drapes over the backpack. The poncho's fit and protection can be improved by tying the backside's corners in a knot around one's waist. A poncho is not as effective as a pack liner or waterproof stuff sacks, but it is more effective than a pack cover, because it covers the gap between the user's back and the backpack.

Organization

My backpack is very deliberately packed and well organized. I'm less likely to lose or ruin gear and supplies—and I can more quickly find what I need—if I know where everything is supposed to be and if I store it all neatly in stuff sacks, containers, and bags. I keep almost everything in the main compartment of my pack, rather than divided among a top lid and separate compartments or pockets. This system is both lighter and more time-efficient.

Repackage supplies in smaller containers, jars, and bags to help save weight.

Stuff sacks

I keep my sleeping bag, cook pot, tent stakes, sunglasses, and loose accessories—including my toiletries, compass, flashlight, flint and steel, first aid, and wallet—in separate nylon stuff sacks, which are lightweight, durable, and relatively inexpensive. The weight savings of stuff sacks made with ultralight fabrics like Spinnaker Cloth and Cuben Fiber are not worth the cost and loss of durability, I believe. For my accessories, I prefer a stuff sack with a large opening so that I can get my hand down inside it. My shelter, bivy sack, and extra clothing are not kept in stuff sacks. Instead, I use them to fill empty areas of my pack.

Containers

I use 0.25-ounce capacity balm jars (available online and at REI) to store toiletries like sunscreen, Sportslick, and Hydropel, instead of keeping these items in their original tubes. I decant liquids like DEET, Dr. Bronner's soap, and Aquamira into 0.25-ounce dropper bottles. The balm jars and dropper bottles save the weight of at least a few Snickers bars, considering that the original containers of these items weigh one to six ounces each.

Storage bags

I store medications (e.g., ibuprofen, Tylenol, and antidiarrheal), single-use bacitracin packets, a needle

In some high-use bear-inhabited areas, hard-sided canisters are required.

and thread, and fishing hooks and line in two-by-three-inch zipper bags. I have two waterproof five-by-four-inch Loksak Aloksaks ($6 for a three-pack, 0.2 oz each). One contains toilet paper, matches, and cotton fire-starter tabs; the other I use as a wallet. On shorter trips, inexpensive plastic zipper bags can be used, but they are not waterproof or durable.

My maps, guidebook sections, and mileage charts are critical, so I take measures to protect them from water and dirt. I store most of my paperwork in a waterproof 12-by-12-inch Loksak Aloksak bag ($4 each, 1 oz). On shorter trips, when durability is not as critical, a gallon-sized zipper storage bag (e.g., Ziploc) works okay. Expect to replace an Aloksak after a month of daily use; the seal usually fails around then.

I place paperwork for which I need regular and easy access—specifically, my current map—in a quart-size Ziploc freezer bag, which I keep in the side pocket of my pack or in a shirt/pants pocket. Freezer bags are cheap, effective, and conveniently sized; but they are only water-resistant, so in really wet conditions, I keep my map inside my rain jacket or double bag it. I have used six-by-nine-inch Aloksak bags as map sleeves, but they are much more expensive than freezer bags, and their performance is no better.

Food storage

After making camp and eating dinner, one of my pre-sleep tasks is separating out tomorrow's daytime rations (breakfast and snacks) from the rest of my food. I store the meals in a quart-size freezer bag; I like Hefty OneZip bags, which have a wider opening than the quart-size Ziploc bags. When I pack up in the morning, I keep this bag near the top of my pack for easy access throughout the day.

How I store the remainder of my food depends on the local wildlife (particularly bears) and/or local regulations. If wildlife is an insignificant concern and if there are no food-storage regulations, I use nylon stuff sacks, which are lightweight and durable.

Animal-resistant storage

If I'm concerned about rodents, I may hang my nylon stuff sack in midair, on

part (2)

a nearby tree branch, or perhaps from the roof of an Adirondack lean-to (via a nail). As far as raccoons are concerned, I'd rather just sleep next to my food bags; raccoons do not seem to be as bold as mice.

In bear-inhabited country, it is prudent—and sometimes required—to take additional food storage measures. Personally, I think *preemptively avoiding* bear encounters is the best way to avoid bear problems.

So I will not camp where I cook; I will not carry or make strongly scented foods like bacon; and I will not camp in established sites or near high-use corridor trails.

In bear-inhabited locations where there are no storage regulations, I use polyethylene, odor-proof, 12-by-20-inch Loksak Opsak bags ($4 each, 1 oz), which help to minimize wafting food odors. This, at least in theory, will lower the odds of a bear wandering into my camp. An Opsak holds about five days of food for me, at 4,500 calories and 2.25 pounds per day. I replace an Opsak after about one month of use, when its seal usually fails.

Animal-proof storage

In some high-use areas—including California's High Sierra, the Adirondack High Peaks, and Washington's Olympic Peninsula—it may be mandated that backpackers carry their food in an approved hard-sided bear canister. For a list of approved models, visit the land manager's website; for the Sierra, visit *www.SierraWild .gov*. Bear canisters are made of plastic or carbon fiber and feature a removable lid that bears cannot open. They weigh 1.5 to 3.5 pounds, hold three to nine days of food (depending on your diet), and cost $75 to $275; rentals are available.

I do not carry a canister unless I have to. They are heavy and an additional trip expense; and, if I'm using a small frameless backpack, they fit awkwardly and cause bruising at body–canister contact points (unless somehow cushioned). My preferred canister is the Wild Ideas Bearikade, which has the best weight-to-volume ratio; there are two models, the Weekender ($225, 31 oz, 650 cu in) and the Expedition ($275, 37 oz, 900 cu in). Two lightweight, more economical options are the Bear Vault BV450 ($65, 33 oz, 440 cu in) and Bear Vault BV500 ($80, 41 oz, 700 cu in). Heavier, inexpensive models are available from Backpackers Cache, Bear Keg, and Bare Boxer.

If a hard-sided canister is not required in a bear-inhabited area, I keep my food in Opsaks, minimize my odds of a bear encounter, and hope for the best—a recipe that has worked thus far. But you might find greater peace of mind by using an Ursack S29 AllWhite ($65, 8 oz, 650 cu in), a soft-sided bear-resistant stuff sack made of Spectra fabric, which is the same material used in bulletproof vests. I do not recommend using Ursack's optional Aluminum Liner ($20, 11 oz)—it only helps prevent your food from being crushed; it does not improve the bear resistance of the Ursack.

sample

gear kits

 194
EASTERN FORESTS

 198
MOUNTAIN WEST

 202
DESERT SOUTHWEST PACKRAFTING

 206
NORTHERN WINTER

 210
PHILMONT SCOUT RANCH

In preparing for a multiseason, multi-thousand-mile trip, I spend days perfecting my gear lists. For a weeklong trip, I still spend at least an hour on my gear list. A chart helps to: 1) ensure that I am sufficiently prepared—and not over- or mis-prepared—for the conditions I expect to encounter; 2) compare all the options, and select the items that have the best combination of performance, weight, comfort, durability, reliability, value, and environmental impact; and 3) eliminate redundant functions within or between product categories.

The five gear lists in this section represent *what I would likely pack* for the trip described, but certainly other combinations of gear would work. I recommend that you use these gear lists as *guides*. Because we may have different skills and preferences, I do not necessarily recommend you follow them verbatim.

Taking bearings with GPS unit, Wyoming

eastern forests

When I am backpacking in three-season conditions in the eastern United States' extensive woodlands, my gear kit usually assumes frequent precipitation, high humidity, persistent mosquitoes and/or black flies, dirt-covered trails, and generous shade and wind protection (save for a few alpine summits in the Appalachians). The one factor that notably varies within this region—e.g., between the Smokies, White Mountains, and Porcupines—is temperature.

Trip objectives

I would like to hike the 270-mile Long Trail (LT), which runs the length of Vermont from Massachusetts to Canada through the Green Mountains, which are a subrange of the Appalachian Mountains. In fact, the LT's southernmost 100 miles are shared by the Appalachian Trail. I want to center my trip around the summer solstice, so I will start on June 15.

Environmental & route conditions

The LT is deceptively difficult. Its high point is just 4,395 feet, but it averages 500 vertical feet of gain or loss per mile for its entire length; it's also often rainy, muddy, rooty, and buggy.

Temperatures. In Rutland, Vermont, in one of the milder parts of the state, average June temperatures are lows around 52°F and highs around 78°F; extreme temperatures are lows around 32°F and highs around 95°F. At the summit of Mount Mansfield, which probably receives the state's worst weather, average June temperatures are lows around 46°F and highs around 62°F, and extreme temperatures are lows around 7°F and highs around 84°F. Source: NOAA

Precipitation. In Rutland, average rainfall in June is 3.8 inches. On Mount Mansfield, average rainfall is 6.9 inches. There are nearly 70 shelters along the trail where I can get out of the rain. Source: NOAA

Daylight. Daylight will be abundant—16.5 to 17 hours per day. Source: U.S. Naval Observatory

Ground cover & vegetation. The trail is mostly dirt, with a lot of exposed tree roots; some of the high peaks are covered in granite slabs. The trail's tread is obvious and marked with frequent white blazes. The trail is heavily forested except for a few windswept peaks and ridges. Source: photos on Trail Journals.com

Sun exposure. Tree cover, low elevation, and rainfall leave me unconcerned about sun exposure.

Water availability. There are few water sources at the range's crest. At lower elevations, water is not a concern. Source: *Long Trail Guide*

Wildlife & insects. Shelters can be plagued by pesky rodents like mice, raccoons, and squirrels; bears are not a concern. Black flies and mosquitoes will be a constant annoyance for the duration of the trip. Source: Green Mountain Club (GMC) website

Remoteness. The LT and its 175 miles of side trails are very popular among both weekend warriors and thru-hikers. Road crossings are frequent. Source: GMC website and topo maps

Natural hazards. The LT's high points have notoriously unpredictable weather. Source: *Long Trail Guide*

sample gear kits

CLOTHING & ITEMS WORN	DESCRIPTION	WEIGHT (oz)	COMMENTS
Base layer, top	S/S merino wool, 150 g/m², chest zip	5.0	Warmer than polyester when wet and less stinky
Base layer, bottoms	Running shorts, polyester, 3/4 split	2.5	Great ventilation, breathability, freedom of movement
Headwear	Visor, polyester with spandex band	2.0	Keeps rain, sweat, and hoods out of eyes
Footwear	Trail-running shoes, not waterproof	28.0	Lighter, more comfy, and dry faster than boots
Daytime socks	Liner-like, merino wool, crew cuff	2.0	Cooler and absorb less moisture than thick socks
Gaiters	Short, no instep strap, stretch nylon	2.0	Keep feet cleaner and avoid stops to empty shoes
Trekking poles	Fixed-length, carbon fiber, no straps	9.0	Takes pressure off legs, improves traction
Watch	Altimeter, barometer, and thermometer	2.0	To help dead reckon, gauge pace, and pinpoint location
Sunglasses	None	0.0	Little sunlight due to forest canopy and cloud cover
TOTAL		52.5	

OTHER CLOTHING	DESCRIPTION	WEIGHT (oz)	COMMENTS
Shell or alt base layer	L/S nylon travel shirt with permethrin	8.0	Wear as base layer when bugs are bad
Pants	85% nylon, 15% spandex	10.0	Wear over shorts in camp and when bugs are bad
Rain gear, top	WP/B, 3-layer, fully featured	7.0	Best rain gear for this trip, but don't expect to stay dry
Insulated top	300-weight fleece, hooded	12.0	OK warmth for temps; warmer when wet than puffy
Gloves, liners	300-weight fleece, not windproof	3.0	For cool mornings and nights, and cold rain
Gloves, shells	WP/B rain mitts	5.0	Otherwise will quickly lose dexterity when cold and wet
Headband	Merino wool and spandex blend	1.0	Keep ears warm without overheating my head
Sleeping shirt	L/S polyester, lightweight	4.0	Extra weight worth a good night's rest
Sleeping pants	Polyester, lightweight	6.0	High odds of pulling into camp soaked
Sleeping socks	"Hiking sock" thickness, merino wool	3.0	For overnight recovery, feet must be warm and dry
TOTAL		59.0	

SHELTER & SLEEPING	DESCRIPTION	WEIGHT (oz)	COMMENTS
A-frame tarp	Sil-nylon, 7' at head, 5' at foot	9.0	Spacious, excellent ventilation; wind breaks abundant
A-frame nest	WP floor, no-see-um mesh upper	9.0	Roomier and better ventilation than WR bivy
Guylines	30' of 3-mm cord	1.0	Sufficiently strong; inexpensive and slightly reflective
Stakes	8 aluminum Y stakes	4.0	Much better hold than titanium skewers in soft ground
Poles	None	0.0	Use trekking poles
Sleeping bag	Quilt, synthetic insulation, 45-degree	13.0	More versatile than mummy; more reliable than down
Sleeping pad	Closed cell foam roll, torso-length	4.5	Warmest for weight; soft campsite improves comfort
TOTAL		40.5	

COOKING & WATER	DESCRIPTION	WEIGHT (oz)	COMMENTS
Pot, mug, and bowl	900-mL Ti pot, short and wide, with lid	3.5	600-mL okay for soloist with smaller appetite
Stove	Homemade with 3-oz cat food can	0.5	Will not break or clog; ultra-cheap and ultra-simple
Windscreen	Homemade with aluminum foil	0.5	Critical role in stove's fuel efficiency
Fuel bottle	8-oz "disposable" plastic bottle	1.0	Need about 0.7 oz/meal; fuel widely available
Ignition	Matches, 20-count book	0.5	Can light stove without burning fingers
Pot grip	None	0.0	Use gloves or shirt, or let pot cool down
Utensil	Polycarbonate (plastic) spoon	0.5	Large shovel, cut in half to fit inside pot
Water storage	2 x 1-L soft-sided collapsible bottles	2.0	Unbeatable weight-to-volume ratio; Nalgene 6x heavier
Purification	Chlorine dioxide liquid drops	1.0	Very light, fast, and effective; decant into small bottles
TOTAL		9.5	

part 3

SMALL ESSENTIALS	DESCRIPTION	WEIGHT (oz)	COMMENTS
Toiletries	Toothbrush, Dr. B's, floss	2.0	Dr. B's multipurpose; prefer natural TP
Foot care	Salve or Hydropel, mole skin, bunion cushions, Leukotape, Krazy Glue	2.0	Preemptively treat foot problems before they develop. Dry them out during rest breaks, and for 8+ hours at night.
First aid	Roll gauze, antibiotic ointment, meds (ibuprofen, Tylenol, Benadryl, and antidiarrheal)	2.0	For field-treatable injuries—e.g., blisters, small cuts or burns, muscle aches. In event of non-field-treatable injury, I must self-evac or call for help.
Knife	3-tool: 1.5-in blade, scissors, file	1.0	Have never needed more
Lighting	80-lumen LED, handheld with brim clip	1.0	Given long days, will only use for camp chores
Fire starter	Lighter plus Vaseline-soaked cotton	2.0	Make fire to dry out, warm up, or in an emergency
Communication	None	0.0	Will be found quickly by other hikers if hurt
Repair	Urethane-based glue, needle, thread	1.0	Not expecting to use, but may
Head net	Mosquito netting	0.5	Much less stuffy than no-see-um netting
Bug repellent	High-concentration DEET	0.5	Perhaps more eco-friendly option: lemon eucalyptus
Maps, guide-books	Long Trail guidebook and databook	4.0	Cut apart and ship ahead sections not yet needed
Navigational aid	None	0.0	Trail very well marked; no way to get lost
Camera	Compact, wide-angle lens, RAW	7.0	Not necessary, but nice for post-trip slideshows
Journal and pen	Half sheets of resume paper	2.0	Lighter than bound journal
TOTAL		**25.0**	

PACKING	DESCRIPTION	WEIGHT (oz)	COMMENTS
Backpack	50-L, frameless, Dyneema nylon	24.0	Load-carrying capacity of framed pack unnecessary
Pack liner	Heavy-duty plastic bag	2.0	Ultralight, inexpensive, simple, and effective
Stuff sacks	Sil-nylon, not waterproof	2.0	For accessories, quilt, pot, and food
Plastic storage bags	2 quart-sized freezer bags	0.5	For current maps and day's food
Wallet	5-by-4-in waterproof plastic bag	1.0	ID, cash, credit card, health card
TOTAL		**29.5**	

WEIGHT TOTALS	LB	COMMENTS
(A) Gear worn or carried on body	3.3	A+B = combined weight of gear listed in charts above
(B) Gear carried in pack ("base weight")	10.2	
(C) Water weight at start	0.0	Water at Mi 1 and 5; start well hydrated and carry none
(D) Food weight at start	6.8	4.5 days @ 1.5 lbs/day to reach Jonesville, at Mi 80
(E) Fuel weight at start	0.2	4 dinners @ 0.75 oz/dinner
(F) B+C+D+E = Pack weight at start	17.2	
(G) A+F = Skin-out weight	20.4	

sample gear kits

197

mountain west

Most of my favorite backpacking destinations—notably the High Sierra, North Cascades, Wind River Range, and Colorado Rockies—are in the Mountain West. The prime season is short: The winter snowpack doesn't melt off until June or even July, and the earliest winter storms return in October. But it's glorious: Sunshine is abundant; humidity is minimal; and bugs are fleetingly fierce. Year-round, of course, the scenery is world-class.

Trip objectives

I would like to thru-hike the entire Sierra High Route (SHR), a rugged 195-mile off-trail alternative to the John Muir Trail that begins in Sequoia-Kings Canyon National Park and finishes just outside of Yosemite National Park. I will start September 1 and resupply once, at Red's Meadow at Mi 118.

Environmental & route conditions

The SHR stays mostly above 10,000 feet, where there is intense sunshine and scant protection from thunderstorms. Some of its 100 off-trail miles are across endless boulder fields.

Temperatures. At the bottom of Kings Canyon in September, average temperatures are 42° to 82°F. At Gem Lake, at 9,000 feet, average temperatures are 40° to 65°F, which translates to about 30° to 55°F at the route's highest passes at 12,000-plus feet.

Precipitation. Average precipitation in September in Kings Canyon is just

0.3 inch. At Gem Lake, average precipitation is 0.7 inch.

Daylight. Including civil twilight, I will have almost 14 hours of daylight when I start.

Ground cover & vegetation.
The ground cover is a mix of granite slabs, granite talus, and grassy tundra. The forested sections cross stands of whitebark and lodgepole pine. Topographical maps show a few permanent snowfields; otherwise, the route should be mostly dry by this time of year.

Sun exposure. My route is high, there is little shade, and it'll probably be sunny for most of the trip.

Water availability. The route passes dozens of alpine lakes and small streams, so water will be relatively abundant.

Wildlife & insects. I find a Wilderness Food Storage Requirement Map on *www.SierraWild.gov*. About half of the SHR travels through areas where a hard-sided bear canister is required.

Remoteness. When I called Yosemite National Park to get my backcountry permit, I asked if I should expect to see anyone else during my trip. The ranger told me that backcountry traffic fades quickly after Labor Day, and that it's possible I will not see anyone on the off-trail sections of my route.

Natural hazards. The guidebook written by Steve Roper mentions only one deep ford, across a slow-moving lake outlet. The National Park Service website says that lightning storms are common, but mostly earlier in the summer. It also says that I should purify all of my water. Avalanches are unlikely given the amount and stability of snowpack in September.

CLOTHING & ITEMS WORN	DESCRIPTION	WEIGHT (oz)	COMMENTS
Base layer, top	L/S merino wool, 150 g/m², chest zip	10.0	Nicer feel and less stinky than polyester
Base layer, bottoms	Short tights, polyester/spandex	4.0	Warmer than running shorts; function as undies
Headwear	Visor, polyester with spandex band	2.0	Keeps rain, sweat, and hoods out of eyes
Footwear	Trail-running shoes, not waterproof	28.0	Sensitivity and sticky rubber helpful on talus fields
Socks, pair 1	Liner-like, merino wool, crew cuff	2.0	Cooler and absorb less water than thick socks
Gaiters	Short, no instep strap, stretch nylon	2.0	Keep feet cleaner and avoid stops to empty shoes
Trekking poles	Fixed-length, carbon fiber, no straps	10.0	Lets arms help power me up the huge climbs
Watch	Altimeter, barometer, and thermometer	2.0	To rule out false summits and forecast weather
Sunglasses	Polarized, photochromic lenses	2.0	Abundant sunshine; lots of glare off rocks, water
TOTAL		62.0	

OTHER CLOTHING	DESCRIPTION	WEIGHT (oz)	COMMENTS
Shell top 1	Water-resistant wind shirt, hooded	4.0	For additional warmth, windy ridges, and passes
Shell top 2	WP/B, 2-layer, minimalist	6.0	Rain should be infrequent and short-lived
Shell pants	Nylon trekking pants	10.0	For cool a.m. and p.m., cold daytime temps up high
Insulated jacket	800-fill down, hooded	12.0	Warmer for weight than synthetic or fleece
Gloves	Liners, merino wool, silicone grips	2.5	For cool a.m. and p.m., cold daytime temps up high
Headband	Merino wool and spandex blend	1.0	Less restricting and noisy than hoods on jackets
Socks, pair 2	Liner-like, merino wool, crew cuff	2.0	Put on halfway through day, then wash pair 1
TOTAL		37.5	

SHELTER & SLEEPING	DESCRIPTION	WEIGHT (oz)	COMMENTS
A-frame tarp	Sil-nylon, 7' at head, 5' at foot	9.0	Storms rare; can complement with natural protection
Bivy sack	Water-resistant top, WP floor	8.0	Frequently will use alone at night to "cowboy camp"
Guylines	30' of 3-mm cord	1.0	Tie off w/trucker's hitch-like system; no fixed knots
Stakes	8 aluminum Y stakes	4.0	Much better hold than Ti skewers in soft ground
Poles	None	0.0	Use trekking poles
Sleeping bag	Quilt, 800-fill down, 5" loft	24.0	More versatile than mummy; warmer than synthetic
Sleeping pad	Closed cell foam roll, torso-length	4.5	Warmest for weight; soft campsite improves comfort
TOTAL		50.5	

COOKING & WATER	DESCRIPTION	WEIGHT (oz)	COMMENTS
Pot, mug, and bowl	900-mL Ti pot, short and wide, with lid	3.5	600-mL okay for soloist with smaller appetite
Stove	Homemade with 3-oz cat food can	0.5	Has worked fine for me at elevations up to 13,000 ft
Windscreen	Homemade with aluminum foil	0.5	Critical role in stove's fuel efficiency
Fuel bottle	8-oz "disposable" plastic bottle	1.0	Need about 0.7 oz/meal; fuel widely available
Ignition	Matches, 20-count book	0.5	Can light stove without burning fingers
Pot grip	None	0.0	Use gloves or shirt, or let pot cool down
Utensil	Polycarbonate (plastic) spoon	0.5	Large shovel, cut in half to fit inside pot
Water storage	2 x 1-L soft-sided collapsible bottles	2.0	Unbeatable weight-to-volume ratio; Nalgene 6x heavier
Purification	Chlorine dioxide liquid drops	1.0	Very light, fast, and effective; decant into small bottles
TOTAL		9.5	

SMALL ESSENTIALS	DESCRIPTION	WEIGHT (oz)	COMMENTS
Toiletries	Toothbrush, Dr. B's, floss, sunscreen	2.0	Cut toothbrush in half to make more packable
Foot care	Salve or Hydropel, mole skin, bunion cushions, Leukotape, Krazy Glue	2.0	Preemptively treat foot problems before they develop. Dry them out during rest breaks, and for 8+ hours at night.
First aid	Roll gauze, antibiotic ointment, meds ibuprofen, Tylenol, Benadryl, and antidiarrheal)	2.0	For field-treatable injuries—e.g., blisters, small cuts or burns, muscle aches. In event of non-field-treatable injury, I must self-evac or call for help.
Knife	3-tool: 1.5-in blade, scissors, file	1.0	Have never needed more
Lighting	80-lumen LED, handheld with brim clip	1.0	Very difficult to hike off trail at night; will try to avoid
Fire starter	Lighter plus Vaseline-soaked cotton	2.0	Make fire to dry out, warm up, or in an emergency
Communication	SPOT Satellite GPS Messenger	5.0	No cell reception and unlikely to be found by other hiker
Repair	Urethane-based glue, needle, thread	1.0	Not expecting to use, but may
Bug repellent	None	0.0	Bugs gone by this time of year
Maps, guide-books	USGS topo maps at 1:24k and 1:100k	5.0	Created with National Geographic TOPO! software
Compass	Baseplate, adjustable declination	1.0	Terrain features super obvious; doubtful will need
Camera	Compact, wide-angle lens, RAW	7.0	Not necessary, but nice for post-trip slideshows
Journal and pen	Half sheets of resume paper	2.0	Lighter than bound journal
TOTAL		31.0	

PACKING	DESCRIPTION	WEIGHT (oz)	COMMENTS
Backpack	70-L, frame: 2 aluminum stays	32.0	Need extra load-carrying for heavy food load
Pack liner	Heavy-duty plastic bag	2.0	Ultralight, inexpensive, simple, and effective
Stuff sacks	Sil-nylon, not waterproof	2.0	For accessories, quilt, pot, and food
Plastic storage bags	2 quart-sized freezer bags	0.5	For current maps and day's food
Wallet	5-by-4-in waterproof plastic bag	1.0	ID, cash, credit card, health card
Bear canister	Carbon fiber, 650 cu in	31.0	Required by Park Service; manufacturer does rentals
TOTAL		68.5	

WEIGHT TOTALS	LB	COMMENTS
(A) Gear worn or carried on body	3.9	A+B = combined weight of gear listed in charts above
(B) Gear carried in pack ("base weight")	12.3	Includes 2-lb bear-resistant food canister
(C) Water weight at start	0.0	First source; Copper Creek at Mi 4. Start hydrated.
(D) Food weight at start	12.0	8 days @ 1.5 lbs/day to reach Red's Meadow, at Mi 118
(E) Fuel weight at start	0.4	8 dinners @ 0.75 oz/dinner
(F) B+C+D+E = Pack weight at start	24.7	
(G) A+F = Skin-out weight	28.6	

desert southwest packrafting

If I wish to go hiking between the months of November and May, when my beloved mountain West is still buried in snow, I head to the Southwest's arid valleys, basins, and steppes. I especially enjoy the Colorado Plateau, which is scattered with textbook-quality geological features and amazing canyons, notably the Grand Canyon. The Southwest is generally a friendly backcountry locale—it's warm, bug-free, and sunny—but it can also be dangerously hot, bone dry, and shadeless.

Trip objectives

After a long winter on Colorado's Front Range, my friends and I are tired of skiing. We agree to spend the three-day Memorial Day weekend backpacking in Canyonlands National Park near Moab, Utah. We identify an ambitious loop through the Needles and Maze districts that includes a short Class I packraft float on the Colorado River.

Environmental & route conditions

Our route has an exciting mix of trail, off-trail, and river components.

Temperatures. Historical averages range from 50° to 85°F, with extremes of 30° and 100°F. When we check the five-day forecast before leaving Denver, we see that temperatures will be above average. It will be difficult for us

part 3

to acclimate to this heat because it's been a cold and wet spring in Colorado. Source: NOAA

Precipitation. The five-day forecast says there is only a 10 percent chance of precipitation.

Daylight. Civil twilight starts at around 5:30 a.m. and ends at around 9:00 p.m., giving us 15.5 hours of daylight total.

Ground cover. We scan Landsat images using Google Maps. Our route is mostly over rock. The topographical maps indicate that the creek bottoms are sandy.

Vegetation. Online photos and the Landsat images reveal scant vegetation.

Sun exposure. Significant. Clouds will be nonexistent, and the sun will

be high in the sky; our route is 4,000 to 5,000 feet above sea level. Sun exposure will be significant.

Water availability. Very limited. There are only two reliable water sources on our route—the Colorado River and Big Water Spring. Source: National Park Service

Wildlife & insects. It is wise to keep an eye out for snakes and scorpions, especially in the mornings and evenings when they are most active.

Remoteness. At our route's turnaround point, we are about 25 miles from the entrance station.

Natural hazards. The Colorado River is swollen with spring runoff and is unsafe to swim at this time of year. Instead, we opt to bring packrafts.

CLOTHING & ITEMS WORN	DESCRIPTION	WEIGHT (oz)	COMMENTS
Base layer, top	L/S merino wool, 150 g/m², chest zip	10.0	Wool prolongs evaporative cooling after soaking.
Base layer, undees	Boxer briefs, polyester/spandex	2.0	Quick dry and cool. Fit nicely under pants.
Base layer, pants	85% nylon, 15% spandex	10.0	Stuffy, but need sun protection
Headwear	Ball cap with drape, polyester	3.0	Sun protection for top of ears and neck
Footwear	Trail-running shoes, not waterproof	28.0	Cooler than boots in hot temps; dry fast
Socks, pair 1	Liner-like, merino wool, crew cuff	2.0	Cooler than thick socks and absorb less moisture
Gaiters	Short, no instep strap, stretch nylon	2.0	Keep feet cleaner and avoid stops to empty shoes
Trekking poles	3-piece collapsible, CF, no straps	14.0	Compactibility helpful when packrafting
Watch	Altimeter, barometer, and thermometer	2.0	To rule out false summits and forecast weather
Sunglasses	Polarized, photochromic lenses	2.0	Abundant sunshine; lots of glare off rocks
TOTAL		75.0	

OTHER CLOTHING	DESCRIPTION	WEIGHT (oz)	COMMENTS
Shell top 1	Water-resistant wind shirt, hooded	4.0	Offers a few minutes of protection in drizzle
Rain gear	None	0.0	Rain very unlikely, and any storm will be short-lived
Insulated jacket	800-fill down, hooded	12.0	Cools off quickly; no humidity or clouds to trap heat
Socks, pair 2	Liner-like, merino wool, crew cuff	2.0	Put on halfway through day, then wash pair 1
TOTAL		18.0	

SHELTER & SLEEPING	DESCRIPTION	WEIGHT (oz)	COMMENTS
Shelter	None; will use packraft if have to	0.0	Taking a chance; nighttime rain very unlikely
Bivy sack	Water-resistant top, WP floor	8.0	To "cowboy camp" without losing groundsheet, wind pro
Sleeping bag	Quilt, 800-fill down, 3" loft	24.0	More versatile than mummy; warmer than synthetic
Sleeping pad	Closed-cell foam roll, torso-length	4.5	Warmest for weight; soft campsite improves comfort
TOTAL		36.5	

COOKING & WATER	DESCRIPTION	WEIGHT (oz)	COMMENTS
Pot, mug, and bowl	900-mL Ti pot, short and wide, with lid	3.5	600-mL okay for soloist with smaller appetite
Stove	Homemade with 3-oz cat food can	0.5	Even in hot temps, still like hot meal for dinner
Windscreen	Homemade with aluminum foil	0.5	Critical role in stove's fuel efficiency
Fuel bottle	8-oz disposable plastic bottle	1.0	Need about 0.7 oz/meal; fuel widely available
Ignition	Matches, 20-count book	0.5	Can light stove without burning fingers
Pot grip	None	0.0	Use gloves or shirt, or let pot cool down
Utensil	Polycarbonate (plastic) spoon	0.5	Large shovel, cut in half to fit inside pot
Water storage	3 x 2-L soft-sided collapsible bottles	4.0	12 mi-long dry stretches; may have to dry camp
Purification	Chlorine dioxide liquid drops	1.0	Filters clog quickly due to Colorado River's silt
TOTAL		11.5	

PACKRAFT	DESCRIPTION	WEIGHT (oz)	COMMENTS
Packraft	1-tube inflatable boat	64.0	Changes route options; changes up pace
Spray deck	None; not necessary for this use	0.0	Usually use; improves warmth, splash resistance
Paddle	4-piece, carbon fiber, fixed-length	26.0	Could use lighter paddle, but it's what I have
PFD	Double-wall vest and 2-L Platy bottles	8.0	Just-in-case PFD; not Coast Guard-approved
Inflation bag	Large stuff sack with male nozzle	3.0	Not taking = "stupid light"; saves lots of time
Lashing system	2 x 60-in webbing straps with buckles	2.0	Very secure, easy to adjust even with cold hands
TOTAL		103.0	

SMALL ESSENTIALS	DESCRIPTION	WEIGHT (oz)	COMMENTS
Toiletries	Toothbrush, Dr. B's, floss, sunscreen	2.0	Not much natural TP in this landscape
Foot care	Salve or Hydropel, mole skin, bunion cushions, Leukotape, Krazy Glue	2.0	Preemptively treat foot problems before they develop. Dry them out during rest breaks, and for 8+ hours at night.
First aid	Roll gauze, antibiotic ointment, meds (ibuprofen, Tylenol, Benadryl, and antidiarrheal)	2.0	For field-treatable injuries—e.g., blisters, small cuts or burns, muscle aches. In event of non-field-treatable injury, I must self-evac or call for help.
Knife	3-tool: 1.5-in blade, scissors, file	1.0	Have never needed more
Lighting	80-lumen LED, handheld with brim clip	1.0	Lots of daylight; not expecting to night-hike
Fire starter	None	0.0	Not planning to make fire on this trip
Communication	SPOT Satellite GPS Messenger	5.0	Would take a while to get help, even with 3 people
Repair	Urethane-based glue, needle, thread	1.0	Unlikely that raft will puncture, but need a fix
Bug repellent	None	0.0	No bugs at this time of year
Maps, guide-books	USGS topo maps at 1:24k and 1:100k	5.0	Created with National Geographic TOPO! software
Compass	Baseplate, adjustable declination	1.0	Terrain features super obvious; doubtful will need
Camera	Compact, wide-angle lens, RAW	7.0	Not necessary, but nice for post-trip slideshows
Journal and pen	Half sheets of resume paper	2.0	Lighter than bound journal
TOTAL		29.0	

PACKING	DESCRIPTION	WEIGHT (oz)	COMMENTS
Backpack	70-L, frame: 2 aluminum stays	32.0	Need extra load-carrying because of heavy raft
Pack liner	Heavy-duty plastic bag	2.0	Ultralight, inexpensive, simple, and effective
Stuff sacks	Sil-nylon, not waterproof	2.0	For accessories, quilt, pot, and food
Plastic storage bags	2 quart-sized freezer bags	0.5	For current maps and day's food
Wallet	5-by-4-in waterproof plastic bag	1.0	ID, cash, credit card, health card
TOTAL		37.5	

WEIGHT TOTALS	LB	COMMENTS
(A) Gear worn or carried on body	4.7	A+B = combined weight of gear listed in charts above
(B) Gear carried in pack ("base weight")	12.9	Only 6.5 lbs without 6.4-lb packraft system
(C) Water weight at start	3.0	First source: Colorado River at Mi 12. Start hydrated.
(D) Food weight at start	4.5	3 days @ 1.5 lbs/day
(E) Fuel weight at start	0.1	2 dinners @ 0.75 oz/dinner
(F) B+C+D+E = Pack weight at start	20.5	
(G) A+F = Skin-out weight	25.2	

sample gear kits

northern winter

Winter's long nights, sub-freezing temperatures, stormy weather, and bottomless snow present a challenging set of conditions that many backpackers intentionally avoid. Those willing to venture into the frozen backcountry are rewarded with uninterrupted solitude even in high-use backpacking areas, the learning of winter-specific skills (e.g., traveling in avalanche terrain), and access to winter-only routes (e.g., across nasty talus and frozen lakes).

Trip objective

My friends think I'm nutty: Starting in early February, I want to do the entire 277-mile Superior Hiking Trail (SHT), which parallels the North Shore of Lake Superior from Duluth, Minnesota, to the Canadian border. I expect to average about 15 miles per day, though I will need to factor in a few "weather days" if/when the conditions are unsafe for travel. If I had the time, this trip could be extended by tacking on the Border Route and Kekekabic Trails.

Environmental & route conditions

This trip is intentionally scheduled in the teeth of winter.

Temperatures. Historical weather data near the SHT are available from the Midwestern Regional Climate Center. In Two Harbors, average temperatures in February are 10° to 25°F, with extremes of -36°F and 59°F.

Precipitation. February is the driest month of the year in northern

part (3)

Minnesota. An average of only 0.8 inch of precipitation falls in Two Harbors, and 0.9 inch at Gunflint Lake, farther north and inland.

Daylight. I will have a mere 10.5 to 11 hours of daylight.

Ground cover & vegetation. Based on historical GIS maps from the National Operational Hydrologic Remote Sensing Center, the North Shore seems to have about 20 to 40 inches of snow by early February. The SHT is entirely forested, with a mix of deciduous and evergreen trees.

Sun exposure. Even if it's a sunny day, the weak sun will likely be at my back, because my primary direction of travel is northeast.

Water availability. When I called the Superior Hiking Trail Association, I was told that large rivers like the Gooseberry and Temperance will be running, but getting water from them may be a challenge because they will be covered in snow and ice. Lakes, ponds, and small creeks will be frozen solid.

Wildlife & insects. No concerns at this time of year.

Natural hazards. The frigid temperatures will be my biggest challenge.

CLOTHING & ITEMS WORN	DESCRIPTION	WEIGHT (oz)	COMMENTS
Base layer, top	L/S, merino wool mid-weight, hood	10.0	Hood not lose-able; thumb loop cuffs insulate wrists
Base layer, undies	Compression shorts, lightweight	4.0	Form-fitting so don't get caught on pants
Base layer, pants	Tights, poly/spandex, mid-weight	7.0	Enough warmth for temps >10°F when moving
Liner gloves	Merino wool with silicone grip pads	3.0	Nice balance of dexterity and warmth; durable
Headwear 1	Balaclava, polyester, lightweight	2.0	Insulates jaw and cheeks
Headwear 2	Visor, polyester	2.0	Keeps hoods and snow out of eyes
Footwear	Running shoes, not waterproof	28.0	Generally much more comfortable than boots
Overboot	3-mm neoprene, integrated gaiter	12.0	Shoe and overboot warmer than boot of same weight
Snowshoes	Al frame and nylon decking, 9-by-30-in	45.0	Probably faster than skis on SHT's rolling terrain
Socks, liner	Merino wool, lightweight	2.0	Lightweight wicking layer to buffer trapped moisture
Socks, VBL	Nonbreathable fabric	1.0	Prevents foot sweat from wetting shoe and freezing
Socks, insulated	Merino wool, mid-weight	3.0	Warmest layer; protects VBL from shoe abrasion
Trekking poles	Fixed-length, carbon fiber, baskets	11.0	5 cm longer than 3-season poles
Watch	Altimeter, barometer, and thermometer	2.0	To rule out false summits and forecast weather
Sunglasses	None	0.0	Weak sunlight, gloomy cloud cover, and back facing sun
TOTAL		**132.0**	

OTHER CLOTHING	DESCRIPTION	WEIGHT (oz)	COMMENTS
VBL, top	Sil-nylon, hooded, many vents	6.0	Prevents perspiration from soaking insulation and bag
VBL, pants	Homemade, sil-nylon, 3/4 leg zips	5.0	Mostly wear only at night, plus on coldest days
VBL, gloves	Mitts, synthetic insulation	9.0	Clip to shoulder strap with carabiner when not using
Shells	None	0.0	Redundant with VBL layers
Insulated jacket	800-fill down, 7-oz fill, hooded	24.0	Warmer and more packable than synthetic insulation
Insulated pants	800-fill down, 2-oz fill, 3/4 leg zips	9.0	Moisture not a concern; dry air, have VBLs
Insulated hat	Wool knit earflap hat	4.0	More comfy and better fit than "puffy" hat
TOTAL		57.0	

SHELTER & SLEEPING	DESCRIPTION	WEIGHT (oz)	COMMENTS
Shelter	Mid tarp, fully enclosed, sil-nylon	16.0	Amazingly storm-resistant for weight, pitched with poles
Stakes	None; will use deadman anchors	0.0	No shortage of sticks; don't have to dig up in a.m.
Guylines	24 ft of 3-mm cord	1.0	4-ft lengths for 6 anchor points
Guyline tensioners	6 x aluminum figure 8	1.5	Allows tightening of guylines without taking off mitts
Sleeping bag	0-degree, 800-fill down, wide cut	48.0	Wear all clothes to bed to extend comfort range
Sleeping pad	Closed-cell foam, full length, 0.75-in	19.0	Warmer and more reliable than air pad
Shovel	Poleless design, pliable plastic	6.0	To dig out floor and bed, and to gather snow for melting
TOTAL		91.5	

COOKING & WATER	DESCRIPTION	WEIGHT (oz)	COMMENTS
Pot, mug, and bowl	2-L titanium	9.0	More efficient than 1-L when melting snow for water
Stove	Remote canister with preheat tube	7.0	More user-friendly than liquid fuel; doesn't clog
Fuel bottle (empty)	80/20 isobutane/propane blend	4.0	Canister must be upside down for liquid feed
Windscreen	Heavy-duty aluminum	2.0	Worth weight; extensive stove use, very cold temps
Ignition	Matches, 20-count	0.5	Easier operation with gloves than a lighter
Pot grip	Aluminum, comes with stove	0.5	To lift and pour pot full of water
Utensil	Polycarbonate spoon, full-length	0.5	Full-length to help melt snow, reach pot bottom
Water storage	2 x 48-oz wide-mouth soft-sided	5.0	Spout more freeze-resistant; easier to pour into
Purification	Chlorine dioxide, tablets	1.0	Some open water likely; liquid drops freeze at 15°F
TOTAL		29.5	

part 3

SMALL ESSENTIALS	DESCRIPTION	WEIGHT (oz)	COMMENTS
Toiletries	Toothbrush, Dr. B's, floss, sunscreen	2.0	Re sunscreen, use balm; extra skin protection
Foot care	Salve or Hydropel, mole skin, bunion cushions, Leukotape, Krazy Glue	2.0	Preemptively treat foot problems before they develop. Dry them out during rest breaks, and for 8+ hours at night.
First aid	Roll gauze, antibiotic ointment, meds (ibuprofen, Tylenol, Benadryl, and antidiarrheal)	2.0	For field-treatable injuries—e.g., blisters, small cuts or burns, muscle aches. In event of non-field-treatable injury, I must self-evac or call for help.
Knife	3-tool: 1.5-in blade, scissors, file	1.0	Have never needed more
Lighting, spot	80-lumen 1-LED handheld, brim clip	1.0	For camp chores and seeing far down trail
Lighting, flood	50-lumen 4-LED, laced on waist belt	3.0	Worn at waist level to improve depth perception
Fire starter	Lighter plus Vaseline-soaked cotton	2.0	Make open fire to warm up and make nights less long
Communication	SPOT Satellite GPS Messenger	5.0	Not remote area, but could quickly get in trouble
Repair	Urethane-based glue, needle, thread	1.0	"Just-in-case" clothing or equipment tears or breaks
Maps, guidebooks	SHT guidebook and maps	4.0	Mail ahead whatever sections are not needed
Compass	None	0.0	Trail is well marked and signed
Camera	Compact, wide-angle lens, RAW	7.0	Need lithium batteries in cold temps
Journal and pencil	Half sheets of resume paper	2.0	"NASA created space pen. Russians used pencils."
TOTAL		32.0	

PACKING	DESCRIPTION	WEIGHT (oz)	COMMENTS
Backpack	70-L, frameless, Dyneema fabric	32.0	Large but light load; use Snowclaw as "virtual frame"
Pack liner	Heavy-duty plastic bag	2.0	In the event of wet snowstorm
Stuff sacks	Sil-nylon, not waterproof	2.0	For accessories, quilt, pot, and food
Plastic storage bags	2 quart-sized freezer bags	0.5	For current maps and day's food
Wallet	5-by-4-in waterproof plastic bag	1.0	ID, cash, credit card, health card
TOTAL		37.5	

WEIGHT TOTALS	LB	COMMENTS
(A) Gear worn or carried on body	8.3	A+B = combined weight of gear listed in charts above
(B) Gear carried in pack ("base weight")	13.5	
(C) Water weight at start	6.0	No running sources on Day 1. Start well hydrated.
(D) Food weight at start	4.5	3 days @ 1.5 lbs/day to reach first resupply
(E) Fuel weight at start	0.6	3 days @ 3 oz/day for melting snow and making dinner
(F) B+C+D+E = Pack weight at start	24.5	
(G) A+F = Skin-out weight	32.8	

sample gear kits

philmont scout ranch

Philmont, located within the Sangre de Cristo Mountains in northern New Mexico, is one of three national High Adventure Bases run by the Boy Scouts of America. Since its founding in 1938, almost a million Scouts and leaders have backpacked and camped there. Most Scouts consider Philmont a highlight of their Scouting experience.

Note: This Philmont-specific gear list fulfills gear requirements specified by the Boy Scouts. If this trip were just beyond Philmont's borders, I would probably modify the gear list some.

Trip objective

My fictitious nephew's troop has asked me to join them at Philmont next July as an adviser for their 12-day trek, during which we will hike 106 miles in 10 days. After reaching camp each day, the Scouts hope to still have time and energy left over for some evening programs like archaeology and horseback riding.

Environmental & route conditions

The Sangre de Christo Mountains are a subrange within the Rocky Mountains near Cimarron, New Mexico. Elevations range from 6,500 feet to 12,000 feet. Resupply points during our ten-day trip are never more than four days apart.

Temperatures. There is a NOAA weather station on the Philmont Ranch at 7,600 feet. Average temperatures for July are highs around 82°F and lows around 49°F. Assuming a 3°F drop for every 1,000 feet, average temperatures atop Mount Baldy (elev. 12,441 feet) should be a high of about 65°F and a low at around 35°F.

Precipitation. About three inches of precipitation fall in July at Philmont, mostly in the form of afternoon thunderstorms that frequently include lightning, hail, and, occasionally, snow (which melts very quickly).

Daylight. There is ample daylight—about 15.5 hours.

Ground cover & vegetation. Philmont's trail system and campsites are heavily used. The earth is hard-packed and denuded of soft materials like pine needles and leaves. The terrain includes grassland, Ponderosa pines, lodgepole pines, Engelmann spruce, and subalpine fir, depending on the elevation and slope aspect.

Sun exposure. Significant, given the high elevation, abundant sunshine, and open forest canopy.

Water availability. Water is readily available at designated campsites, as well as from many natural sources. Staffed camps provide treated water.

Wildlife & insects. There is a healthy black bear population on the ranch, but Philmont's policies have been very successful in avoiding incidents. Mosquitoes are mostly gone by July, and they are not active during the cold nights. Because of extreme concentrated use, many campsites have problems with "minibears"—chipmunks, ground squirrels, and deer mice.

Natural hazards. The afternoon monsoons can include violent thunderstorms. Beware of vertical cloud development when summiting the high peaks.

Camping and orienteering merit badges are two of more than 100 that Boy Scouts can earn.

sample gear kits

CLOTHING & ITEMS WORN	PERSONAL DESCRIPTION	WEIGHT (oz)	COMMENTS
Base layer, top	L/S merino wool, 150 g/m², chest zip	10.0	Full sun protection; alt is polyester (cheap but stinky)
Base layer, bottoms	Polyester/spandex boxer briefs	2.0	Great breathability and stretch fit well under pants
Pants	Nylon convertible trekking pants	10.0	Shorts: daytime hiking; pants: cool temps and bugs
Headwear	Ball cap with drape, polyester	3.0	Sun protection for top of ears and neck
Footwear	Trail-running shoes, not waterproof	28.0	Lighter, more comfy, cooler, and faster-drying than boots
Socks, pair 1	Liner-like, merino wool, crew cuff	2.0	Cooler and absorb less water than thick socks
Gaiters	Short, no instep strap, stretch nylon	2.0	Keep feet cleaner and avoid stops to empty shoes
Trekking poles	Fixed-length, carbon fiber, no straps	10.0	Take weight off legs; cheap alt is aluminum ski poles
Watch	Altimeter, barometer, and thermometer	2.0	To help dead reckon, gauge pace, and pinpoint location
Sunglasses	Polarized, photochromic lenses	2.0	Abundant sunshine; in and out of shade in forests
TOTAL		**71.0**	

OTHER CLOTHING	PERSONAL DESCRIPTION	WEIGHT (oz)	COMMENTS
Shell top	WP/B, 2-layer, minimalist	6.0	Rain should be infrequent and short-lived
Insulated jacket	800-fill-down insulation, hooded	12.0	Alternatives: 300-weight fleece or synthetic insulation
Insulated hat	None; jacket has a hood	0.0	Take for cool a.m. and p.m. temps if jacket lacks a hood
Gloves	Fleece, not windproof	3.0	Simple and warm; not expecting to use often
Socks, pair 2	Liner-like, merino wool, crew cuff	2.0	Swap midday with pair 1; hand-wash at staff camps
TOTAL		**23.0**	

SLEEPING	PERSONAL DESCRIPTION	WEIGHT (oz)	COMMENTS
Sleeping bag	Mummy, 800-fill down, 40-degree	24.0	Alt: synthetic fill (cheaper but less compressible)
Sleeping pad	Inflatable air pad, 2.5 in thick	14.0	Campsites very hard; need plush pad to sleep well
Sleeping pad, alt	Closed-cell foam	0.0	Much cheaper; okay comfort for Scouts
Sleeping clothes	Polyester shirt and pants	10.0	Required by Philmont; not needed in Southwest, in my opinion
TOTAL		**48.0**	

part 3

SHELTER	GROUP (for 4 crew members) DESCRIPTION	WEIGHT (oz)	COMMENTS
Shelter	Pyramid-shaped tarp, floorless	48.0	Excellent storm resistance and space for weight
Center pole	Sturdy aluminum, adjustable	12.0	Trekking poles not strong enough for shelter this size
Ground sheet	2 x polyolefin, 72 in by 96 in	3.0	Plenty durable for length of trip
Guylines	None	0.0	Shelter has adjustable stake loops
Stakes	8 aluminum Y stakes	4.0	Better hold and strength than Ti skewers
Spare stakes	4 aluminum Y stakes	2.0	Impatient young men can break them in hard ground
TOTAL		69.0	
PER PERSON WEIGHT		17.3	

COOKING & WATER	PERSONAL DESCRIPTION	WEIGHT (oz)	COMMENTS
Water storage	2 x 2-L soft-sided collapsible bottles	3.0	Carry <1L during day; have extra volume for dry camps
Purification	Chlorine dioxide tablets	1.0	Very light, fast, and effective
Eating bowl	24-oz Glad or Tupperware bowl	1.0	Ultralight and inexpensive
Utensil, spoon	Polycarbonate or Lexan	0.5	Large shovel, cut in half to fit inside bowl
TOTAL		4.0	

COOKING & WATER	GROUP (for 4 crew members) DESCRIPTION	WEIGHT (oz)	COMMENTS
Pots	2 x 2-L, aluminum	16.0	Fast and efficient; get Scouts quickly to p.m. programs
Stove	2 remote canisters	14.0	More stable than uprights; cleaner than liquid fuel
Windscreen	Heavy-duty aluminum	2.0	Worth weight; extensive stove use
Fuel bottle	80/20 isobutane/propane blend	4.0	Canisters can be purchased at trading post
Ignition	Bic lighter	0.5	Has long-lasting flame and infinite sparks
Pot grip	Aluminum, comes with stove	0.5	To lift and pour pot full of water
Serving spoon	2 plastic, large ladle	5.0	Less messy than pouring water into bowls
Other cooking gear	Soap, sponges, strainer, etc.	5.0	Issued by Philmont. Lighter alternatives available.
Dining fly	8-by-10-ft sil-nylon	10.0	If need to cook in rain; pitch with trekking poles
Shelter guylines	30 ft of 3-mm cord	2.0	Pitch as lean-to or A-frame
TOTAL		59.0	
PER PERSON WEIGHT		5.9	

SMALL ESSENTIALS	PERSONAL DESCRIPTION	WEIGHT (oz)	COMMENTS
Toiletries	Toothbrush, Dr. B's, floss, sunscreen	3.0	Repack in smaller bottles, or share among group
Lighting	LED, handheld with brim clip	1.0	For camp chores and navigating camp at night
Bug repellent	None	0.0	Bugs gone by now; if earlier, bring some DEET
Camera	Compact, wide-angle lens, RAW	7.0	Not necessary, but nice for post-trip slideshows
Journal and pen	Half sheets of resume paper	2.0	Lighter than bound journal
TOTAL		13.0	

sample gear kits

SMALL ESSENTIALS	GROUP (for 10 crew members) DESCRIPTION	WEIGHT (oz)	COMMENTS
First aid	Roll gauze, antibiotic ointment, meds, CPR mask, blunt-tip scissors	8.0	
Foot care	Salve or Hydropel, mole skin, bunion cushions, Leukotape, Krazy Glue	8.0	
Knife	Multitool with pliers	4.0	With large group, likely need increases
Fire starter	Lighter plus Vaseline-soaked cotton	2.0	Make fire to dry out, warm up, or an emergency
Communication	SPOT Satellite GPS Messenger	0.0	Lets parents follow along, but unnecessary
Repair	Glue, needle, thread, duct tape	1.0	Not expecting to use, but may
Map	Philmont map, 1:24,000 scale	3.0	Shared among group
Compass	Baseplate, adjustable declination	1.0	Unnecessary, but Scouts should know how to use
Bear ropes	6-mm cord	8.0	Lighter cord available but easiest to use Philmont's
Trowel	Philmont-issued	0.0	Unnecessary; latrines throughout backcountry
Trowel, backup	Y stake, aluminum	0.5	Lighter than Philmont shovel or "garden" trowel
Pack liner, spare	20-gal trash compactor bag	2.0	Likely that at least one Scout will destroy in 10 days
TOTAL		37.5	
PER PERSON WEIGHT		3.8	

PACKING	PERSONAL DESCRIPTION	WEIGHT (oz)	COMMENTS
Backpack	50-L, frameless, Dyneema ripstop	24.0	Pack so light that rigid frame is unnecessary
Pack liner	20-gal trash compactor bag	2.0	Keeps all contents dry; no need for additional protection
Stuff sacks	Sil-nylon, not waterproof	2.0	For accessories, quilt, pot, and food
Plastic storage bags	2 quart-sized freezer bags	0.5	For current maps and day's food
Wallet	5-by-4-in waterproof plastic bag	1.0	ID, cash, credit card, health card
TOTAL		29.5	

WEIGHT TOTALS	LB	COMMENTS
(A) Gear worn or carried on body	4.4	
(B) Personal gear carried in pack	7.3	
(C) Share of group weight carried in pack	1.7	
(D) B+C = Total gear carried in pack ("base weight")	9.0	A+D = combined weight of gear listed in charts above
(E) Water weight at start	2.0	First water source 4 mi away. Start hydrated.
(F) Food weight at start	6.0	4 days @ 1.5 lbs/day
(G) Fuel weight at start	4.0	4 days @ 1 oz/day per person
(H) D+E+F+G = Pack weight at start	21.0	
(I) A+H = Skin-out weight	25.5	

gearing up on a budget

Retail prices for backpacking equipment and supplies can be outrageous. For that much money, it seems like the gear should do the walking for you. The net total can be especially prohibitive for incomeless thru-hikers, Boy Scouts, and a-few-times-a-year backpackers. To help reduce costs:

Do not purchase unnecessary stuff. I try to avoid walking into a grocery store if I'm hungry and/or I don't have a list because I end up buying too much. Similarly, before you visit an outdoor retail store or shop online, determine what you truly need by consulting more experienced backpackers and reviewing relevant gear lists like those in Part 3.

Use what you already own. It may not be perfect or exactly what you want, but it might save you from another purchase. Most people already have a lot of clothing, most likely including a base layer top, ball caps, wind shell, non-cotton athletic socks, and running shoes.

Buy discounted, closeout, and used gear. If you are willing to be seen in last year's styles and colors, you can find excellent deals at Sierra Trading Post, REI-Outlet, Steep and Cheap, Campmor, and eBay. And if you are making large-volume purchases (e.g., backpacks for an entire Scout troop) call up the manufacturer to see if it is willing to give a volume discount; often it will.

Share gear among a group. A group needs only one shelter, one stove and cookpot, one water purification system, et cetera.

Find inexpensive alternatives. See chart below.

sample gear kits

BUY THIS	FOR	INSTEAD OF THIS	FOR UP TO
Fleece jacket	$50	Down-insulated parka	$200
Synthetic-insulated sleeping bag	$125	Down-insulated sleeping bag	$300
Closed-cell foam sleeping pad	$12	Self-inflating or inflatable air pad	$150
Rectangular tarp and bug nest	$100	Double-wall tent	$300
Homemade alcohol stove	$1	Canister or white gas stove	$80
Aluminum pot	$15	Titanium pot	$45
Disposable water bottles from recycling bin	$0	Nalgene or Platypus bottles	$10
Fixed-length aluminum ski poles	$20	Collapsible trekking poles	$150
Frameless backpack	$125	Large-volume suspension back	$300

glossary & list of hikes

Alcohol stove: An ultralight, trustworthy, and inexpensive model usually made from a cat food or soda can. The most widely available fuels for it are denatured alcohol (available in the paint department of most hardware stores) and HEET (the yellow bottle).

Base weight: The weight of a full backpack, minus food, water, and fuel, plus clothing and other equipment that is worn or carried on the body. This oft-cited measurement provides apples-to-apples comparisons of pack weight regardless of trip length.

Breathability (aka moisture vapor transmission rate): The ability of a material to permit the passage of moisture through it. For example, glass is nonbreathable; mosquito netting is breathable. Breathability differs from ventilation, which is the transfer of air.

Durable water repellent (DWR): A fluoropolymer-based coating commonly applied to polyester and nylon (including the exterior layers of waterproof-breathable fabrics) in order to improve water-resistance. When new, DWR will cause water to bead up and roll off. But it is easily degraded by dirt, body oils, and abrasion, and it must be restored regularly.

Environmental and route conditions: Temperatures, precipitation, daylight, ground cover, vegetation, sun exposure, water availability, wildlife and insects, remoteness, and natural hazards. This is key information that may affect itinerary, gear, and necessary skills.

Gear list: A bare-bones chart of every item that will be taken on a trip. Gear lists are useful for ensuring that all needs are addressed, for comparing all available options, and for eliminating redundancies.

Layering: A time-tested strategy for developing an effective clothing system. There are three types of layers: base layers, shells, and insulation. Each layer type excels in a particular function. Base layers manage moisture; shells provide resistance against the elements; and insulation offers warmth.

Polyurethane (PU): A polymer that is frequently used in backpacking equipment, for instance as the waterproofing agent for shelter floors.

Stupid heavy: A very common practice whereby a backpacker carries a completely unnecessary item (or items) given trip objectives, conditions, and skills. Examples include a boom box or a four-season tent for a July trip in Virginia.

Stupid light: A fairly common practice whereby a backpacker does not carry an item (or items) necessary for given trip objectives, conditions, and skills. An example includes not carrying rain gear or a shelter despite a forecast calling for 35°F and rain.

Tarp system: A multipiece tarp-based shelter that is augmented with an inner bug nest, ground sheet, bivy sack, head net, or some other item that offsets the inherent shortcomings of a tarp.

Three-season: Spring through fall, the conventional backpacking season throughout most of the country, when conditions are relatively hospitable and gear need not be winter-worthy. In the Southwest, "three-season" includes the winter but not the summer.

Ventilation: The transmission of air. Ventilation is helpful in a clothing system because it replaces the warm and moist air near the body with relatively cooler and drier air. It is helpful in a shelter system because it reduces condensation inside the shelter.

Waterproof: A nonbreathable fabric through which moisture cannot pass. With enough abrasion and UV light, waterproof fabrics can cease being waterproof and begin to leak.

Waterproof/breathable (WP/B): A type of fabric commonly used for rain gear and marketed as—miraculously—impervious to moisture while also allowing moisture to pass through it. Although these fabrics are constantly improving, for now, they are more accurately described as being highly water-resistant and somewhat breathable.

Water resistant: A type of fabric that, when new, will temporarily shed light precipitation, usually courtesy of a durable water repellent (DWR) finish, which is degraded by abrasion, dirt, and body oils.

Select list of author's hikes

Appalachian Trail: 2,175 miles, Georgia to Maine. May-August 2002.
Colorado Trail: 480 miles, Denver to Durango. July 2004, August 2006.
Sea-to-Sea Route: 7,775 miles, Quebec to Washington State. August 2004-July 2005.
Pacific Crest Trail: California. 38 miles per day for 45 days. June-July 2006.
Ultralight in the Nation's Icebox: 385 miles, Duluth to Ely, MN. January 2007.
Great Western Loop: 6,875 miles around the West. April-November 2007.
Sierra High Route: 200 miles, Sequoia-Kings Canyon National Park to Yosemite National Park, CA. July 2008.
Iceland Traverse: 550 miles, coast to coast. July 2008.
Hayduke Trail and Grand Canyon Traverse: 800 miles, Arches National Park, UT, to Supai, AZ. February-March 2009.
Alaska Mountain Wilderness Classic: 180 miles, Gerstle to McKinley Village. July 2009.
Alaska-Yukon Expedition: 4,700 miles in giant loop. March-September 2010.

glossary

217

illustrations credits

All photos courtesy Andrew Skurka unless otherwise noted:

Cover (Clockwise from top left), Courtesy Victorinox Swiss Army; Courtesy GoLite; Courtesy Black Diamond; Courtesy GoLite; Courtesy GoLite; Courtesy La Sportiva; Courtesy Jetboil.

Spine, Courtesy Victorinox Swiss Army.

4 (A), Courtesy Snow Peak; (B), Courtesy of Cascade Designs; (C), Courtesy GoLite; (D), JuGa/Shutterstock.com; (E), Courtesy La Sportiva; (F), Courtesy Black Diamond; (G), Courtesy Headsweats; (H), Courtesy REI; (I), Courtesy RBH Designs; (J), Courtesy Integral Designs; (K), Courtesy Black Diamond; (L), Courtesy Black Diamond; (M), Courtesy GoLite; (N), Courtesy Suunto; 7, Ryan Day Thompson; 8, Frans Lanting/Corbis; 11, Michael Christopher Brown/National Geographic Stock; 14 (ALL), Ryan Day Thompson; 18, Danny Warren/iStockphoto.com; 21 & 22, Michael Christopher Brown/National Geographic Stock; 23, NOHRSC/NOAA; 25, Alex Treadway/National Geographic Stock; 28, Matthias Breiter/Minden Pictures; 31, Noah Couser/Wild West Photos; 35 (LE), A. Syred/Photo Researchers, Inc.; 35 (CTR), SPL/Photo Researchers, Inc.; 35 (RT), Michael Abbey/Photo Researchers, Inc.; 42, Noah Couser/Wild West Photos; 44, Jeff Diener/Wild West Photos; 45, maigi/Shutterstock.com; 51, Wikimedia Commons; 52, GIPhotoStock/Photo Researchers, Inc.; 54, Anatol Jasiutyn/Panoramafactory; 56, Courtesy RBH Designs; 57, Courtesy Integral Designs; 61 (UP), Courtesy Headsweats; 62, Courtesy DeFeet; 63, Jose Gil/Shutterstock.com; 64, Chris Christie/All Canada Photos/Corbis; 66, Paul Willerton; 67, andesign101/Shutterstock.com; 69 (UP LE), risteski goce/Shutterstock.com; 69 (UP RT & LO), Courtesy La Sportiva; 70,

Michael Christopher Brown/National Geographic Stock; 74, MarFot/Shutterstock.com; 75, Miriam Stein; 76, JuGa/Shutterstock.com; 79, Courtesy of NEOS; 80, Ace Kvale; 84 (UP), Jeff Diener/Wild West Photos; 84 (LO), Courtesy GoLite; 86, Courtesy MusucBag; 88, Courtesy of Cascade Designs; 92, Tony Wong; 92 (RT), Tom Grundy/Shutterstock.com; 95, Courtesy REI; 98, Courtesy Sea to Summit; 102, Courtesy GoLite; 103, Courtesy TarpTent; 104, Michael Christopher Brown/National Geographic Stock; 106-107, Courtesy Black Diamond; 109, Tony Wong; 110, Peter Muller/Getty Images; 114, NG Maps; 117, Michael Christopher Brown/National Geographic Stock; 120 (LE), Courtesy Suunto; 120 (RT), Courtesy Garmin; 125 (UP LE & RT), Courtesy Black Diamond; 125 (LO), Courtesy Black Diamond; 126, Anatol Jasiutyn/Panoramafactory; 137, Jeff Diener/Wild West Photos; 140 (LE), ck./Shutterstock.com; 140 (RT), Courtesy Snow Peak; 141, Courtesy Jetboil; 142, Ryan Day Thompson; 143, Ryan Tansey; 144, Miriam Stein; 146, DenisNata/Shutterstock.com; 153, Courtesy of Cascade Designs; 160, Jeff Diener/Wild West Photos; 165 (LE), Courtesy Black Diamond; 165 (RT), Courtesy Mammut; 167, kenkistler/Shutterstock.com; 169, Michael Christopher Brown/National Geographic Stock; 170, 2011 Google-Map Data; 173, Courtesy Joby; 175, Alaska Stock Images/National Geographic Stock; 177, Ryan Day Thompson; 182, Ryan Day Thompson; 184, Courtesy GoLite; 189, Miriam Stein; 192, Ocean/Corbis; 194, drewthehobbit/Shutterstock.com; 202, Vlad Ghiea/Shutterstock.com; 206, Dean Pennala/iStockphoto; 210, Laurence Parent; 212, Keith Courson.

acknowledgments

Neither the adventures on which this book is based, nor the actual writing and production of it, would have been possible without the help and support of many others, a few of whom I would like to especially thank here.

At the very top of the list are my parents, Bob and Karen, who never would have chosen this path for me but who nonetheless support me in any way they can. They've been willing to send me supply boxes via General Delivery full of chocolate, fresh shoes, and new maps; to console me over the phone when I can no longer internalize the stresses of solo wilderness travel; and to offer practical life and career guidance if I ask for it. My sisters, Kerri and Christine, and brothers-in-law, Ryan and Matt, are less hands-on but equally reliable supporters.

Two women on Colorado's Front Range are also deserving of my deepest gratitude: my longtime friend Elizabeth, who has always been generous with her rational advice as well as her home, where my belongings usually reside rent-free during my prolonged absences; and my girlfriend, Amanda, who has been a coveted sounding board during the writing process and who, more important, balances me with her warmth, lightheartedness, style, and beauty.

The book's content is mostly based on what I have learned through my trips, while both planning for and doing them. But I have consulted other sources to round out my views and to gain clarity on subjects with which I was not intimately familiar. The all-star crew of Phil Barton, Buzz Burrell, Alan Dixon, Roman Dial, Howard Friedman, Jeffrey Jacobs, and Don Wilson were immensely helpful, as were two online resources, *Backpacking Light* magazine and REI's Expert Advice.

Finally, I would like to thank National Geographic Books—notably Barbara Brownell Grogan, Barbara Noe, Cameron Zotter, Ruthie Thompson, Miriam Stein, Heather McElwain, Judith Klein, Leslie Allen, and especially my editor, Larry Porges—for taking the project to another level, as would be expected of anything that earns the yellow border.

index

ISEINDEX

Published by the National Geographic Society
1145 17th Street N.W., Washington, D.C. 20036

ISBN: 978-1-4262-0920-8

The National Geographic Society is one of the world's largest nonprofit scientific and educational organizations. Founded in 1888 to "increase and diffuse geographic knowledge,"
the Society's mission is to inspire people to care about the planet. It reaches more than
400 million people worldwide each month through its official journal, *National Geographic,*
and other magazines; National Geographic Channel; television documentaries; music; radio;
films; books; DVDs; maps; exhibitions; live events; school publishing programs; interac-
tive media; and merchandise. National Geographic has funded more than 9,600 scientific
research, conservation and exploration projects and supports an education program pro-
moting geographic literacy.

For more information, visit www.nationalgeographic.com.

National Geographic Society
1145 17th Street N.W.
Washington, D.C. 20036-4688 U.S.A.

For information about special discounts for bulk purchases, please contact
National Geographic Books Special Sales: ngspecsales@ngs.org

For rights or permissions inquiries, please contact National Geographic Books
Subsidiary Rights: ngbookrights@ngs.org

Interior design: Cameron Zotter, Ruthie Thompson

The text on hiking fast on pp. 18–19 and on vapor barrier liners on pp. 56–60 is adapted
from articles that originally appeared in *Backpacking Light* magazine and is reprinted here
with permission.

Printed in the United States of America

11/QGT-LPH/1